SECOND HELPINGS

A Taste of The Glenfiddich Awards

SECOND
HELPINGS

A Taste of The Glenfiddich Awards

COMPILED BY GEORGE THAW

FOREWORD BY DEREK COOPER

Good Books

PUBLISHED FOR WILLIAM GRANT & SONS LTD
BY GOOD BOOKS (GB PUBLICATIONS LTD)
LAGARD FARM, WHITLEY, MELKSHAM, WILTS SN12 8RL

A CATALOGUE RECORD FOR THIS BOOK IS AVAILABLE FROM THE BRITISH
LIBRARY.

ISBN 0 946555 41 9

EDITOR: GRAHAM TARRANT
COVER AND INTERIOR DESIGN: DESIGN/SECTION, FROME

PRINTED IN ENGLAND BY CLAYS LTD, ST IVES PLC

CONTENTS

DRINK

For over a quarter of a century The Glenfiddich Awards have recognized and celebrated excellence in writing, publishing and broadcasting on the subjects of food and drink. During this time, the Awards have consistently attracted the highest levels of accomplishment within these three disciplines, and we are now pleased to bring you a selection of the winning entries.

Each year, the process of judging The Glenfiddich Awards becomes more demanding. With a choice of twelve categories, a panel of five judges, and upwards of 600 entries, it is an enormous undertaking just to consider the wealth of submitted material – let alone decide which should be singled out for individual recognition. Without the dedicated support of our judges there would be no Awards, and I would like to take this opportunity to record my heartfelt thanks to all those who have made this invaluable contribution over the years. My thanks also go to the many writers, photographers, broadcasters and publishers who have entered the Awards and have allowed us to reproduce some of the winning material in this anthology.

This book stands as a tribute to the combined efforts of both judges and contributors. Though each of the extracts stands alone as a valuable source of information and pleasure, together they make the compelling point that The Glenfiddich Awards have achieved something quite remarkable over the past twenty-five years. In encouraging and recognizing the very best in this field of writing and journalism, they have made a profound contribution to the nation's appreciation and enjoyment of fine food and drink. This volume celebrates both the Awards and those who have made them possible.

David Grant
Chairman of The Glenfiddich Awards Judging Panel

FOREWORD

It is now over a quarter of a century since The Glenfiddich Awards were inaugurated. The presentation of the first Trophy was done discreetly behind closed doors and the press were not invited to the lunch party for eight at the Dorchester where a bottle of '61 Château Rausan-Ségla was still to be had for £3. Those were the days when a carafe of rosé was 50p in the Savoy Grill and a five-course dinner at Sharrow Bay was £2.50.

It was an adventurous move on the part of William Grant & Sons even to contemplate giving prizes to food and wine writers. They produced neither food nor wine themselves and in those days not much was being written about whisky; indeed in 1973 there were no worthy entries at all in the category "writer most contributing to the appreciation of malt whisky" and the judges made no award.

What is remarkable about the enterprise is that not only have Grant's continued to underwrite the awards for over twenty-five years, but they have been run without a break by the same member of the family who first conceived them, David Grant. Thanks largely to his enthusiasm the Glenfiddichs have become the major event in the food and drink writers' year, the gastronomic equivalent of the "Oscars".

The awards themselves have multiplied to reflect the growing importance of food and drink in the public consciousness. David Grant's original modest proposal was to present a trophy to the Wine and Food Writer of the Year and silver and bronze medals to the two runners up. There was a case of Glenfiddich as well and an envelope containing a cheque.

In the second year came three new categories – the best article by a provincial journalist, the best book and the best piece of writing on malt whisky. A special prize for a young writer was added in 1974; in 1977 restaurant criticism was given a class of its own and in subsequent years came awards for trade press journalism, radio, television, publishing, photography and illustration. The expansion of the awards to the present dozen categories reflects the authority and respect which the Glenfiddichs now command – a dust jacket boasting a "Glenfiddich Awards Winner" does wonders for sales.

Back in the early 1970s no one could have foreseen the astonishing national popularity which the subject of food would kindle, much of it fuelled by the insatiable appetite of the television channels. Food not only looked good on the small screen, it was good for the ratings. Along with snooker and darts cooking has become a compulsive spectator sport; film crews roam the world gathering material for culinary documentaries; chefs have become cult figures and even the smallest radio station has its food guru. Food and wine magazines are big business in the shopping malls, supermarkets now sell fine wine, gourmet foods and the books to go with them.

To match this enthusiasm and keep it informed and entertained we now have not only a Circle of Wine Writers but a Guild of Beer Writers and a 250-strong Guild of Food Writers. Wine appreciation classes and cookery courses, food quizzes and competitions in which aspirant amateurs prepare elaborate dishes in front of master chefs are all part of the emergence of food as a fashionable manifestation of lifestyle.

The showbiz potential of food, its Sunday supplement appeal, has perhaps obscured a much more serious concern about the role of food in society, recognized by special Glenfiddich awards to campaigning groups like Common Ground and the Food Commission. The last twenty-five years have seen intense debate about factory farming, the standardization of produce, the loss of regional diversity and the effect of agribusiness on the quality and integrity of our food and drink. By recognizing and encouraging excellence in writing, publishing and broadcasting in this field the awards have made a significant contribution to improving the standards and choice of what we eat and drink.

All this is mirrored in the anthology. The menu moves from the simplicities of cod and cabbage, peanuts and seaweed, to the *grands crus* of Bordeaux, the wider attractions of the classic malt and the cooking in country houses.

The first winner of the Glenfiddichs, Pamela Vandyke Price, is here, and the most recent, Nigel Slater. Between them all manner of writing from some of the best palates and pens of the age.

Elizabeth David buttering crumpets and muffins, Jane Grigson savouring pears, Cyril Ray sparkling on champagne and Arabella Boxer slicing rose petal sandwiches for afternoon tea. Alan Davidson makes marmalade, Colin Spencer dissects the British sausage, while Jancis Robinson turns a scholarly eye on fashions in the world of wine.

There has never been anything elitist about the awards. A eulogy of Château d'Yquem sits comfortably alongside a chip butty. Classical scholar Margaret

Visser ponders on the semiotics of an ice cream with the same objective delight that Richard Olney bestows on the raw materials of a stew.

There has never been anything insular either. Yan-Kit So on Chinese cuisine, Pierre Koffmann in Gascony, Julie Sahni at a wedding feast in India, George Lassalle catching fish in Greece and Elisabeth Luard in Granada affirm the universality of good food.

If there is a common theme in these second helpings it is a respect for food in all its joyous abundance. Those of us who write about such matters owe a debt of gratitude to the Grant family for the steadfast and generous support they have given over the years to the appreciation and enjoyment of both food and drink.

Derek Cooper

OUT OF THE SEA

MAGNIFICENT OBSESSION

GEORGE LASSALLE

I first fell in love with fish at the age of thirteen, in a village called Twelve Crows Nest on the eastern edge of Loch Corrib in Connemara. There I was taught to get up at dawn and, before Mass and breakfast, catch a tinful of daddy-long-legs for the day's fishing on the loch. As breakfast was either a brown trout caught the day before or an inch-thick lump of fat bacon swimming in its own grease, the incentive to a day's fishing was overwhelming.

We would set out – the priest, the old gillie and I – at about nine-thirty, equipped with rods, artificial flies and lures, the big tin of now buzzing "daddies" and a bigger tin of sweet brown bread. Half a dozen Guinness bottles were left to swish around in the bilge. In such circumstances, miracles could be expected to happen, and that year the sun shone every day, though in a chequered sort of way, the threat of rain only rarely being fulfilled, and then not for long. The old gillie baited our lines with the live daddies, and the priest and I flogged the lake in front of us as we drifted slowly backwards, broadside on. Suddenly the trout would begin to jump and every strike would lose a daddy or take a fish. They were small – none as large as a pound in weight – but we seldom took less than a dozen at a go when they were rising. Then, for perhaps an hour, there'd be no sign. We would be trolling, our lines streaming out behind the boat, baited with glittering, twisting silver minnows. We would be into the Guinness and brown bread, and suddenly the ratchet would scream and . . . We never saw what the old cook did to them, but our catch would come to us smoking hot and barred brown and black. The taste of the exquisite pink flesh (we consumed them seasoned only with butter and a little salt) is with me still. By the end of a week, I was totally committed – and doomed thereafter to ten long years of growing frustration before I would experience any comparable gastronomic thrill.

It was indeed almost exactly ten years later, in Greece (in the middle 'thirties, between two minor revolutions), when I was staying on the islet of Aghios Nikolaos in the narrow waters between Euboea and Boeotia, that I first began to cook. The one-armed cook, Ervin, a refugee from Hitler's Brownshirts, was frequently unable to attend to his duties and on these occasions, sacred to Bacchus, I managed, with the assistance of two peasant boys, to provide not only the regional diet for the island's nine resident labourers, but also tolerable meals for the frequent guests of its lovable and eccentric owner. Ervin's repertoire was limited (he had previously been an electrical engineer at Siemens), and on the rich and heavy side for the heat of a Greek summer. The guests ranged from young German *Wandervögeln* to near-apoplectic American profs of Eng Lit; from minor diplomats to touring English dilettanti. They were animated, one and all, by an intense curiosity to confirm Athenian gossip of bizarre happenings on Aghios Nikolaos. I naturally tried to spare this motley flow of Private Eyes the rigours of Prussian cooking and, with the aid of a battered Mrs Beeton, I started my apprenticeship. Supplies of fresh vegetables, fruit and wine were brought in by rowing boat from the large mainland village of Khalia (literally, rubbish dump) while meat and groceries involved a weekly trip to the nearest big town, Khalkis. But our immediately available larder was the sea all around us which teemed with fish, the best of which, for our purposes, were the red and grey mullets – the latter being of exceptional size. *Zargana* (garfish of the green bones), *caponi* (gurnard) and many other varieties – apart from octopus, squid and sepia – were plentiful. For all of these we hunted by night, four to a boat, with wide-shaded acetylene lamps overhanging the stern, and armed with ten-foot trident-topped poles and long iron swords (these were for the garfish). When the dynamiters were out, we would rush towards the sound of the explosion to hijack their catch. On the first of these expeditions, we hijacked a number of stunned red mullet; these were of about the same size as my Loch Corrib trout. We cooked them just as they were, scales and all – after rubbing them with oil – on a large, flat, iron griddle, over the wide opening of a wood-fired range; after turning them three times, at three-minute intervals, the skins were almost charred, but still intact, even though the scales had been jumping off throughout the cooking. Hungrily I opened my fish down the back, and the aroma which came up at me almost sent me into shock. It was the experience of Loch Corrib all over again, but with something added which was not just the gamy flavour which has earned the mullet the title of woodcock of the sea. I had eaten mullet many times before in the tavernas of Athens, but never any as large or as fresh. Perhaps my overwhelming reaction to this particular fish was quite subjective, brought on by the excitement of my first night-fishing expedition and the tremendous hunger it generated. The fact remains that that red mullet closed all the exits from an obsession which I have never since wished to escape.

FROM *THE ADVENTUROUS FISH COOK* (1976)

NORWEGIAN WAYS WITH COD

ALAN DAVIDSON

The day which I spent with Professor Fægri in Bergen included a demonstration of how fresh cod is prepared and cooked there.

At 08.15 the Professor was in the fish market, examining the cod and saithe which were swimming about in the fishmonger's tank. Some of the cod had recently spawned and were deemed unsuitable because of their "spent" condition. But there was one fine seaweed-coloured specimen which swam with vigour and was fat round the neck, as a cod should be. He chose this and the fishmonger netted it. It weighed 3.7kg (8lb), just about right for six people. It was immediately killed and gutted and the tail fin cut off, to facilitate bleeding. The Professor had correctly foreseen that it would have no roe but a large liver. This was kept separately. The Professor then took the fish to the Botanical Museum, where he had work to do, and allowed it to "rest" for a full hour, explaining that this repose was a desirable element in its preparation. At 10.00 he laid it on its back and cut it into steaks about 1½ cm across, not quite completing each cut, so that the fish would be easier to carry. The fish was then left under cold running water, to keep its temperature down and to leach out the remaining blood, until the time came (14.30) to take it home.

At home, salted water (three per cent salt, like sea water) was brought to the boil and half the cod steaks, now completely severed from each other, were put in. Once the water came back to the boil, the pot was removed from the fire. Five or six minutes later, the cod was judged to be ready and was served with floury boiled potatoes and melted butter. The liver, cut in pieces, had meanwhile been poached for a shorter time in a half-and-half mixture of vinegar and water, with a couple of bay leaves and some whole peppercorns. It was served at the same time.

While we ate the first batch of cod steaks, the remaining ones were made ready in the same way, to provide second helpings. The fish was snow-white, tender and delicious. The Professor pointed out that its subtle flavour would be obscured by the addition of almost any second vegetable; he preferred to take a little lettuce afterwards. He also observed that he had not salted the fish at all before cooking it; and that if he had had some whey he would have cooked the cod in that instead of water, thus making the fish even whiter and firmer. In the north they would actually prefer cod a day old but cooked in whey to fresher cod cooked in water.

I have never eaten cod so good.

FROM *NORTH ATLANTIC SEAFOOD* (1979)

A CURE FOR KIPPERS

JANE GRIGSON

The mildest of all cured herrings is the kipper. As you would expect, it's the latest comer. John Woodger of Seahouses, in Northumberland, decided in the 1840s to adapt the salmon-kippering process to herrings. He split the fish down the back and gutted it, soaked it briefly in brine – half an hour or more depending on the fatness of the fish – then hung it up on hooks fixed to long rods or "tenters" to be smoked over slow oak fires for six to eighteen hours. His methods are still followed by the small family firm of Robson at Craster down the coast from Seahouses, by a firm or two on Loch Fyne, and by all kipperers on the Isle of Man.

Larger concerns cheat time and loss of weight, and make up for the skill of individual judgement, by dyeing the kippers to various shades of mahogany. The browner a kipper is, the more pains you should take to avoid it. This is not crankiness on my part. Try a silvery brown kipper from one of the places I've mentioned, or from the Hamburg fish shop in Brewer Street in Soho; at the same time try one of those sunburnt objects from a deep-frozen package, and you will see what I mean. (Canned kippers I find disgusting: they do not come into it at all.) The practice of dyeing was introduced during the First World War, when it was excusable to pass off inferior kippers because people were hungry. The dye disguised the fact that the kipper hadn't been smoked for long enough: which meant that it had lost less weight, so it took fewer kippers to fill the boxes. Good kippers are sorted out after the curing is over: dyeing disguises the poor ones, and so lessens the need for skilled sorters who know what a kipper should be.

In *The Herring and its Fishery*, W C Hodgson remarks: ". . . in fairness to many respectable curing firms, it is true to say that, *provided the fish are properly smoked*, a little added colour will do no harm, but at the same time it is difficult to see why if colour was unnecessary in the 'old days' it should be necessary now. However one looks at the problem, there is always the chance that the colour will be used to speed up the processing of the herring."

Kippers may be grilled, skin side to the heat, baked in foil, fried, or jugged – ie put into a large pot, with a kettleful of boiling water, and left for ten minutes. I like them best raw, arranged in strips round the edge of some well-buttered rye bread, with an egg yolk in the middle as sauce . . .

Two hints from Mr Hodgson:

"Put a pair of kippers together, flesh to flesh, in the frying-pan with a small piece of butter between them. Fry very slowly, turning them over from time to time, but always keeping them together like a sandwich. In this way the oil runs continually from one kipper to the other and the result is excellent. Incidentally mustard is good with kippers, and mustard sauce is correct with most kinds of cooked fresh herrings."

"Many people object to eating kippers because they have difficulty with the bones . . . Eating a kipper is quite simple if it is laid correctly on the plate to start with, that is, with the skin uppermost . . . With the head towards you, lift up the skin from half of the kipper by running the point of the knife along the edge and fold the skin back. This exposes the flesh *on top of the bones*, and it is quite easy to remove it in fillets, leaving the bones untouched. When this side has been eaten, turn the kipper round on the plate so that the tail is towards you and repeat the process on the other side." This works.

FROM *FISH COOKERY* (1973)

THE END OF THE ROAD FOR A DONEGAL DELICACY

NIKI HILL

Go up a certain mountain track in Donegal – forget about the lumps and bumps in the road and the underside of your car – follow through a long mountain valley steep and gloomy on either side, past a deep brown trout lake, and on to the sea.

Nestling in a gulf in the cliffs is a village, watered by a swift-flowing bog-coloured stream, with a stony beach and a concrete pier sticking out into a dark seaweedy sea. All about is silence.

There are four houses in the village, all – until one recent summer – totally deserted and in decay, walls open to the sky, grey and crumbling, stones in untidy heaps. The fields about are patterned with that strange corrugation that betrays the years of potato "lazy beds", yet still smooth and green, for once the toil of removing the stones was done, the grass grew fertile and uninterrupted. The pathways to and fro around the fields and the houses are now moss-grown, cluttered too with straying stones.

And yet outside a house you will see a large flat boulder, where someone used to sit in the sun looking at the mountain and the sea and waiting for a boat to come home. Sitting in a ruddy twilight that you only seem to see when you look out across that broad Atlantic, sitting knitting at the door, with a big turf fire smoking quietly behind, the lamp lit already, the table set and the kettle on the black hook over the fire, knitting those thick woolly socks for the handsome sum of two shillings a dozen pairs; so the women waited. They waited for the lobstermen to come home. The boulder is smooth through generations.

This and their children and the odd trip to the nearest village some seven or so miles away to buy bacon, flour and sugar and maybe a bit of tea if they could afford it, were the limits of their horizons.

If you walk up the side of the cliffs at the village you will find a little cabin set in a fold of the hillside, with a square or two of fields about it filled with cabbage rows, or oats, or potatoes, and a cow grazing. And in the corner of one of the fields a tiny stone house maybe eight paces square where a certain wild Welsh poet stayed and wrote in 1935, "Here are gannets and seals and puffins flying and puffing and playing a quarter of a mile outside my window where there are great rocks petrified like the old Fates and destinies of Ireland and smooth white pebbles under and around them like the souls of the dead Irish. There's a hill with a huge echo. You shout and the dead Irish answer from behind the hill."

Old Dylan Thomas got that feeling there, staying in that little house lent him by Tom and Rose who lived in that other cabin nearby.

And it was of this strange place that another poet, or so it is said, wrote "up the airy mountain and down the rushy glen" which drums into our heads as children.

The story of the place is indeed a strange one. Before the Second World War the main occupation was lobster fishing. The rugged rocky coastline with all that swirling ribbon seaweed was an ideal habitat for the lobster. Eat in the finest restaurants in Paris, it was said, and the chances were that your lobster came all the way from this enchanted spot.

But the war, like all wars, changed everything. Lobsters could no longer be exported and the villagers could no longer find profitable work to support them.

One day two bright boys, so the story goes, in an inspired moment, bade farewell to their families and emigrated to the land of hope for so many Irish – America.

Here the story varies. The version I prefer says they found their way to a west coast fishing centre and there found another lobster fishing industry to work in. Maybe that is my wishful thinking. At any rate the outcome was that after a time, with a little help from their new-found friends, they had saved enough money to bring out the entire village of thirty-seven souls, to a new country and a life of opportunity.

I wonder how they fared in that hustling, bustling land so far from their own solitudes.

So the village was deserted and lay thus for many years. Except for the odd curious visitor.

Anyone who knows this spot will claim it as their special place.

There is a certain charm about a place you can be really alone in.

To walk along the beach and throw those rounded pebbles into the tide, just you and the sea and that feeling of the company of unseen others that still haunt the place.

Last year somebody managed to buy one of the houses, and has rebuilt it in that solitary place. So there's a smell of turf smoke once again amongst the old stones. The lobsters are still fished but by people who come from a neighbouring village. They are of fine and remarkable size, so if occasionally a friend brings me one, I think long and enjoy my lobster that bit more.

FROM *THE BELFAST TELEGRAPH* (1973)

FLEUR DE SEL

MICHAEL RAFFAEL

It is a very rare and capricious flower. Unless the wind is blowing from the east it will not grow. Sometimes, it has a scent of violets, but not always. Freshly gathered, it is a frosty flamingo pink: within a day it turns a dull off-white. It will not be ready for the table for a year. After that it will keep almost indefinitely. *Fleur de sel* – flower of salt – is one of the last great unadulterated ingredients of the world.

The salt bays in the Guérande marshes, near St Nazaire, are the last haven of a dying craft. A century ago, Brittany and the south-west coast supplied half of France with salt, a figure that has dwindled to half a per cent. Almost all of that is the delicious unrefined, grey sea salt beloved of leading French chefs and bakers. A tiny amount of the harvest, like cream on top of the milk, is the *fleur de sel*.

There is much to recommend the comparison. Seawater flows through a network of canals into a set of clay-lined bays, built like miniature paddling pools. As the sun and wind evaporate the moisture, salt begins to form. Most of it sinks to the bottom. A thin, crystalline slick – the *fleur* – spreads across the corner of each pan. Skimmed off with a *lousse*, a tool like an outsized croupier's rake, it is the salt-farmer's precious bonus.

According to François Lecallo, president of the Guérande Producer's Co-operative, it is an unpredictable crop. "If the winds are too strong, the crystals sink. If the direction changes, the crust breaks up. When it rains, the crystals don't form. You can have an average *sel gris* harvest and almost no 'flower'."

Lecallo is a *paludier*, a man of the marshes. He farms two *salines*, the mazes of channels, drains and ponds where the salt evaporates. One of them has not altered since it was built in 1536.

He has no time for the whiter-than-white refined salts which most of us buy. "Industrial salt," he says, "is bitter. It deforms the taste of food, whereas an unrefined salt adds to it."

Do not be taken in by the words "sea salt", he warns. Most of it is pure, manufactured sodium chloride. "When they refine salt, they take out all the other minerals, like magnesium, potassium and iron. Guérande salt is similar in composition to the water in the human body and it's more easily assimilated." He does not go so far as to claim that his natural salt reduces blood pressure, but he is convinced it is less likely to raise it.

He may be right. *Fleur de sel* contains a high level of humidity. It has the lowest sodium chloride level of any salt. Because its flavour is so pronounced and interesting, cooks use much less of it.

Harriet Helliwell is one of the first cooks in Britain to try it. She started buying it soon after opening her Crosse Farm Bakery at Cheriton Bishop, near Exeter, this year. "We've cut our consumption of salt by a third since we switched to it."

She dissolves it in water and brushes it on the crust of foccacia halfway through baking, or adds it as a flavouring to potato and oatmeal crackers, with fresh marjoram and pumpkin seeds.

Her model is the celebrated Paris bakery, Poilâne, which has always relied on Guérande salt. "A difficult customer to satisfy." Lecallo admits, "When the *saline* from which they bought salt changed hands, they noticed the drop in quality at once and complained."

At the moment Guérande salt enjoys a cult following in France. Three-star chefs such as Paul Bocuse, Pierre Troisgros and Alain Senderens serve it. However, they tend to buy the best grey sea salt for cooking and put the finer more expensive *fleur de sel* on the table as a condiment.

The attention it has attracted is timely, because it was fast becoming an endangered species. The number of full-time professional *paludiers* has dipped to around 100. Although the marshes cover about 4,000 acres, there are twice as many salt pans lying abandoned as there are being exploited.

The revival owes something to the formation of a co-operative in 1989. Since then, its salt has obtained Label Rouge status, the French mark of quality food. Some co-operative members also have the right to bear the *Nature et Progrès* symbol, the equivalent of the Soil Association's emblem. It deserves its green image: the only energy required is the electricity needed to sift it before packing.

One of the first actions of the co-operative was to construct *salorges*, large warehouses for stocking the salt. The level of production depends entirely on the weather. In a rainy summer, as with a cereal crop, the yield is low. When it is gathered, the salt is humid. It takes a year drying out before it is ready for sale.

With the infrastructure in place, the co-operative has started exporting to America and now to England.

Southwick Country Herbs, in Devon, supplies the trade. At £2.75 for a 500g bag, though, *fleur de sel* has not made many converts among the public. "But tasting is believing," said Martin Menist, the proprietor.

In a backhanded way, it is a good thing that salt should again be valued. The price of a slave-girl in Timbuctu market used to be twenty blocks of salt. Gold renaissance salt-cellars by the likes of Cellini show the place it once had on the rich man's table. Gathering *fleur de sel* is a painstaking, labour-intensive task.

The *salines* really do smell of violets. It is an elusive and transcient scent. Lecallo recalls the first time he smelt the flower: "'Funny,' I said, 'it smells of salt.'"

At home, like the wine-maker who keeps a few priceless bottles to impress his friends, he stores salt from special vintages, days when the elements combined to provide salt of perfect fineness, texture and flavour.

They can be years old. "These are the salts you keep for your friends, because they symbolize the pride you take in your work."

FROM *THE SUNDAY TELEGRAPH* (22 AUGUST 1993)

SECRET OF SUPERIOR SEAWEED

JOHN McKENNA

"You need to be like a hare to do this," says Frank Melvin, hurdling and jumping from stone to stone on the Long Rock in west Co Sligo with the agility of a high-wire specialist. "You know the fellows that you would come across on the foreshore – and you might surprise them – and they'd be away like mad."

Frank springs and leaps amid the lumpen outcrop of the Long Rock in pursuit of edible seaweeds, in particular the fine sea-salty dilisk (known as dulse in Northern Ireland) and the tangly, khaki-brown restorative which is carrageen moss.

Packed in small plastic bags with the promise "Harvested in the North West of Ireland" on the label, the weeds are found mainly in health-food shops throughout the country. In comparison with other weeds which are produced on a large scale, Mr Melvin's seaweeds are finer and more complete in both texture and taste.

The secret of the high quality of his seaweeds lies not just in the suitability of the Long Rock and its neighbouring outcrops, but also in his method of drying the weeds: "The weather will do the bleaching," Frank says. "All you need to do is pitch it out, for ten days. But, I believe, to do it right, it must be bleached all around, from the point of view that I can sell that and it won't go soft or go bad at room temperature. If I don't bleach it there will be a tendency that what won't get bleached will go soft."

Originally a fisherman, Frank later became the harbour pilot in nearby Ballina before the container ships dried up and died away, forcing him to look for a new method to earn a living. "I like to work with the sea – the funny thing is if I could make a living I'd work every day at the sea. It's a very healthy place, and there's great peace of mind down there: no one to fight with but the sea urchins!"

But if the shore is a peaceful place, it is also, to the outsider, a place of strange surprise. Summon up the nerve to gambol amidst the rocks with Frank and a tour of the Long Rock becomes not unlike a tour of Burgundy vineyards.

Over here, just near the water's edge, is a place good for dilisk with fine, long, dark strands – a *grand cru* site, perhaps. Over there, further out on the water, is where the shorter strands of a type of dilisk known as *crannach* grows, the fronds of the weed sprouting from tiny shells.

"That's the one the old folk prefer," Frank says, "they would just walk out and collect it by the handful and eat it." Its penchant for blooming from the shells, however, means that it is not a good commercial proposition as the strands are too short.

Then, in a *premier cru* site, one finds the carrageen. "It's at a different water-level, but not far removed," he says, "and it's possible to get it on a day when you won't get dilisk, it's at a higher level. You would only get it in very small proportions when there's a weaker tide, simply because the water is on it."

With the dilisk, he says, "Most of the people that I know just chew it, straight from the bag," though a handful of the chopped weed added to a soda bread mixture makes for a cake of bread that is particularly good with cheese.

The carrageen is used for cooking – the inevitable nursery school, blancmange-style pudding, of course – "though a lot of the people I sell it to use it for colds and 'flus, for the chest. There are many families even who I supply in the Ballina-Sligo area and they use a huge amount, give it to their kids and bring them up with it, they reckon they never have colds or sickness or anything, they swear by it."

As a restorative, indeed, carrageen is unbeatable, the weeds soaked and brewed up in water, then strained and mixed with honey and lemon juice. On Aran, notes the writer Tim Robinson, "Next to whiskey it is the people's most trusted cure for coughs and colds."

A drop of the hard stuff tilted into some brewey carrageen, of course, is surely the perfect recipe for health and happiness.

FROM *THE IRISH TIMES* (11 JULY 1992)

TALENT TO AMUSE

RICHARD STEIN

The correct name in the catering trade for the small pre-dinner morsels . . . is *amuse-gueule*, which means "an amusement for the palate". We regard these as a very important part of the meal, since the first thing one eats when one is hungriest is likely to be remembered above all else.

ANCHOVY ICE CREAM IN PUFF PASTRY

I am fond of putting ice cream in warm puff pastry for a sweet, and we have adapted that idea for a savoury *amuse-gueule*. It is very good indeed.

> *2 small tins of anchovy fillets (total weight 3½ oz [105g])*
> *1 egg yolk*
> *2 teaspoons (10ml) olive oil*
> *pinch of cayenne*
> *2½ oz (75g) double cream*
> *1 lb (450g) puff pastry*
> *1 egg (for egg wash)*

Put the anchovy fillets, egg yolk, olive oil and cayenne in a food processor and blend till smooth. Now pour in the cream, keeping the blender on for no more than 15 seconds. Pour out and freeze.

Roll out the puff pastry so that it is ⅛ inch (3mm) thick. Cut into little parallelogram shapes with sides 2 inches and 1 inch (5cm and 2.5cm). Lay on a baking tray and chill them till you need them.

Set the oven at 450°F (230°C; gas mark 8).

Brush the tops of the pastry cutouts with beaten egg and bake in the oven for 6 to 8 minutes.

Leave to cool a little on a wire rack, then slice each one in half horizontally.

Sandwich a teaspoon of the anchovy ice cream between the two layers of puff pastry and serve at once.

FROM *ENGLISH SEAFOOD COOKERY* (1988)

NATURAL PRODUCE

COOK'S GOLD

PHILIPPA DAVENPORT

It is early morning at the end of October. We have been driving across the plain of La Mancha for what seems like hours. I am cold and sleepy. The coach stops, a man gets on and the air is suddenly filled with the unmistakable smell of roast saffron. Paco Martinez is a saffron buyer and the scent of the spice he deals in clings to him as tenaciously as the reek of tobacco to a heavy smoker. It is a pungent, sweet, musky aroma with a background hint of burning tyres, not entirely pleasing per se perhaps but its association with good eating prompts instant salivation.

Saffron is the world's most expensive spice, "worth its weight in gold", once measured in carats, now retailing at about £90 per ounce in the UK. The threads or filaments, as tawny-red as the hair of a Pre-Raphaelite beauty, are in fact the three-pronged stigmas of *Crocus sativus Linnaeus*, which flowers in the autumn (not to be confused with the poisonous *Colchicum autumnale*, commonly known as meadow saffron or autumn crocus). To yield just 1lb of dried spice more than 80,000 saffron blossoms are needed.

Ironically, this costly spice is the product of a cottage industry, grown in some of the poorest parts by families cultivating strips of rented land – in India, Iran, Turkey, Greece, Spain and Italy. Saffron from La Mancha is generally considered the finest, though the Iranians claim that saffron from the Qum plateau is second to none.

Wherever saffron is grown the land must be freed of stones, weeded, watered and fed. The corms must be lifted, divided and replanted each year to cajole them into flowering. The returns diminish with time as the land becomes exhausted and each corm produces fewer flowers. In Iran saffron is grown on the same spot for nine consecutive years, then the fields are left fallow for seven. In Spain alternative crops are introduced after four years and saffron is not replanted there for twenty years.

Saffron flowers are as pale, frail and short-lived as the spice is potent. They appear almost overnight, as though by magic, like mushrooms, painting the

October landscape with ribboned patches of lilac haze. Each corm throws up a new bloom on two, three or four consecutive days; the season lasts little more than a fortnight. But what a time of frenzied activity it is for the crokers (saffron growers). Saffron flowers do not close at night and must be picked on the morning they appear, while they are still in bud, before the sun, wind or rain can spoil the stigmas clasped inside them. They have to be picked by hand, the stigmas hand-plucked and carefully dried – all within twenty-four hours for top quality.

The plain of La Mancha is inhospitable. The temperature can reach -20°C in winter, +40°C in summer. Now, as Paco Martinez takes me to meet a family harvesting their saffron garden, it frets with rain and the wind runs through our ears like a sword. The family have been at work since dawn. Bent double, each croker straddles three rows and shuffles forward picking the flowers from all three rows, dropping them into an esparto basket that brushes the freshly picked middle row. They pick swiftly and deftly, like grazing animals munching their way across pasture. When they stop for a five-minute break to stretch their backs and sip coffee, the efficiency of their labour is evident. Ahead lie fat buds of lilac bloom. In their wake is a silvery snail trail of spears – tomorrow's embryonic flower buds.

By about 10 o'clock the day's harvest should be finished. The baskets, soft and shallow to prevent compacting the blooms, are taken home and plucking begins. "Time to swap backache for a stiff bum" as one jolly matron put it. The first basket of flowers is emptied on to a table. Practised fingers dart with grace and speed delicately opening the petals and drawing out the fiery-red stigmas. The stigmas are dropped into saucers or old tuna fish tins (each person has his or her own receptacle) and the spent flowers fall into aproned laps or onto a drugget. Slowly the heap of fresh flowers grows smaller and the tins fill up. Fingers damp with petal juice gradually turn inky blue as though from writing with leaking fountain pens.

The most experienced woman present does the roasting: the critical task of drying the saffron until reduced to one-fifth its weight, in which state it keeps well. Too much heat and the saffron may go up in smoke. Too little and it may rot in storage. Each batch of plucked filaments is checked for foreign bodies, spread on a hair sieve and placed over a steady source of heat for about fifteen minutes, probed gently, turned and left for another ten minutes or so. Everything is judged by eye and touch. No weighing, no clock-watching. In one house I visited the sieve was placed over a wood-burning stove; in another it was balanced on a Heath Robinson projection from a Calor gas heater. The dried and cooled saffron – which looks disconcertingly like roll-your-own shag – is packed into a leather pouch or an airtight plastic bag. It may be offered to a dealer or used as barter, sold soon or saved to pay for, say, a wedding. Meanwhile nature's alternative to krugerrands will probably be stashed under a mattress like any other currency.

Plucking parties are convivial affairs. Friends and neighbours call by to offer words of encouragement, to deliver titbits of gossip, to bring sweetmeats or to lend a hand for a few hours. By tradition only men and boys are paid in cash; women helpers receive a proportion of the saffron they have plucked.

Food is vital fuel to keep the workers going. Chickpea soup with chorizo, rabbit stew and baked pumpkin were offered in the houses I visited. Cakes and biscuits are appreciated for the quick energy boost they bring, particularly to those who may have gone to the fields without breakfast in the belief that it is easier to bend double on an empty stomach than a full one. No time to linger over meals, however, and no time for siestas. "No time even to scratch ourselves," one croker wagged. They work on till midnight, or later if need be, before falling into bed. Then back to the fields at crack of dawn to begin the picking, plucking and roasting cycle all over again. And so it goes on until florescence ends.

By tradition the spent flowers from the previous day are taken back to the fields next morning, "to water the fields" one person told me. "There is probably some old religious significance," suggested another. Mounds of them line the roadside, pale mauve milestones darkening to purple as the petals wither. The smell of them is sweet, fresh and pretty, at odds with the smell of the spice. It is narcissus-like and the honey fragrance intensifies with time. I brought home a handful. Now, ten months later, the petals are ghostly pale, but the scent of them seems richer and deeper than ever.

Saffron boasts a long history of use as a medicine, perfume and dye. One Sassanian king even used saffron dissolved in rose-water as ink. But above all else, saffron is important in cooking. Say saffron and most people think of paella, risotto Milanese, bouillabaisse and our own Cornish saffron cakes and buns. These last are all that remain of our earlier grand passion for colourful and fragrant food. Francis Bacon believed that saffron promoted vigour, and that its use in broths and sweetmeats was what made the English so sprightly – a good reason, surely, to reconsider some old saffron recipes and to explore new ones. Apples fried in saffron batter with a grinding of pepper for extra zip is a dish worth reviving. Fish- and saffron-scented *arroz abanda* is Spain's most exquisite rice dish. Tripe as cooked in Albi with bacon, garlic and saffron is marvellous; hare welcomes the same treatment. Consider also cooking small birds and pastries endored with saffron and egg yolk. Try pumpkin baked with saffron and cinnamon, Indian almond sweetmeats seasoned with saffron and fennel, saffron ice cream, and a compote of dried fruits in saffron syrup served with gilt gingerbread. Ideas like these appeal to me as much as the saffron-mashed potato and saffron-flavoured oils currently so chic in chef circles. But the greatest saffron discovery for me has been learning about classic Persian rice cookery. Whereas other cuisines employ the obvious trick of stirring saffron into a whole pot of rice, the Iranians mix it with only a very small portion of the rice. The egg-yolk yellow grains look stunning scattered over a mound of pure white rice and this combination makes seductive eating, each mouthful offering not a mishmash blend but two distinct aromas and tastes, the pleasure of one heightening the enjoyment of the other.

In comparative tastings I have found Iranian saffron threads to be shorter, more brittle, more forcefully odorous and darker in colour than Spanish – ox-blood red rather than fiery golden-red – perhaps due to higher roasting. Spanish saffron is classified as Mancha, Rio or Sierra, depending on whether the saffron has been plucked to include virtually none, a little or quite a bit of the style as well as the stigmas. The style (the yellow-white "stem" that links the stigmas to the ovary) is, so to speak, dead weight as it contains no picrocrocin, crocin or saffranal, the components that give the spice its distinctive flavour, colouring power and aroma. That is why Mancha costs the most and Sierra costs the least of the three grades.

A commodity as valuable as saffron is prone to adulteration by unscrupulous vendors. Caveat emptor. If you are offered saffron that seems "unbelievably cheap", it is probably no bargain. Pure saffron costs the same whether it is sold as powder or strands. But powder is easier to cheat, so I buy strands (packed loose in a small glass or plastic container, not in sachets which mean extra packaging costs) and I stick to reliable Spanish brands.

European Union inspection is now obligatory and in December 1993 the ISO (International Organization for Standardization) introduced regulations to control saffron quality – as was previously done for olive oil. To be classified as Mancha grade, saffron must possess a minimum of 70 picrocrocin, 190 crocin and 20 saffranal. The requirements for Rio are 55, 150 and 20, and for Sierra 40, 110 and 20 respectively. Standard grade saffron tests at 30, 80 and 20.

If you buy ready-prepared saffron rice and saffron cake, always check the ingredients label: some products contain more E-number colorants than they do saffron, notably anatto (E160B), the notorious azodyes tartrazine (E102) and sunset yellow (E110).

The amount of saffron needed for a dish is generally too tiny to measure precisely. One sachet or a pinch is the usual directive. How much is a pinch? If in doubt err on the mean side for, though a little saffron can work wonders, even a touch too much can be disagreeable in a bitter, medicinal sort of way.

Maria José Sevilla, on whom I rely for advice in all Spanish culinary matters, suggests when cooking rice that you allow the saffron of one bloom (ie one three-pronged stigma) per person plus one for the pot. Pound the threads well with mortar and pestle then infuse them in liquid, as though brewing tea. But first, if uncertain of the age of the spice, place the threads in a spoon over a flame for five seconds to drive off any moisture. I use a mini brass mortar dedicated to saffron. It looks a bit twee but its small size is important. No other instrument is more effective for pulverizing and thus for extracting maximum colour, flavour and aroma from this most precious spice, the cook's gold.

MOURTAIROL

Bouillabaisse is France's great contribution to saffron cookery so far as international fame is concerned but I confess I prefer the soothing comfort of this ultra-simple soup from the Tarn, where saffron was once grown when the city of Albi was a centre of the spice trade. A bowl of mourtairol looks as beautiful as it is good to eat. Followed by lots of fresh fruit it makes the sort of light supper I need to counterbalance blow-out meals at Christmas. The quality of stock is crucial here: only the best will do. Serves 4

2 pints pure rich chicken broth
a good pinch of saffron and ½ lb stale bread
2 tablespoons chopped parsley
a few small snippets of cooked chicken meat (optional)

Pound the saffron and soak it in a little of the hot stock. Break the bread into chunks and put them into a warmed soup tureen, scattering the scraps of chicken meat (if used) among them. Bring the rest of the stock to the boil. Stir in the parsley and pour it into the tureen. Cover and leave in a low oven for 5 minutes or so before serving so the crumb softens and swells with the fragrant liquid.
FROM *COUNTRY LIVING* (JANUARY 1995)

COOKING WITH FLOWERS

NATHALIE HAMBRO

At first thought this might sound precious or unpractical, but it is only a question of using the imagination. Edible flowers are readily available and very easy to use.

PURPLE OMELETTE

In spring, gather a few of the purplish-blue flowers of the chive plant. They taste delicately of onion. The contrast between the colour of the flowers and the colour of the eggs makes for a very bold effect.

5 eggs
2 tablespoons soda water
½ teaspoon sea salt
a dash of cayenne pepper
2 tablespoons chopped parsley
1 handful of chive flowers

Separate the spiky petals of the flowers and reserve. Prepare the omelette in the usual way, using all the other ingredients. (The soda water makes the omelette lighter.) At the last minute, scatter the petals over the pan. Fold the omelette, and transfer to a warmed serving dish.

NASTURTIUM AND AVOCADO SALAD

This is a salad of contrasts: first the green and vermilion colouring, secondly the bland and piquant taste, and lastly the smooth and crunchy textures. Nasturtium leaves have a tartness similar to those of the Good King Henry plant, a few of which can be added to the salad.

2-3 ripe but firm avocado pears
5 nasturtium flowers
a few nasturtium leaves (optional)
3 tablespoons emulsified vinaigrette
sprinkling of cayenne pepper

Prepare this salad at the last minute, as the peeled avocados will discolour quickly. In any case, cover and refrigerate until serving.

Cut the avocado pears in half lengthways, then peel and stone them. Cut in long slices. On a round serving dish of contrasting colour, spread the slices in a circle, like the petals of a flower. Spoon over the dressing. Arrange the nasturtium flowers on the top. If you are using them, chop the leaves in thin strands and sprinkle over. Dust with cayenne pepper.

MARIGOLD AND CAULIFLOWER

Shakespeare's "winking mary-buds" are marigolds (*Calendula officinalis*) which are found in many gardens. The taste has a slight aromatic bitterness.

Marigold petals were used as a herb long ago and the marigold's dense colour gave many dishes their golden hue. In fresh and dried form it appeared in puddings, cakes and salads. Nowadays it is used mainly as a natural colorant for butter and cheese. For the winter, you can get dried flowers from a herbalist. Their orange petals will enliven a green salad or brighten an egg dish.

1 medium-sized cauliflower [or equivalent quantity of broccoli]
1 tablespoon dried marigold petals, crushed
2oz (60g) butter
2 sprigs fresh parsley, coarsely chopped
a few fresh marigold petals
salt and pepper

Cut a cross in the bottom of the cauliflower stalks to ensure that it cooks evenly. Lower it into a saucepan filled with salted, boiling water. Add the crushed dried marigold petals and cook for 10-12 minutes. The cauliflower should be tender and still crisp, and lightly coloured by the petals. Drain and put into a hot dish. Smear with fresh butter and season. Scatter here and there the chopped parsley and the fresh petals.

FROM *PARTICULAR DELIGHTS* (1981)

SCARLET FRUITS AND BERRIES

NIGEL SLATER

Raspberries, mulberries, loganberries, redcurrants, blackcurrants and strawberries form the backbone of fast summer fruit puddings. Nothing good will come of fancy recipes for these glorious fruits. Raspberries with blackberries and soft white Petit Suisse cheese, blackberries crushed and folded into double cream with toasted hazelnuts, or a hot crumble made with blackcurrants and mint is sophisticated enough.

I try not to add anything to these fruits that will interfere with their fragrance. I see little point in adding *framboise*, the raspberry liqueur, to the fresh fruit, though blackcurrants are assertive enough to benefit from a touch of cassis. A sharp cream such as *crème fraîche* or *fromage blanc* is a favourite accompaniment, though even better, I think, is a half-and-half mixture of thick natural yoghurt and softly-whipped cream. The cream should barely hold its shape and the yoghurt must be a thick Greek one, perhaps a strained sheep variety. Sweet wines, especially the muscats and Sauternes, and a few peppery herbs such as basil and mint are other natural partners for red fruits.

With figs, muscat grapes and peaches, I think of the raspberry as among the finest fruits we have. I often eat a handful balanced on fresh white bread spread with soft fresh cream cheese such as Ricotta or Mascarpone. At their most heady and luscious, raspberries need no sugar or cream, just a white bowl and a spoon.

Strawberries need more help than the softer berries. Deeply-flavoured berries are a rare find nowadays. A squeeze of lemon juice or a splash of rose water will lift a slightly dull berry though there is little that will improve an out-of-season berry if it is really not ripe. The fact strawberries can be eaten with cucumber in a salad is hardly news, but have you ever thought of giving them a richer flavour with a sprinkling of precious balsamic vinegar or sharpening their edge with the juice and seeds of a passion fruit?

On a sunny day there can be few better ways of eating these deeply-perfumed rich scarlet and purple fruits than setting them out on the table under the shade, in their punnets, with a bowl of *crème fraîche* and a glass of muscat wine for those who wish for it.

CHERRIES

I am sure that cherries, yellow- and red-tinged, are at their best eaten straight from the greengrocer's brown paper bag. I remain unconvinced that their flavour is better for the application of heat. Crumbles are better made with plums, pies with apples and blackberries, and tarts are surely the vehicles for soft scarlet fruits. The stones, which take up most of the cherry, drive me quite mad.

I find the next best way to eat this fruit is: stone a handful of slightly sour cherries per person. Put half of the fruit in the bottom of a large wineglass. Two-thirds fill the glass with a soft fresh cheese such as a French *fromage frais*, then pile on the remaining fruit. Toast a few flaked or shredded almonds until they smell nutty and turn light brown in colour, and sprinkle them over the top.

FROM *REAL FAST FOOD* (1992)

A LESSON IN EATING PEARS

JANE GRIGSON

At Trôo, we had a good friend who helped with the hard labour of the house. One autumn day at lunch we were eating some beautiful pears, when suddenly he laughed, and went on laughing until his eyes were rimmed with tears. "*Une de ses poires*," he would say, then begin laughing again. At last he quietened down and told us the tale. His father, Lucien, had been coachman to a wealthy *curé* in the small market town where we had seen the bright red pears. The *curé* was very fond of Lucien, and they often had their meals together in the presbytery.

One such time the lunch included two fine pears which Lucien had brought in, by way of the stables, from the *curé's* garden. The *curé* took one of the two pears from the fruit stand and bit into it with great enjoyment, without peeling it. When he had finished, Lucien took the other pear and started to peel it with some attention. The *curé* suddenly realized what he was doing.

"*O, Lucien, qu'est-ce que tu fais là? Pour déguster un bon fruit, il faut manger avec le peau.*"

"*Mais oui, M. le Curé, je le sais bien, mais il y a une de ces poires qui a tombée dans la merde, et je ne sais plus laquelle.*"

Of course, the *curé* was right – you should eat a pear, skin, core and all. But wash it first, thoroughly.

FROM *JANE GRIGSON'S FRUIT BOOK* (1982)

SAVOY FARE

JOHN TOVEY

Maybe I was lucky, but my childhood memories of cabbage were entirely favourable: they focused on my Nan's bubble and squeak (cabbage and mashed potatoes), which was invariably served on Mondays for the hectic washday dinner, cooked in the dripping from the Sunday lunch and moistened with the melted jelly from the juices. Perhaps luckier still, I spent my early working life abroad, in a country where cabbage simply did not feature in the diet.

So tales of the smell of over-boiled cabbage and the horrors of washed-out helpings were just hearsay. That is, until I returned to Britain and found myself in a succession of theatrical digs. These institutions had a unique way with cabbage (which I will not go into) and compounded it whenever we were late, which was frequently, by plating it over pans of simmering water to keep warm and therefore dry up.

It was only when, as a poverty-stricken stage manager, I moved away from the digs and into a flat that cabbage rehabilitated itself. Minced meat and vegetable leftovers, I discovered, made super supper dishes when wrapped in blanched cabbage leaves to form a kind of rissole. I would brown these in equal parts of olive oil and butter, then reheat them when I needed to.

But the true versatility of this vegetable, in all its forms, only dawned on me fully when I opened my own hotel in the beginning of the Seventies. One of the first recipes I did there was to pan-fry savoy cabbage in oil, garlic and juniper – a beautiful combination that remained a firm favourite. Nowadays, I prefer to deep-fry it and use it in a recipe with sesame seeds and buttered eggs – it's delicious.

Thinly sliced green cabbage also stir-fries well and, served with slices of various smoked meats and fresh fruit (I love banana, peach and pineapple), makes a lovely simple supper dish. A warmed French dressing of your own making turns it into a feast!

Coarsely grated white cabbage, on the other hand, goes brilliantly in salads. It may not be authentic, but add some to the celery and apple in a Waldorf salad and see what a difference it makes. If you want to go right over the top, you can spice it up further with the addition of halved, pipped grapes, a few sultanas, some grated carrot, diced preserved ginger, sliced strawberries, honey-roasted peanuts and croutons. Serve it with a dollop of *crème fraîche* to which you have added grated lemon or orange rind, whichever you like.

Red cabbage is the only type that can be baked. To do this, slice it thinly and cook in a lightly oiled or buttered casserole in a low oven for 2-3 hours, depending on the texture you like. Many recipes add sliced apples, oranges, wine and spices. Recently, I did it with sliced "tough as Tarzan" pears along with redcurrant jelly, and actually added a ham knuckle to the casserole during the cooking time. Stunning.

There's no end to what you can do with cabbage – it saved one of my recent dinner parties from disaster. An extra, unexpected guest suddenly turned up – the two people with whom she was staying each thought the other had phoned to see if they could bring her along. No problem. It just meant rearranging the table and giving everyone a smaller portion of the quiche starter. My calmness was premature, however, because as I was passing round the hot mini sausage rolls with drinks, she declined, saying she was both vegetarian and on a gluten-free diet!

That evening, I proved the old adage that necessity is indeed the mother of invention. I ran over to my neighbour's allotment and cut a firm white cabbage. Back in the kitchen, I turned it on its side and cut out a one-inch-thick circle, which I painted with hazelnut oil and baked in the oven. It emerged looking like a pizza and I finished it off with melted Roquefort cheese. It has now become part of my repertoire.

My only partial failure with cabbage has been in the garden. I recall seeing literally acres of the vegetable when I was working in Japan: not in agricultural plots but as decorative garden pieces on numerous traffic islands and endless pedestrian crossing approaches. They were obviously hardy enough to stand up to the great volume of carbon monoxide, but I doubt if any were ever picked, cooked and eaten. When I returned home I decided to have a similar centrepiece in the garden. It never compared to the ones I had seen in Japan, but it survived – until it attracted the attention of the neighbouring rabbits. At around 1 a.m., Ozzie, my blind Old English sheepdog, would hear the syncopated crunching from outside and break into a volley of barking that shut them up, but only until they realized that the dog never gave chase. Oh well, I like to see God's creatures enjoying their food.

FROM *SAINSBURY'S **THE MAGAZINE*** (OCTOBER 1994)

PARSLEY

SIMON HOPKINSON (WITH LINDSEY BAREHAM)

I shall never forget a children's story I was told when I was little:
Once upon a time there was a dear old lady who lived in a chocolate box cottage at the end of a leafy lane. Her garden was a riot of beautiful flowers and shrubs, which she tended and cosseted with love and care from dawn till dusk.

At the end of each day, after her chores, she would trip down to the bottom of the garden for a natter with the fairies and pixies who, quite naturally, lived there. They loved the old lady and all the flowers that she grew in her garden, for it was their playground.

Time passed and, as is the way of things, the old lady died and some horrid city folk moved in to her lovely cottage. They didn't want flowers in their garden, they wanted to fill it full of vegetables. So, out came the nasturtiums, the lupins, cornflowers and roses. No more hollyhocks, lavender, Canterbury bells (the fairies use them for hats, you know), or forget-me-nots. In their place went cabbages, carrots and sprouts, swedes, potatoes and horrible old turnips, together with row upon row of parsley. And this particular parsley grew and grew in huge bunches all over the place.

Well, as you can imagine, the fairies and pixies were none too pleased about this, so they decided one night to cause a little mischief. There was a full moon and plenty of light and one by one they scampered up and down the rows of parsley, pinching it as they went with their spindly little fingers, over and over and over again, until they could pinch no more.

And that, dear reader, is how we come to have curly parsley. The flat-leaf variety of parsley is infinitely finer and has much more flavour than the "pinched" stuff. The problem is, though, that few people realize just how much of it is needed. For example, white sauce with a few flecks of green floating in it is not parsley sauce. For a small panful, I would use a whole bunch. A wonderful soup can be made from it, requiring many more bunches, and is one of the nicest soups I know. Parsley stuffings are delicious, too. For instance, little forcemeat balls, dense with parsley and chopped lemon rind, are a wonderful partner to braised rabbit or a jugged hare.

I've even used parsley as a vegetable. Gently stewed in a little butter for a few moments with a sliver or two of garlic, it is very good with grilled chicken. For this, however, you do have to use the curly variety as, irritatingly, the flat type sticks to the sides of the pan and doesn't absorb the butter well. You need the curly type of parsley if you want to deep-fry it, too. I adore deep-fried parsley. It is simplicity itself to prepare. Just drop some well-dried sprigs into hot fat for a few seconds. (One of those electric deep-fryers with a basket is ideal.) Lift the parsley out, drain it on absorbent kitchen paper, and sprinkle with salt. It's a shame you don't see it used as much as you used to, accompanying old favourites such as fresh whitebait and goujons of sole. Surely dull dishes without their hive of deep-fried parsley?

FROM *ROAST CHICKEN AND OTHER STORIES* (1994)

THE SAD PLIGHT OF A LITTLE NUTCASE

COLIN SPENCER

Have you come across a stressed peanut lately? If the answer is no, it may be because you have not yet developed a peanut flavour consciousness, or been really exposed to a peanut experience. Once you have, there is little doubt that you would recognize that stressed peanut. It suffers from an "off" flavour like "burnt plastic food", which comes from the peanut oil which has oxidized and gone rank.

My peanut consciousness was raised, widened, astonished and even somewhat alarmed at a Peanut Flavour Quality Seminar given by Gail Vance Civille, consultant in the field of sensory evaluation of foods, beverages, pharmaceuticals, paper, fabrics, personal care and . . . take a breath . . . other consumer products.

All this psychology of the inanimate derives from a panel of flavour and peanut specialists who have established a lexicon of flavours, backed by the US Department of Agriculture, no less. Basically, this concordance of unexpected adjectives to describe the characteristics of a nut is to boost the profits of the US Peanut Council, which is doing very nicely already.

But in England, the land of the class system, they are up against a view like that of Peter Fort of the *Financial Times*. "The trouble is", he confided to me, "my mother taught me that peanuts were common. Can't even take that butter. Don't like it."

The US Council forget to label some peanuts as upper class and others as vulgar, though I daresay Mrs Fort would have considered a stressed peanut pretty common. What she would have made of a painty, or a fishy, or a cardboard peanut, is anybody's guess. As for the fruity fermented peanut . . . well, a number of my closest friends could be described as fruity fermented.

But I am here to tell you about the normal peanut, a fresh-faced yuppy peanut, with spring in his step. The normal peanut has "on" flavours, it smells roasted peanutty, raw beany, dark roast, sweet aromatic, and it tastes sweet, salty, sour and bitter; it has a woody hull and skin. This normal peanut is the US Control Peanut.

As in wine tasting, peanut samples are rolled over the palate, swilled around the mouth, and inhaled. Now how you can do that with a gunge beats me; this is the way to lose a filling or displace a denture. As it is, the thick, viscous purée gets lodged into dental crevices like Polyfilla which, to my untutored palate, somewhat blurs the difference between green burnt nutty and sour sweet roasty.

Even what the average consumer calls yum and yuck could be confused when the teeth are coated with a clammy, tacky, gooey, colloidal emulsion that could taste leathery, putrid, mawkish, acerbic, coarse and corked.

All peanuts that do not meet the complex demands of US Control are inferior peanuts. They may even be "off" flavour peanuts: chemical, phenolic, plastic flavours with a metallic feeling factor. This peanut is our old friend, the stressed peanut.

Alas, unlike Ms Vance Civille who must have a distinguished palate and throat, I am not sure I feel aromatic volatiles at the back of the throat being transmitted to the olfactory nerve in the nasal cavity. These could be fruity, dairy, herbal, spicy, vegetative, animal, nutty, roasted, raw, burnt and chemical. And each of these categories can be split into many others.

"But how does a stressed peanut become stressed?" I asked, having an instinctive feeling for the underdog. With immense seriousness, Ms Vance Civille informed me that the plant physiology could be damaged by seasonal malevolence, by gross handling, by insensitive processing and inadequate storage.

Exactly. The environmental influences were not up to standard, so this is a deprived and maladjusted peanut we have here. Sadly, there was none to taste, but there were little jars of peanut butter. I noticed Peter Fort was unable to sample his.

FROM *THE GUARDIAN* (26 NOVEMBER 1988)

40

THE FIRST OF THOSE BLUES

NIKI HILL

There's a time in the year, not St Patrick's Day or the Twelfth of July, when every Ulsterman gets that special feeling. It arrives unheralded, totally taken for granted, and not even the media take note.

It is the day of the first Co Down Blues.

The first sight after weeks of last season's potatoes invariably tired, mashed, and sadly roasted, the soapy Cypriot imports, can take the breath away. Steaming proverbial balls of flour waiting for generous butter and sprinkling of salt, a flavour to titillate any man's tastebuds. Maybe that old familiar feeling is just another reawakening of something old and tribal, something emotional that goes right back to our forebears, to that first time when the potato found its home in our moist black soil.

It hearkens back to thatched cottages, pigs in the parlour, a big black three-legged pot on a hook over the open fire filled full and steaming, aromatic. Even that pot gave our language today that expression "taking pot luck".

What more could you want than a big pot of spuds enriched in any number of ways. Mashed with dark green curly kale for colcannon, with buttermilk and scallions and egg for champ. Or filled with potato soup or Brothchan Foltchep – a rich oaty leek soup.

Put the griddle on and these potatoes can be transformed into boxty with lots of butter, pratie oaten and some potato bread with crisp bacon.

It was Mrs D. who first really introduced me to potato soup.

She had come to the depths of Armagh as an evacuee during the war and far from Belfast, from the narrow streets of redbrick houses each with aspidistra in the windows and china dogs on the mantelshelf, the paintings on the gable walls, and the little corner shops.

And on the days when we could dissuade her from making beds or washing dishes, she would sit and tell us tales of her childhood in Belfast in the hungry Thirties when the great slipways that had built liners like the *Titanic* lay moss-grown and unused, and men and women wondered indeed where the next meal would come from.

It's in days like these when jobs are few and money is short that the potato comes into its own again. Like some old friend it is always there to provide a big nourishing dish that fills the belly and satisfies for a long time. Small wonder when the potatoes rotted away in those years in the last century that famine was the result.

There were nine children in Mrs D.'s family, nine mouths to feed. And when things got really bad Mrs D. and all her brothers and sisters had a small manoeuvre which they made so that there would be something in the pot for tea that night.

There was a shop on the corner, and with all little shops like that which are really a kitchen house converted, the potatoes, carrots, bags of coal, all sit outside in the street, for inside is packed with tins and jars and packets from floor to ceiling.

On the way past the shop, each of the nine children would sneak a potato from the sack outside. Mrs D. always insisted that the shopkeeper knew rightly what they did, for he knew just how short of money the family was, and he never said anything on those days. The family would eat well that night.

Our humble potato has that special magic that only the simplest foods have. No matter what you do with it you can guarantee the dish will be really tasty, and it will not cost too much either.

FROM *THE BELFAST TELEGRAPH* (1973)

DINING OUT

MAKIN' WHOOPEE IN INFLATIONARY TIMES

HUMPHREY LYTTELTON

If, by some curious aberration of fate, I ever find myself in front of a giggling audience being asked by Wilfred Pickles to recall an embarrassing experience, you will not see me tongue-tied. At least two episodes will be right there jostling for precedence.

The first is of little relevance to this column, being an occasion at school when, getting dressed on a Sunday morning, I mislaid my underpants. Being late for chapel I grabbed another pair from the drawer, finished dressing and dashed out as the bell stopped ringing. As a member of the Sixth Form, I had to slow march down the aisle in a traditional procession, watched by five hundred pairs of eyes eager for disaster. It was about halfway down the aisle that the errant underpants made their presence felt, sliding down one trouser leg where they had been lurking all the time. With protocol demanding that my arms should stay rigidly by my sides, there was nothing I could do, and seconds later the entire upper school saw what must have looked for a moment like ectoplasm emerge from my trouser leg and trail along behind me for the rest of my miserable journey.

The other occasion does hold a relevant moral, since it concerns a Spanish restaurant in Paris which my wife and I visited with some friends in 1955. She was expecting our firstborn at the time and was at the queasy stage when quite unexpected things could arouse nausea. The restaurant was on top of a high block of flats and the lift wasn't working, so we trudged panting up flight after flight of stairs until we eventually reached a room garishly designed in a *fiesta* motif and blindingly lit as if by arc-lights. We were the only customers in the place, and we received an effusive welcome from the *patronne* who gave patient assistance while we ordered rather laboriously from enormous hand-written menu cards. Spanish food is not perhaps ideal for someone with a temporary aversion to oil, not to mention a strong pre-natal craving for mint sauce. However, we eventually chose a meal which she could anticipate with equanimity, and settled down to await it. The disaster struck from an unexpected quarter. A Spanish guitarist who had been lurking unseen behind some foliage stepped forward, making threatening tuning-up noises that gave notice that he was about to serenade us. In the event he got no further than two or three thrumming chords before my wife turned green, rose unsteadily with some muttered words about "fresh air" and headed for the door. The rest of us could do nothing but follow, leaving the thwarted minstrel to wonder, perhaps to this day, what it was about his performance that emptied the whole place with such alacrity. The moral here is that music in restaurants is not always the life-enhancing boon that proprietors imagine it to be. Take taped music for example. Tinkling melodies from yesteryear may be all right as a backcloth to the clatter of cutlery and babble of conversation. But was ever a sound more desolate than mechanical music in an empty restaurant?

One Saturday evening about six weeks ago my wife and I dined alone – and I mean alone – at a new restaurant called Le Cochon Noir (26 Motcomb Street, SW1). From a certain amount of publicity in the daily gossip columns, we expected it to be jolly, if not erring on the hearty side. Instead there were the hushed voices of the small staff, some rather disconcerting gastric gurglings from the oxygen plant of an aquarium set into the wall, and the music going round and round, coming back with a dreadful mechanical tactlessness to "Makin' Whoopee" every twenty minutes or so. It may be, of course, that the music was inherited from a restaurant called Davide which, unknown to me, previously inhabited the premises. Whatever the circumstances, it is a mistake, intrusive when the place is empty, redundant when it is full and at all times imparting a square, provincial tone. Without it, Le Cochon Noir looks promising enough with light wood-panelling, mustard-coloured seating, red tablecloths and a touch of originality in the framed cartoons by Emmwood of the *Daily Mail*, if you like mild political comment with your food. According to the publicity, the chef once worked for Edward Heath. I don't know if this applies to the French chef who started there or the Spanish chef who succeeded him, but certainly the amount of salt in the sauces suggested an employer of maritime propensities. The hand-out promised Finest French Cuisine but we didn't find that. Escargots, vichyssoise, the braised pork chump chop in wine sauce which is the house speciality – all were nice enough but betrayed a heavy hand with the seasoning which is anything but finest French, and the *crêpe Mandarin* with Grand Marnier would have failed a breath-test on its own account. The wine list, on the other hand, seems well-chosen and the half-bottles of Sancerre and St Émilion (Château Haut Lavallarde '61, a name not known to me) were very good and well-served.

Le Cochon Noir is owned by Baron Van Baerle, sometime Devon farmer and fashion wig-maker – a name and a description which suggest a certain personality and character which has not yet been imparted to the restaurant. But it is new, and restaurants, like governments, deserve a honeymoon period. I see hope in every aspect of Le Cochon Noir except that ghastly music. Our bill for two, including service, was £7 17s 9d, which one must accept as pretty average these days. I preferred Le Cochon Noir to La Loggia (68 Edgware Road, W2), to which I went the night before with all five members of my family. This is of course quite unfair, because La Loggia is more briskly professional, more strikingly decorated, and provides, within its own terms of reference, better food. It is run by Biagi whose name is bestowed upon the restaurant next door. But while Biagi's is almost a caricature of an Italian restaurant with lobster-pots galore, La Loggia is rather more posh. It's a quite expensive Italian restaurant decorated in Florentine style with walls striped with broad wooden strips, a buff-coloured tile floor and sundry arches and colonnades. I treated myself to a *filet steak alla Loggia*, which turned out to involve a sauce rich in Marsala. There were good reports from the others on the chicken *sorpresa* with a more elaborate and interesting filling than usual.

Why, then, did I not love La Loggia? Well, for one thing, I am always strongly put off by service which wanes in attentiveness and solicitude as the meal progresses. The intervals between courses grew longer as the evening wore on, and I ended up practically pleading for the bill. I am irritated, too, by the foolishness of putting a bottle of white wine in an ice-bucket when, up to that point, it has apparently been stored in an airing cupboard. And I have a deep suspicion of financial booby-traps – for instance, a half-melon unpriced on the menu and out-of-season raspberries, again unpriced, on the sparse sweet-trolley – which between them contrived to pump up quite ordinary antipasto and sweet courses to well over £2 each. All in all, a bill of £12 17s for five, less service and including one spaghetti bolognese as a main course, was on the high side.

Galloping inflation seems to be having its effect on the restaurant scene, as elsewhere, and the food scout must be careful not to go on judging prices by the standard of a year or even six months ago. Looking back over my files I see that one could then eat in quite distinguished style around London for between £5 and £6 for two. The kind of place I have in mind is like Marcel at 14 Sloane Street, SW1 – smallish, French-run, with the dishes of the day displayed on a blackboard in addition to an à la carte menu. The cooking is simple but subtle – my *fricandeau de veau* with fresh spinach and a salad satisfied without crippling me for the afternoon. Was it all worth a bill for two of £8 10s? By today's inflationary standards, I suppose the answer is "yes". But eating out will lose a lot of its pleasure if one's only dining companions are exporters with heavy expense accounts.

FROM *HARPERS & QUEEN* (NOVEMBER 1970)

THERE'S A CONRAN IN MY SOUP

CRAIG BROWN

The Conrans – Terence Conran and Shirley Conran (and wasn't there a Caroline Conran at one stage?) and Jasper Conran and the other Conran who does something like design furniture and all the various other Conrans here and there – are so omnipresent in British life that I sometimes feel that if I investigate my birth certificate more closely it will emerge that I, too, am a Conran. We are all Conrans now. It seems to me a bit too close to *The Night of the Living Dead*, in which perfectly normal-looking people turn out to be inhabited by alien beings, though now it would have to be re-named *The Night of the Living Designer*, with ordinary men and women suddenly spouting enthusiasm for the design of this toaster or that step-ladder before gradually revealing themselves as sisters or cousins or aunts of The Conran.

Design this, Design that: at one stage in the Eighties you couldn't get away from Design. Picking up a pencil, it was *de rigeur* to coo over its contours, its bold colour, the cleverness with which the lead was surrounded by wood, the brilliance with which it was sharp at one end and blunt at the other, and so on. By the end of the decade, everyone was rattling on about it. Mrs Thatcher gave speeches about it, Prince Charles gave awards for it, and newspapers printed special supplements in celebration of it. Earlier in the decade, I had felt rather fashionable to be a journalist, but towards the end I was thinking seriously of changing my job description to Verbals Designer so that I, too, might enjoy a place in the sun.

Oddly enough, with the advent of 1990, the conversation switched, and nobody seemed to be bothered about Design any more. It seems appropriate that by this time a Design Museum should have been built, just as there will soon be an SDP museum too.

The Design Museum [Butlers Wharf, SE1] opened a year or so ago in a blaze, or at least a camp fire, of publicity, with pictures galore of Sir Terence, but I had heard no more about it until the other day, when someone suggested that we all set off to have lunch there, at the Blueprint Café. As prospects go, it sounded like utter misery. Something about that name and those surroundings suggested self-service, raw carrots, mineral water, uncomfortable steel chairs, ostentatiously bald men in zip-up jackets and modern jazz. I tried to argue against it, but was overruled.

The Design Museum is not far from Tower Bridge, on the south of the river, bang on the waterside. To enter the museum itself you have to pay an entrance fee, but if you don't pay an entrance fee you are let off going round the museum and you can head straight upstairs to the Blueprint Café without further ado.

My first emotion was relief that it was quite obviously upmarket and non-puritanical. Every table seemed to carry a bottle of wine and there wasn't a raw carrot or a self-service tray in sight. There were babies everywhere – so many, in fact, that at first I thought they might be on the pudding menu. Generally, a restaurant which has employed top designers is instantly recognizable for two reasons. First, it is impossible to sit down comfortably. Second, the menu will contain nothing like a proper meal. Happily, the Blueprint Café (why this new insistence that expensive restaurants are in fact cafés?) breaks this rule. From top to toe it is riddled with Design, but somehow in the end it's none the worse for it.

Design features include red formica table-tops with black rubber mats, white plastic beams with circular glass shelves containing jars of what look like pickled aubergines in mauve water, white walls and ceilings, deep blue wall seats, and – gasp – blue bottles of mineral water which have, of course, won Design Awards.

There are just two Design features of the Blueprint Café that I could have done without. The first is a rather gloomy selection of chiaroscuro photo-portraits of short-haired men with funny glasses and mad eyes, all of them presumably Top Designers. The second is a porthole in the wall which looks through to someone doing the washing-up. Perhaps this is an egalitarian gesture. If so, it is misplaced, for a restaurant is the least egalitarian place in the world, and to have the poor washer-up staring out at people stuffing their faces, and vice versa, can only induce revolution on the one side and embarrassment on the other, and just about every variety of emotion in between.

Who designed the Thames? I trust he has won a few awards for it, as it is one of the most effective Design features of the Blueprint Café. Like its close counterpart, the River Café in Hammersmith, the Blueprint Café is right on the river but, unlike the River Café, the Blueprint Café has a view of the river unimpeded by a concrete wall. On a sunny day, it is possible to eat on a terrace with a clear view of Tower Bridge. Even on a damp day, our lunch was greatly cheered by our view of a race of longboats struggling past. There is nothing like the sight of other people needlessly exerting themselves to make one feel cosy. When a team of sea scouts overturned headlong into the river, we felt the least we could do was to smile.

The food at the Blueprint Café is quite outstandingly good. In a moment of aberration, I ordered a plateful of aubergines, courgettes, dried tomatoes and so on (£4.25). Normally, I would run a mile from such ostentatiously healthy stuff, but these were quite delicious, rich, fresh and juicy. Other winners included a warm salad with a good runny poached egg (£5) which didn't taste of vinegar; fine smoked salmon with marscapone (£5.25), and shitake mushrooms with garlic (£4.75) which, said their consumer, did need a little salt, "but then everything does these days".

Nor did the main courses let us down. Liver and spinach – what better dish for a Saturday lunchtime? – was a complete success (£9.25). "Really, really lovely – had I not been with you I'd have licked the plate," was the verdict. Spinach kept cropping up elsewhere, too: my perfect salmon was served on a bed of spinach (£8), and someone else had spinach with squashed and charred chicken (£8.25) ("herby and very tender and with a fashionably small portion of potatoes"). Only the lamb stew (£8) was spinachless, but this did not seem to affect the purrs of pleasure it produced.

By this stage, helped by a crisp New Zealand white wine, we all felt in our element, so much so that we even toyed with going around the Design exhibition afterwards. Coincidentally, just as we were mooching over the pudding menu, one of our number caught sight of what she was pretty sure was a Conran. "It's . . . erm . . . could it be Sebastian? You know, the one married to John Boorman's daughter." All this was news to me. Presumably there is a Conran married to Arthur Scargill's daughter, and another married to Reg Varney's son: life is too short to keep up with the Conrans, but quite obviously every home should have one.

Back to the food. Having had aubergines and then salmon, I ruined my health kick by going for a wide, low, crisp, creamy and horribly plentiful crème brûlee (£3.25). The others had first class tarte tatin (£3.50), nicely burnt on the top, a slightly bland chocolate mousse cake (£3.50) and a runny tiramisu (£3.50). All this was served by efficient waitresses in white shirts with thin black stripes. They are overseen by a maître d' of quite spectacular trendiness who is, I suspect, going to be entered for a major design award before going on permanent display in the Tate.

I hope I haven't made The Blueprint Café sound too prissy: we were able to lounge around perfectly scruffily without being made to feel awkward, and the food tastes every bit as good as it looks. For anyone who lives or works nearby, it's a godsend, and everybody else should have a high old time too, Design permitting.
FROM *THE SUNDAY TIMES* (13 OCTOBER 1991)

DOING THE BISTRO BUSTLE

JOHN McKENNA

Eight-thirty on a Friday morning and Colin O'Daly, in crisp clean chef's whites, is already about his business in Roly's Bistro. "Sleep is like rat poison," he says. "After a while you get immune to it."

Mr O'Daly is taking to this poison rather well. Any possible bitterness from lack of sleep seems leavened by the fact that the success of Roly's Bistro, in the two years since it opened, must be sweet as honey from the hive.

That success has been built on a fundamentally simple principle. It must be possible, reckoned Roly Saul, John O'Sullivan and John Mulcahy, the three partners behind the Bistro, to combine volume, value and good food. Put them together and you hit the ground running, and then build up speed.

During the course of a day observing the entire operation of Roly's Bistro, I was struck by the fact that what Mr O'Daly calls the octopus – "it has arms all over the place" – operates efficiently because of the interplay of the principal characters – executive chef Colin O'Daly and partners Roly Saul and John O'Sullivan – with the secondary characters – John Kenny the hatch man and John Coleman the floor manager upstairs, Gerry Butler and James Mulcrone in the basement kitchen; head chef Jean Michel Poulot; Joyce Flood and the rest of the squad who work the floor.

"We're like John Rocha a bit," said Mr O'Daly. "You go from a corner shop to a department store, but you keep the service and the quality of a corner shop, and you keep your own style."

By the time Roly Saul arrives, followed shortly afterwards by John O'Sullivan, the basic preparations of the day are in full, quiet swing. The prawns – for the day's special, Fricassee of Dublin Bay Prawns with Vanilla Sauce – are being shelled, one by one. Cranberries are being sunk into the game pies and the pastry helmets neatly ringed around their tops. Vast volumes of broccoli are being par-cooked.

The lunch menu is a clever arrangement of achievable cooking. There are five starters, two of which are soups. The half-dozen main courses are Roast Leg of Lamb, Game Pies, Chicken Niçoise, Salmon Trout with a Fennel and Saffron Sauce, a Smoked Fish-Cake and a Crêpe stuffed with Spinach, Oyster Mushrooms, Swiss Cheese and Sesame Seeds as the vegetarian choice.

This balance between dishes shows the influence of partner John O'Sullivan. Mr O'Sullivan, whose previous restaurants include Rafters in Rathmines and the original Blakes in Stillorgan, is a real figures-man. Shortly after his arrival, his wife Angela brings in the print-outs for the previous day: every cutlet and caramel can be accounted for, the consumption of every bottle of Sancerre and glass of Smithwicks is revealed.

To Mr O'Sullivan, the matter is simple: you give people what they want. If there is something they don't want, they won't order it. Everything is standing up well, however, which creates a problem for the planned menu-change in a week or so. If everything is shifting, then what do you replace? They will sort it out at the weekly management meeting on Tuesday.

By mid-morning, the phone has commenced its mantric persistence. "Hello, Roly's; may-I-help-you?" and then the book is lifted and consulted, the names and numbers taken, the floor plans opened and the names committed. It is here, perhaps, that we see one of the most remarkable features of Roly's: Mr Saul's Seating Situations.

Roly Saul is a peerless people-handler. He is a restaurant critic's nightmare, for he cannot forget a face and one's chances of sliding in here anonymously are almost zilch. He combines efficiency with the correct degree of professional nonchalance and command. "Mr Cassidy, sir, are you well?" "Good afternoon, welcome." "Would you like to come with me?" Whether those pushing the swing doors are celebs or ordinary decent folk, Mr Saul's word of welcome is one of the vital ingredients of Roly's.

But just as vital is his ability to play "3-D chess". This mind-boggling concept is the name Mr Saul gives to the business of who sits where. If you have a super-keenly-priced lunch – and at £9.50 plus ten per cent service Roly's is a steal – then you need a large volume of customers at all times. Fall down on this bit and your kitchen staff will be becalmed, your floor staff bored, and you will be quickly bankrupt.

Mr Saul plays 3-D chess by knowing who is where at any and all of the many tables in Roly's at any given time of the day. If there is a cancellation or a no-show, then he must fill the table with folk who turn up with no reservation. If he knows that some customers will eat early and be gone, then he can sell the table twice in an evening. If he makes a mistake, then the consequences don't bear thinking about. If he gets everything right, then he keeps this extraordinary business ticking over at maximum speed.

By late morning, the wine delivery is being tucked away, the floor staff are arriving. In all, about fifty people are employed in Roly's, a business the size of a small factory. "It's like factory management here," says Mr O'Daly, hopping from floor to floor as the kitchens are assembled after their scrub-down, as the deliveries are checked in – "except we're all on the factory floor".

Mr O'Daly's ability to coin an aphorism is as sharp as his skills in the kitchen. In the success story of Roly's, his ability to evolve from highly-wrought, individualized cooking to barn-storming brasserie master-minding has been indispensable. I thought, when he got the job, that Roly's had got the wrong man. After many visits to the Bistro, I relish eating my words every bit as much as I relish eating his food.

What Mr O'Daly does, aside from cooking and consulting, is to direct and inspire his staff. In the cruel world of the professional restaurant, where chefs can so easily find their vision and ambition crushed, Mr O'Daly continues to be excited, continues to enjoy the whole business of cooking. His staff (fortunate for them) get this lesson for free.

In a standard Friday lunchtime, the restaurant will serve some 150 covers. People begin to come through the doors about 12.20 p.m. In the kitchens on both the ground and first floors, the roasted legs of lamb are wrapped in foil after they are taken out of the roasting pans. The great trays of potato gratin bubble like hot lava as they are lifted out. The yellow dockets with the orders scribbled on them begin to arrive and are posted above the hatches, where they flutter in the heat.

Even before the punters really begin to hit the seats, Colin O'Daly is bouncing up and down on his toes in the kitchen, eager for engagement. Downstairs, Jean Michel Poulot, by contrast, is cool, unfazed. Anyone who has ever worked in a kitchen knows this time well; the last breath of normal time before the assault is complete. There is the last chance to check things, the last chance for the plongeurs, with their ubiquitous pasty-complexions (I was one once – I had that complexion) to stack plates, check crockery, the last chance for the floor staff to see things are aligned correctly.

Then, suddenly, we are in the inferno. It is about 12.45 p.m. The noise is shocking, the language between the staff incomprehensible: "How many prawns?" "Four prawns. There's seven on it." The kitchen has been transformed into an ice-hockey game, the blur of movement, the astonishing violence of speed, the roar of energy. Except that, here, no one bumps into anyone else. The choreography of a good kitchen is a thing of beauty. Intuitive, understood, startlingly efficient, and everything is accomplished in double-quick time.

Outside, the contrast is sublime. A few yards from the ice-hockey game, we have an afternoon at Glyndebourne. This is the great secret, and the great truth, of restaurants. Without the maelstrom of the kitchen, with its pumping adrenalin and its hyperventilating staff, you cannot have the concordance of the dining room, with its relaxed customers and its ordered calmness. It's Friday afternoon, the October sunlight dithers through the blinds and, with work for the week almost done, you can smell the craving for this womb of greetings and G&Ts, feel the hunger for that first sip of cool white wine with a plate of stuffed mussels, in this singularly elegant dining room.

In the kitchen, nobody walks, everybody runs: Mark Ryan literally slides across the floor on his clogs. Joe the plongeur scrambles to the sink to clean up a new batch of pans. *The noise.* "Would you quit socializing over there?" "Very hot plate." "John, how's 22?" I realize, standing there as all this goes on, that my heartbeat has increased dramatically. "Joe, I need a pan, please." "I don't wanna hear you don't know. Get me some flat-leaf parsley." The staff slake their thirsts with pint-glasses of orange squash. The puddings and parfaits begin to go out, then coffees. "That's okay, Colin." "Are we over the hill?" "We're on the home stretch."

It has taken forty minutes. The ticker-tape of yellow dockets over the hatch has dwindled and migrated over to where James is doing desserts. At eight minutes past two there is only one docket left, but then a late party arrives: "Two pie, two fish, a prawns, and a lamb".

In the dining room, the plink and plash of celebrating glasses is dwarfed by chatter super-charged with wine. At 2.45 p.m., the dining room upstairs is still largely full. Many of the punters are women, in small groups, in large groups, more relaxed than the more serious tables of businessmen.

Mr O'Daly, having worried his way through lunch, changes out of his whites and has lunch with Mr O'Sullivan and Mr Saul.

By 7.30 p.m., the final lunch party has just left – *We'll go to Kitty O'Shea's! Ah no, I can't. Go on, come on, come on. Aah, one then* – and the staff have returned everything to pristine perfection. Everything which has been done at lunchtime will now be done all over again, except there will be another 250 people involved – 250 people for whom the staff must perform as if this was opening night.

During her break, Joyce has been to see Keanu Reeves in *Speed*. "Yeah, great," she says. "Great effects." "Keanu looks just like Colin," I say. "Chef's better looking," says Joyce.

Chef doesn't laugh. He has a single party of thirty-six French tourists to worry about. "Don't go 'til you're ready," he shouts to Mark and the others in the ground-floor kitchen. "I want bam, bam, bam. I'd rather wait five minutes and have it right." The thirty-six French are not the problem. It is the party of twenty-six due to settle into their seats twenty-five minutes after they leave that is causing anxiety.

The discipline of planning a combination like this is terrifying. The ideal is to get thirty-six main-courses out as close together as possible. To do this, what each diner has ordered is marked on the table plans, so the right waitress takes the right order to the right person and does not have to ask who ordered what.

"Right lads, we're going to go," shouts Mark Ryan, working the evening shift downstairs. Suddenly, the kitchen is a madhouse. "One more after this." "What's next Ronny?" "Three turbot, one beef." The heat level climbs, sweat breaks out on everybody's face. The turbot fillets are placed gently on their beds of spinach, then a sundried tomato and pistou vinaigrette is danced around the plate, dice of tomato scattered on. One after another, after another. The concern shown for the arrangement of food on each plate is amazing. There is a huddle as the veg is readied: colcannon, green beans, carrot purée. The floor staff wait with operating-theatre expressions, then grab plates and chase away quick as teenagers who have been given the car keys.

Downstairs, they are already into tomorrow. A trainee is getting a lesson in how to peel an onion. Later, he will get a lesson in how to cut up a cauliflower. The beef, lamb and chicken stocks simmer away in the corner, in the surreal calm.

Nanci Griffith and the Chinese Circus have given them a hard time. "We got hammered at 6 p.m. . . . going on to the Point and the RDS," says John the floor manager.

"The venison is good. You do get feedback, that's nice. They like it. It's wild."

"You do get a sixth sense in this business. I try to teach them to anticipate people's needs, tell them to treat people the way they want to be treated when they go out."

The character of Roly's Bistro comes into its best at this time of evening, I think. It's not truly a bistro, of course, but a brasserie, and the low lights and chatter of early evening seem to me to be its best companions. Mr O'Daly does a quick tour of the tables at 8.30 p.m., handshakes and how-are-you's. Roly Saul is downstairs, as usual, standing at his podium, welcoming the individuals who quickly congress into groups: "I'm Mary. How are you. A sherry."

Dinner is more difficult than lunch, for every system in the kitchen must work side by side. The quenelles of liver mousse are being prepared as the blow-torch caramelizes the tops of the crèmes brûlée. An eye must be kept on the lamb's-liver and kidney at the same time as the fillets of beef.

This planning – the orchestration of diners and tables, the taking and posting of orders, the timing of starters, main courses and desserts, the checking and correction of orders – would stymie the most sophisticated computer imaginable. In Roly's Bistro, on Friday night, the orchestration is so seamless one might imagine Fred Astaire had taught them how to move and Richard Strauss had scored the melody for the evening.

Maybe Astaire is the wrong comparison. The thirty-six French have been happily fed, and the tables they occupied cleared, cleaned and re-set in a matter – literally – of minutes. Mr Saul is beaming. "It's like Busby Berkeley," he says. Proud as punch. "Marvellous meal," says one man, departing with a handshake.

By 9 p.m., the cacophony of voices from the tables is counterpointed by the quiet efficiency of the kitchens as they simply go about their business: John the hatch man standing in judgment over every plate that goes out; Jean Michel easily marshalling every order; the waitresses drenching the coffee grounds with hot water; the wine orders flowing steadily from the bar downstairs; the youthful runners pegging up and down the stairs like yo-yos. This calmness, of course, is right at the centre of the storm, for the place is buzzing.

Kitchens work by discipline, and intuition, for there is little dialogue other than barked orders. Everybody has to do what everybody has to do. Everybody understands that there are no second acts in restaurant history. There are only bankruptcies.

FROM *THE IRISH TIMES* (22 OCTOBER 1994)

CODE FOR RESTAURATEURS

DEREK COOPER

1 If you own the restaurant put in frequent appearances yourself. Stand at the back, slightly blocking the kitchen door, with a menacing look. A frown never did any harm. The busier and more over-worked the staff are the more important it is for you to resist the temptation to muck-in and help. Limit your interference to occasional teeth-clicking and "tsks" of annoyance.

2 Remember, an un-cheery welcome doesn't cost you anything. Most of your clients will deserve nothing less. All that smiling and bowing and fawning foreigners get up to is most un-British. You should encourage your staff to be as icily correct as yourself. You set the standards, they will follow.

3 Try not to go out for your own meals when the restaurant is crowded. You never know when you'll be needed to sort out a trouble maker, there's one in every party. Hover round any table where revolt may be lurking and keep a close eye on the cutlery – some people will take the table as well if you don't keep them under constant scrutiny.

4 Ideally your premises should be hot and stuffy in summer and cold enough in winter to encourage customers to keep their outdoor clothes on. This will ensure that their stay is minimal.

5 Tables should be as close together as possible and of the smallest available size; eating out should be an intimate occasion. Make sure that your lighting is of the brightest – strong, overhead lighting enables you to see what everybody's up to and makes a dramatic effect when you start flicking the switches just before closing time.

6 Keep your opening hours as limited as possible. The staff may benefit indirectly but this cannot be helped. An ideal time to serve lunches is 12.30 to 1 – keeping food hot after one is uneconomic and encourages people to take advantage of you. Don't forget, you are paying heavy rates and taxes, customers lounging about talking are abusing your hospitality.

7 The staff should be as few as possible. Ideally one person should do all the cooking and all the serving but this isn't always possible. Foreigners with no training and no knowledge of English make the best employees. If you have to have a British staff organize working conditions so that they are in a perpetual state of ferment. This unrest is quickly communicated to the customer which again makes for the shortest possible stay. Your ultimate aim should be to make every customer want to leave as quickly as possible.

8 Decorate the restaurant by all means, if you think it's worth it. Cardboard signs and advertisements are pleasant; so are plastic flowers which, however, are not at their best until they have been *in situ* for a good number of years. If you have to repaint the premises choose gay clashing colours.

9 If you provide toilet facilities – another millstone round your neck – ensure that they are inadequate. Your restaurant is a place to eat in not a comfort station. And remember a little bit of dirt never did anybody any harm.

10 Be wary of foreign tourists. They tend to ask for impossible things like fresh orange juice, glasses of water, green salads and ice. If you can do it without being too ingratiating head them off at the door, say you're fully booked, anything. Remember the best customer (not that there is such a thing as a good customer) is one who doesn't complain, ie, a fellow Briton brought up in the same simple decent traditions as yourself.

11 Deal firmly with complaints. It is unfortunately not possible for you or your staff to assault physically unruly elements but they should be given very short shrift indeed. Let your treatment of them be an object lesson to other diners. It's no good paying lip service to the rule that the customer is always wrong. Let him know.

12 Your customers will prefer to have their menu in English which is a good reason why you should put it in French. As only 3.2 per cent of your clientele will understand even the most rudimentary French you can have an imposing *carte* without having an imposing *cuisine*. Although most people will know what a good beef stew should taste like, you can serve almost anything under the guise of a *ragoût*. Use French creatively!

13 When planning your menus arrange to have the smallest number of portions of the largest number of dishes. This gives an impression of great variety but will enable the staff to cross most of the items off a few minutes after opening. Customers like to find things "off" as it simplifies their choice.

14 Lukewarm food on cold plates, sodden chips, washed-out greens, ·over-

cooked meat never did anybody permanent harm. If your cook is inclined to be slovenly or not very good at his job be patient. Remember there's no shortage of customers, there is a shortage of cooks.

15 Make sure that the portions are small and dainty. If you can get your materials tinned, frozen, dried, bottled or packeted, do so. Convenience foods are there for your convenience. Use them – exclusively if you can. There should be no need for a really intelligent caterer ever to meet his local butcher, baker, greengrocer or dairyman. Get your supplies from the factory – in bulk.

16 Don't forget the wartime slogan about not wasting food scraps. All your old vegetables and meat can be minced into lovely croquettes, pasties, pies, rissoles or *vol-au-vents* (if you've got a classy trade). Re-heat, re-heat and re-heat until it's all gone. Remember the less in the swill the more in the till.

17 If you suspect members of the staff of being on the fiddle try and channel their competitive instincts where they will do the least harm – in the direction of the customer. A really decent customer doesn't quibble over small errors and mistakes in his bill.

18 Buy your wine cheaply and sell it expensively. The cheaper the wine the bigger the mark-up. People like to pay a lot for their wine, it gives them a sense of well-being and gives you a lot of profit for no work at all.

19 Charge as much as you can. Eating out for most folk is an experience. Make it a memorable occasion for them. Remember, too, the little extras that mean so much – cover charge, surcharge, service charge – we all have our own favourites.

20 Don't discourage your staff from stacking chairs on tables and sweeping up noisily as closing time approaches. Your customers would stay all night unless you gave them a mild hint

    and

        don't forget the golden rule

PEOPLE HAVE TO EAT SOMEWHERE

FROM *THE BAD FOOD GUIDE* (1967)

FOREIGN PARTS

GRANADA

ELISABETH LUARD

The spirit of the Moors lives on in the kitchens of Granada, and the cookery of the ancient kingdom of the caliphs remains among the best in Spain. This, the most romantic of Andalucía's cities, was the jewel in the Muslim crown; Christians, Jews and Muslims flourished in harmony under the enlightened rulers of the Nasrid dynasty, and all contributed their expertise to the culinary traditions of the city they called the Gateway to Paradise.

The sybaritic easterners brought snow from the Sierra Nevada to cool their sherbets; imported spices and grew saffron to spice their *al-cuscuzu*; irrigated the surrounding plain and planted almonds and aubergines, broad beans and artichokes, figs, oranges, lemons, grapes and rice.

Granada was the last Moorish stronghold to fall to the Catholic Kings as they reconquered Spain. The boy-sultan Boabdil fled the combined might of Ferdinand of Aragon and Isabel of Castile in the same year that Columbus sailed west in search of a new spice route to the East. He returned with a cargo of New World vegetables, and before long potatoes and peppers, tomatoes and maize, beans and marrows were planted in the market gardens, providing a seed-bed for the rest of Europe.

Today, the ethereal Alhambra, with its intricate arabesques, ice-white halls, marble-ducted snow-water streams, sky-bright pools and lush, shady gardens, soars above the solid granite-grey Spanish city which replaced the Arab souks and silk markets. Exotic as a belly dancer in a downtown rush hour, the caliphs' palace is a reminder of the artistic and architectural skill of the vanished conquerors.

Granadinos still have the eastern taste for mixing the sensual with the spiritual, and maintain literary-gastronomic societies not unlike the more down-to-earth men-only dining clubs of the Basques, to whose territories many of Granada's Moriscos, its converted Moors, were exiled in the 1500s.

As for home-cooking, the city remains true to her patrician origins and keeps a rich bourgeois table. The cheaper cuts of meat and offal furnish the urban poor and the gypsies of Sacromonte with more modest delicacies, and these too are given eastern spicing. The sweetmaking of the Arabs became the province of Christian nuns, who baked delicious confections for saints' days:

There is no wine to speak of: this is not vine-country, and followers of the Prophet were not permitted strong drink. Water is another matter: the springs of the Sierra Nevada supplied the citizens with the clearest, purest and most delicious of refreshment. The legacy of the Moors remains, too, in Granada's magnificent fruit and vegetables. Even its *bouquet garni*, the *ramillete alabaicinero*, is a Moorish combination of mint, parsley and bay leaves. These days it flavours soups and stews enriched with Christian pork, prohibited by both Jewish and Muslim law: but providing proof, if any further was needed, that many cooks make fine broth.

GRAPES IN ANISETTE (*UVAS EN ANIS*)

This is an Andalucían New Year treat – you have to eat one grape for every stroke of midnight if you want good luck in the year to come. What you get, of course, is indigestion and a hangover. And the way to put that right is an egg yolk whipped up with a little of the grape liquor from the night before. This recipe is made with the last grapes of autumn.

1 lb / 500g small sweet grapes
1 bottle anisette (aguardiente),
 or vodka with 1 teaspoon of aniseeds added

Makes a 1¾ pint / 1 litre / 4½ cup jar

Scald a Kilner jar. Snip the grapes neatly off their stalks, leaving a scrap of stalk behind to act as a plug.

Pack the grapes in the Kilner jar and pour in the spirit. Seal and leave for 2-3 months, until it's time to welcome in the next New Year.

FROM *THE FLAVOURS OF ANDALUCIA* (1991)

ARTICHAUTS À LA GRÈQUE.

EDOUARD DE POMIANE

I learned to make *artichauts à la grèque* many years ago in the course of a prolonged journey in the Middle East. From the quay at Piraeus I watched the steamer which had brought me sail away on its course to the Black Sea whilst I remained, for a time at least, in the land of Homer.

Then I turned. The Acropolis was before me. From a distance the Parthenon seemed quite new, pure white beneath the blue sky. Suddenly I was transported from the world of books and legends to that of reality. The whole of Ancient Greece lay before me.

If I had been a Renan I might have recited a prayer worthy of the beauty of the Acropolis. As it was, I could only remain mute and, as a devoted pilgrim, ascend the sacred hill on foot, disdaining the railway and the horses which were offered to me.

I stayed the whole afternoon amidst the burning stones and contemplated the deserted landscape before me, but my stomach recalled me to reality. I had to return to the town and I had to eat.

On the Acropolis, not far from the Parthenon, there was a small restaurant famous for its artichokes. Every day a little donkey carried a load of them to the city and every day people flocked to the restaurant to enjoy them. They even said that King George, *incognito*, sometimes came to eat them on the bare table with its oil stains.

I arrived and sat down on a wooden bench. Immediately, the proprietress called the woman who served as cook and waitress too. "Aphrodite! Aphrodite!" She appeared, but what a disappointment. Aphrodite was blind in one eye and had a limp. She was more than sixty. Venus had aged.

She brought me three artichokes and some broad beans glistening with oil and a glass of *resinata*, a wine prepared, it seems, with a sort of resin. The artichokes were incomparable. The proprietress allowed me to watch Aphrodite and I shall tell you just what she did. If you wish to copy her you will need:

8 small artichokes, 10oz onions chopped very fine, a glass of olive oil, 1 lb freshly-shelled broad beans, chopped parsley and chervil.

Trim the artichokes as in the previous recipes and rub the hollow where the "choke" has been with lemon juice to prevent its turning black. Fill the hollows with minced onions, parsley and chervil and put the artichokes into a flameproof dish, just covering them with cold water. Sprinkle them with salt and pepper, add the broad beans and the rest of the minced onion, and cover the dish. Let it simmer on top of the stove until the beans are cooked and you can easily detach the leaves of the artichoke. This will take at least half an hour.

Take the lid off the dish and let it boil on a hot fire until all the water has evaporated and the oil is beginning to splutter. Now lift it off the fire and stand it to cool for an hour or two, and try to restrain your impatience. The moment will soon come when you can enjoy your cold artichokes and dream. For me they recall sunset and the hard wooden bench of the little inn. Spread beneath me I see Piraeus and the Bay of Salamis; the Temple of Theseus and Hymettus veiled in violet. In the far distance, merging into the rosy sky, Pantelikon catches the last rosy glow of the setting sun.

FROM *COOKING WITH POMIANE* (1993)

DAY OF THE PIG KILLING

PIERRE KOFFMANN (WITH TIMOTHY SHAW)

In early January, when Camille's force-feeding of the second lot of ducks was well under way, it was time to fix the date on which Monsieur Montaud, the Saint Puy pig-killer, would come to the Oratoire to kill Marcel's pigs. This was a great annual event and a long day of very hard work – a ceremony with all its own customs and traditions and also something of a family feast, which we used to enjoy hugely when we were children.

So, on a carefully chosen day in January, when his services were not required elsewhere and when the moon was on the wane, Monsieur Montaud arrived at the Oratoire with his five assistants. My grandfather used to keep two pigs, one of which was always named after the President of the Republic and the other after some prominent politician; they lived in a sty with a small square window next to the stables. Sometimes they managed to loosen their gates and then they escaped into the fields and had to be chased back. This was an event which we greatly enjoyed when we were children, but it was not enjoyed by the adults, especially not by my grandfather, whose running and thwacking and breathless shouting and swearing had to be heard to be believed.

The annual slaughter of the pigs was an important happening, since every scrap of the animals would be used in some way or other, and nothing would be wasted. Hams, *confits*, sausages and fat would be eaten and used all through the year. In addition to Monsieur Montaud's team, three or four women friends of my grandmother's came to help as well, probably the same women who helped with the duck killing. There was plenty of work, enough usually to last for two days at least, and each day there were about a dozen people to be fed at lunch.

It took six very strong men to kill one pig, and both our pigs were killed on the same day. Four men were needed to get a pig out of its sty, each man being put in charge of a different leg; once outside, the pig was rolled over on to its back, its legs were tied together, and everybody hoisted it up until it lay, flat on its back, on the top of a special low, upturned wooden trough. Once the animal was in position, Monsieur Montaud, wearing a black beret and white apron, came forward with his knife and expertly, and in just the right place, cut a thin slit down the side of the upturned throat. Immediately the pig set up a raucous, screaming yell, and blood started to pour from the wound in torrential spurts. It was the job of the sixth man to catch the blood in a large pan.

Once the bleeding had stopped and the pig was finally quiet and dead, the wooden trough was turned right way up and the pig was placed in it to be covered with boiling water from the wash-house copper. All six men then worked together in a huge cloud of steam to scrape its hair off, until at last the animal's skin was absolutely soft, white and clean. Then the pig was heaved up against the wall and attached by its back legs to an iron hook. Monsieur Montaud executed another swift, skilful cut right down the length of the animal's belly, and suddenly the great heap of intestines fell out, steaming, into the winter air.

The women had already taken the blood away into the kitchen, and were busy with their first task of the day of a slaughtering: this was always to make the black pudding and to clean and prepare the right pieces of intestine into which the pudding had to be pushed in order to turn it into a *boudin noir. Boudin* was traditionally the main dish at the lunches, and Camille always served it with a potato purée flavoured with duck fat. It was also the day when she mixed some of the blood with cornmeal to make a special version of the little maize cakes called *miques*.

FROM *MEMORIES OF GASCONY* (1990)

STREET FOOD

CLAUDIA RODEN

The anthropologist Ahmet E Uysal writes in an article on "Street Cries in Turkey" in the *Journal of American Folklore* (1968) that the list of goods sold in the streets and open air bazaars of Turkey from push-carts, baskets and directly off the ground would cover the entire range of human needs. Apart from the usual fruit, vegetables, meat and fish, cooked foods are also available; soups at breakfast time and sweet pastries during festivals. You will also get metaphors, puns, exaggerated descriptions, earthy and salty humour, practical wisdom and frequent appeals to the medicinal properties of the foods. Peddlers enjoy a good deal of licence for insolence and can often be heard pouring outrageous insults on to passers-by or making rude retorts and using words with double meanings. Some set up a lecture platform and demonstration table to attract prospective buyers.

The best of Israeli food is also in the street, a legacy of the Ottomans reinforced by the ways of Arabs and Oriental Jews. It is here that national styles are forged, that young Israelis from different backgrounds form their conception of the food of their land. They have got used to grabbing a cheap snack on their way somewhere at all times of the day, and it is the different foods, which start at the initiative of the vendor and spread quickly into a rash of kiosks, that bring the tastes and ways of the different communities into the common national pool. Often, they are better than the food provided by the trendy restaurants which open one day and close the next. The cactus peeled for you with art, the sesame bread rings sold with the spice mixture zahtar, fish grilled at the harbour, sanbusak and borekas produced at the back of petrol stations and home-made hummus or falafel offered in the market place are the joys of the country which tourists often miss for fear of food poisoning and because they are strange.

For obvious reasons the warmer and the poorer countries are richest in open-air culinary activities. We have little to offer in England these days besides jellied eels and cockles, hamburgers, hot dogs, chestnuts and ice creams and, for a brief three days a year, red mullet and other Jamaican specialities at the Notting Hill festival. When will we have pancakes at street corners as they do in Paris, where you can have a whole meal of crêpes starting with savoury ham and cheese and finishing with sugar and cointreau? It would be so good to stop and buy oysters from a basket and have them opened on the spot and eat them there and then with a squeeze of lemon.

FROM *PICNIC* (1981)

FAT-TAILED SHEEP TAIL-FAT

MARGARET SHAIDA

Most visitors to Iran are intrigued by the sight of the Persian sheep grazing on the central plateau, because they appear to have so little grass to eat and because they have such enormous fat tails. It was noted by M L Ryder in *Sheep and Man* in 1983 that such sheep existed in ancient Iran as long ago as 300BC. Marco Polo was one of the earliest Europeans to give a contemporary report on them when he travelled through Persia in the thirteenth century:

> We find here also sheep that are equal to the ass in size, with long
> thick tails, weighing thirty pounds and upwards, which are fat and
> excellent to eat.

Sir John Chardin also noted in his *Travels in Persia* in the seventeenth century that "there are some of those Sheep which we call Barbary Sheep with great Tails, one whereof weighs about Thirty Pounds".

Like the hump of the camel, the fat tails of the sheep serve as an emergency supply of sustenance for an "arid" day. Since the sheep in Iran have little need for fat to be distributed throughout their bodies to keep out the damp and cold, the meat remains lean, all the fat being stored in the tail to be called upon during periods of drought.

The tail fat unfortunately smells unpleasant while being rendered but, once rendered, it is infinitely more delicate in flavour than body fat, and gives a pleasing fragrance and richness to many Persian meat dishes that is difficult to emulate. As recently as thirty years ago, housewives in Iran would always ask the butcher to add a piece of *donbeh* to their purchase of lamb, and many Iranians recall how, as a child, they relished a sandwich of the crispy remnants of the tail after rendering.

Donbeh has gone out of fashion in recent years, largely because of a shortage of local meat supplies in Iran and also because of the cholesterol threat. It is however interesting that recent research has shown that tail fat appears to be far less likely to clog arteries than body fat.

Since sheep-tail fat is unavailable in the West, the choice of cooking fat in meat dishes is optional. In Iran, *roghan-e nabâti* (vegetable oil) has largely replaced the tail fat. In Europe, many Iranians prefer the solid vegetable oil as being the least offensive, since it has virtually no flavour or odour of its own. But polyunsaturated oil is also popular for everyday use because it is perceived as being more healthy in the long term.

FROM *THE LEGENDARY CUISINE OF PERSIA* (1992)

BLESSED BY THE GODS

JULIE SAHNI

The wedding ceremony, one full day of rituals, feasting, and celebrations, was to take place in a lovely classic structure called a *chattra*, next to a temple of Lord Shiva. The courtyard surrounding the building was lined with the famous coconut and date palms of southern India. The fragrant jasmine and rose patches and the statues of the different deities gave the whole place a feeling of tranquillity.

In the morning the air was filled with the smell of freshly roasted, ground, and brewed coffee. I ate steaming savoury puddings, tiny puffy breads with braised potatoes in a shallot-and-ginger sauce, accompanied again by that wonderful coffee. To beat the heat I sipped a special lemonade made with tamarind water, palm jaggery (unrefined sugar), and the essence of fresh ginger. There were snacks and sweets to munch on all through the day, consisting of spicy chick-pea noodles, griddle cakes, cardamom-laced jaggery and wheat dumplings, silky crepes with fiery dips and spice powders, and ample varieties of asafetida-laced fritters. I ate many of them on disposable plates made of banana leaves.

My sister was missing all this, for she had to attend to the various rituals (*pooja*) in order to be prepared for the great occasion. The auspicious time for the marriage ceremony determined by the holy priest was late morning; hence everyone was busy getting the wedding altar (*mandap*) with its holy fire (*agni*) ready. The sweet pipe and drum music, traditional at weddings, played melodiously in a slow rhythm while the priests gathered sandalwood, turmeric paste, rice, coconut, bananas, betel nut and betel nut leaves, sweets and fruits, holy grass, holy water from the temple, and clarified butter (*usli ghee*, the holy food of the Vedic Aryans, our ancestors). These ingredients were to be offered to the supreme Lord Vishnu to appease him and seek his favour, using the fire god as messenger. The local town gardener brought beautiful garlands of roses, marigold, marjoram, and jasmine that the bride and the groom would exchange. My mother brought silver coins and gold-brocaded silk saris to be offered up to the various gods (these finally ended up with the presiding priest) and to the elderly relatives, to seek their blessing, which in many cases was more important than the blessing of the lower-ranking gods such as the Mouse God (*Chooha Dev*) or the Monkey God (Hanuman).

As the preparations neared completion, the air started becoming thick with the aromas of lentils cooking with turmeric and sesame, tamarind boiling with jaggery, and spices roasting. I followed the scents to the large backyard. There they were – the famous temple vegetarian chefs: bare-chested and barefoot, wrapped from the waist down in gold-brocaded white cloth. They wore a bright yellow sacred thread (*janaeo*) around their necks and across their chests and had holy ash smeared on their foreheads and arms. Gently chanting a Vedic hymn, they stirred large batches of lentil and vegetable stews and braised vegetables, some with fried spices, some with roasted lentils and spices, others with yogurt and herbs, in large gleaming brass and copper pots as big as Japanese bathtubs!

There were helpers grinding coconut and chillies for the relish and stews and pulverizing almonds for the puddings and *halwa*. One person did nothing but crack and grate the enormous pile of coconuts that resembled a small mountain. At Vedic ritual celebrations and associated feasts, all the food has to be made on the premises that day, including combining, roasting, and grinding the spice blends for the many dishes. In Hindu ceremonies the food needs to be blessed by all the appropriate gods, but in fact it ensures absolute freshness and the most perfect taste in the ingredients.

FROM *CLASSIC INDIAN VEGETARIAN AND GRAIN COOKING* (1987)

REDCURRANTS
PHOTOGRAPH BY KEVIN SUMMERS (*OBSERVER LIFE*, 14 AUGUST 1994)

PHOTOGRAPHS BY KEVIN SUMMERS

ABOVE: PESTLE AND MORTAR (*OBSERVER LIFE*, 7 AUGUST 1994)

OPPOSITE: KIPPERS (*OBSERVER LIFE*, 27 FEBRUARY 1994)

FOOD AND ART: PHOTOGRAPHS BY ROBIN BROADBENT (*HARPERS & QUEEN*, JUNE 1991)

ABOVE: "DALI: SELF-PORTRAIT WITH ÉCREVISSE AND ROCK (LOBSTER)"

OPPOSITE: "GAUGUIN: WOMAN WITH RED SNAPPER"

FOLLOWING PAGE: "CARAVAGGIO: THE FEAST"

ROASTED RED PEPPERS STUFFED WITH FENNEL (SEE PAGE 113)
PHOTOGRAPH BY JAMES MURPHY (*DELIA SMITH'S CHRISTMAS*, 1990)

LEARNING CHINESE

YAN-KIT SO

My interest in food is inherited from my father. Although he did not cook himself, he always asked mother to see to it that what was on the table was correct, right down to the last detail: for him, stir-fried dishes had to have "wok fragrance", sugar was to be used very sparingly in marinades; chicken was not to be overcooked lest the flesh became tough; fish for steaming was to be bought live from the market and abalone was to be well seasoned with oyster sauce. Like children in other Chinese families, my brothers, sisters and I joined the grown-ups for dinner from the age of four or five, picking with chopsticks from the dishes served in the centre of the table so it isn't surprising that what has stayed in my mind is delicious well-prepared dishes, seasoned to father's liking, rather than fish-finger nursery food.

From those early childhood days in Hong Kong I also remember father taking us to restaurants where we had delicate hot tid-bits, *dimsum*, or to the boating restaurants in Aberdeen for special seafood. Every year, during the month following Chinese New Year, his *Hong* or import-export trading company, would give a banquet to which our whole family as well as those who worked for him would go. At these banquets the menu would follow a prescribed procedure: two small, hot seasonal dishes followed by shark's fin, either as a soup or braised in a sauce, next a chicken with crispy red skin to augur another prosperous year, then a duck or perhaps succulent pigeons, followed by another soup – turtle or something else equally exotic – then one or two more stir-fried dishes and lastly a whole steamed fish, the pronunciation of which is the same as the word "surplus" which can signify abundant wealth.

Having taken good food for granted, like so many other Chinese, I did not think seriously about it until I became a frugal post-graduate student at the University of London. Short of cash but nonetheless hungry, haunted by the tastes of both home cooked and restaurant dishes, I began to try my own hand at cooking Chinese food. To my delight, I found I was adept at it. One dish led to another, and soon I found that I had become an enthusiast, cooking with zest and satisfying not only my own palate but many others'.

This amateurish approach took a marked turn some ten years ago when I spent a long summer with my young son in Waterford, Connecticut. There I used to entertain my American family and friends with Chinese dishes, and I remember their surprise that the tiny Niantic scallops could be so succulently tender, simply stir-fried; that the Cherrystone clams, delicious served on the half-shell New England style, could make one's mouth water equally, if not more, when cooked in black bean sauce with garlic, and that sea bass and blue fish could be so refreshing steamed with slices of ginger and seasoned with a little soy sauce. They were equally enthusiastic about the strips of pork I roasted then brushed over with a little honey, and with ox tongue braised slowly in soy sauce and sherry. On my part, I found cooking remedial, relaxing and rewarding. The seed of this book was sown then.

Since that time, I have worked with different Chinese chefs in Hong Kong and London, been to China and Taiwan to sample different regional cuisines, entertained at home, and taught and demonstrated Chinese cookery both privately and publicly. The invaluable reactions of friends and students led to much pondering over food and cookery in general, and Chinese food and cookery in particular. I discovered that many people who are very enthusiastic about Chinese food are, unfortunately, in awe of Chinese cookery. They claim it is time-consuming, fiddly and generally incomprehensible. But since every form of cooking takes a certain amount of time and involves some technique, however trivial, the first two points are irrelevant. On the third point, I strongly believe that Chinese cookery can be as comprehensive as any other.

FROM *CLASSIC CHINESE COOKBOOK* (1984)

A JAPANESE MEAL

LESLEY DOWNER AND MINORU YONEDA

In Japan, a tiny three or five line poem – *haiku*, *senryu* or *tanka* – encapsulates a whole experience in the fewest possible words. A poet of the last century, on being confronted with a Western meal, wrote a *senryu* which roughly translated reads, "Western food – every single plate is round!". Having taken your place at table you will find before you something rather different from a traditional Western meal on its single, large plate. Every Japanese meal, no matter how simple, is prepared with the utmost care, the primary aim being to provide delight both to the tongue and eye. While Japanese cuisine is undoubtedly one of the healthiest in the world, this is almost accidental since nutritional considerations have not traditionally played much part in the planning of a meal. Each item of food is chosen for its perfection of form as well as its freshness, and is arranged in an aesthetically pleasing fashion on the plate. While every place setting is identical, within each place setting every item of china is different. The plates and bowls are selected to provide variety of shape, colour, material and even texture, and to complement the visual qualities of the food which they contain.

When the diners have taken their places and refreshed themselves by wiping their hands and faces with the small steaming towel which is folded at each place, they are served first with the hors d'oeuvre (*zensai*). This consists of tiny portions of a variety of seasonal delicacies – fresh prawns, morsels of squid and minute portions of an assortment of vegetables – all exquisitely shaped and elegantly arranged on the plate. The preparation of hors d'oeuvres is largely left to professional chefs in Japan; the home cook will normally omit the hors d'oeuvre or simply serve a light vinegared salad instead.

The hors d'oeuvre is followed by two apparently simple dishes which, to the Japanese gourmet, constitute the high point of the meal. A delicate clear soup (*suimono*), in which tiny morsels of seafood and vegetables hang suspended, is served in the finest of lacquer bowls, usualy red or black, and topped with a domed lid. This is accompanied by *sashimi*, gleamingly fresh raw fish of several different varieties, which is truly the highlight of the meal. The fish is cut into succulent slices, and one portion typically consists of two or three slices of each variety of fish, beautifully garnished with perhaps a seasonal leaf or a few slices of cucumber decoratively cut. It is on the clear soup and the *sashimi* that the chef's reputation rests, and the tiny portions are savoured and the dishes removed before the following course is served.

The central part of the meal consists of a variety of small dishes representing each of the different techniques of Japanese cuisine. Even in the simplest of family meals there is usually a grilled dish and a simmered dish. The diners may be served with a slice of grilled fish or a small whole fish, cunningly arranged on the plate to resemble a fish leaping through the waves. A dish of vegetables, lightly simmered and still crisp and colourful, will be served in a deep bowl. The grilled and simmered dishes are frequently served at room temperature. During the meal some hot dishes, perhaps a savoury steamed custard (*chawan mushi*) in a small cup with a lid and some crisp deep-fried fish or seafood, may be served. Very soft foods, such as *chawan mushi*, are eaten with a spoon and the lid of the cup is replaced to indicate that the dish is finished.

In the winter, be it in a restaurant or a private home, the central part of the meal may consist of a one-pot dish (*nabemono*). Some of Japan's most famous dishes, such as *sukiyaki* and *shabu shabu*, are one-pot dishes. The table is loaded with platters of immaculately fresh vegetables or paper thin slices of the finest beef, and formality is forgotten as the diners help in the cooking, taking cooked foods directly from the cooking pot. Some restaurants are designed solely for one-pot cooking, with tables consisting of great iron griddles heated from beneath. *Sake* is an essential accompaniment of such meals, and the evening is likely to end with singing.

When all the dishes are cleared away, rice is served, steaming hot, in small white porcelain bowls. A few hot or salty pickles are eaten with the rice, and a bowl of *miso* soup completes the meal. It is considered quite unforgivable to leave even a single grain of rice, for rice is food itself and should never be wasted. The meal is followed by green tea and tiny portions of fresh fruit, artistically cut into bite-sized pieces and served with a tiny fork or cocktail stick. Fruit is never picked up with the fingers.

When the meal finally ends, the diners murmur "*Gochiso sama deshita*", to express their appreciation of the meal to both the deities and the host or hostess or even the waitress. Even after receiving a simple cup of tea it is customary to give thanks in this way.

FROM *STEP-BY-STEP JAPANESE COOKERY* (1985)

THE BELLY OF ITALY

PHILIPPA DAVENPORT

Emilia-Romagna is a food lover's paradise. It is the belly of Italy, where rich alluvial soil yields some of Italy's finest ingredients and the cooks of the region, drawing on a historical mix of court grandeur and farm kitchen simplicity, produce exquisite recipes.

Orchard fruits and soft wheat flourish here. So do all manner of vegetables and fungi. The area is famed for its egg-yoke yellow pasta, richly sauced or lavishly stuffed, and for balsamic vinegar, one of the most fashionable flavourings of our times. Above all else, this is the land of the pig and Parmigiano-Reggiano cheese.

Do not think, though, that Emilia-Romagna is famous only for its food. There are romanesque cathedrals, medieval abbeys, Byzantine basilicas, the ceramics of Faenza, the mosaics of Ravenna and paintings by Correggio. It is also the home of Ferrari, Maserati and Lamborghini cars.

Bologna is the greedy capital and contains the oldest university in Europe, hence its nickname "the fat and the learned". It is a city of joyfully noisy, hotly competitive gourmandise – a legacy probably derived from medieval times when the rich demonstrated their power by giving gargantuan feasts and constructing towers bigger and better that those of rival families.

Paolo Atti, near the basilica of San Pietrono, is never without a queue for its crusty loaves made half-and-half with wheat and maize, its heavyweight cakes that appear to be composed almost entirely of glistening glazed fruits and nuts, and its pastas.

Huge and delectable tortelloni are stuffed with fresh artichokes or pumpkin.

Little tortellini are stuffed with a mixture of fresh pork, chicken, *mortadella*, Parma ham, eggs and Parmesan, dextrously folded and twisted into rings (the shape was supposedly inspired by the navel of Venus). Served in a rich broth with globules of fat floating on the surface, or sauced with scalded cream, they epitomize the sumptuous glory of Bolognese cooking.

Prize items in the herb and vegetable market on the morning I was there were *porcini*, brought in fresh from the woods. Their sight and smell drew crowds, and even those who did not buy relished watching others make their selection from the three grades on offer.

For a late-night supper that evening at the Ristorante Diana in the via dell' Indipendenza, I succumbed to a potato *porcini* and Parmesan *gratin* finished with a grating of truffle – not one helping but two.

Elsewhere in the market there were chickens split to reveal the unlaid eggs inside them (it is their deep golden corn-fed yolks that give the local pasta its rich colour). Strings of little *cacciatore salamis*, suspended in rows, swung like bead curtains – dwarfed by *mortadella* sausages, some as big as punch-bags at the gym.

Mortadella is a cooked sausage of ancient pedigree, a smooth forcemeat of high quality pork studded with fat and spices, so beloved of its creators that it is sometimes simply known as Bologna sausage – which British travellers of earlier centuries called baloney.

FROM *THE FINANCIAL TIMES* (10 DECEMBER 1994)

BACK TO THE LANGUEDOC

FRANCES BISSELL

Twenty-five years after leaving, I returned to Albi in the Tarn, south-west France, on a gastronomic and vinous pilgrimage. A few years ago I made some negative comments about the wines I remembered from that area, and I was invited back to see how they had evolved in the ensuing years.

It took only a few lunches and dinners, accompanied by a wide range of Gaillac and Côtes du Tarn wines, together with a visit to the main man of Gaillac, Robert Plageoles, and another to Martine David at Château Clement Termes at the foot of the *côteaux* near Lisle sur Tarn, to convince me that things have changed. We drank the superb 1990 reds, lively and fruity 1993 whites and the unique Mauzac *nature* – softly sparkling wine made by the 1,000-year-old *méthode gaillacoise*.

One of the most appealing features of Gaillac winemakers is that they do not aim for copycat chardonnays and cabernets. The mauzac, the duras, the l'en de l'el, and the ondenc are all local grapes, which give the wine its typicality.

As with the wine and winemakers, so with the food. There are dishes still available on menus that you will find nowhere else. And a group of chefs, with Claude Izard as their president, has formed Les Tables Gourmandes Tarnaises under the auspices of the French Ministry of Tourism and the Restaurateurs de Métier des Provinces Françaises. Their aim is to preserve the culinary patrimony, and also to work with local growers and farmers to obtain high-quality produce. It seems to be a very happy relationship and one that could well serve as a model elsewhere.

The Tarn is a tucked-away agricultural *département*. No beaches, no high mountains, no tourist hot-spots, no famous dishes, and wines that are just beginning to make their way once more outside France – it is little wonder that most visitors pass this area by. Let them. Sitting on my balcony one soft, sunny morning, above the lawns at La Réserve that lead down to the cool, silky, dark-green river Tarn, or on the Terrace at L'Echaugette in Giroussens, high above the river Agout, watching the sun go down, refracted in the mist from the irrigation sprays, I wouldn't have given tuppence for the Côte d'Azur.

And now my kitchen smells like an Albigeois kitchen. I caught the garlic market at Lautrec just as the last transactions were being carried out in the back of the growers' *camionnettes* and was able to buy a couple of kilos to bring to London.

Out comes the box of saffron, too. Five hundred years ago this part of the Languedoc was famous for its woad production, supplying the rest of Renaissance Europe with the high-quality blue dye. This crop was then replaced by saffron, which became an important ingredient in many dishes of the region, particularly the *gras double à l'albigeoise*: today's recipe is a pale copy, as tripe in England is bleached and processed almost beyond recognition.

This is not olive oil country. Food is fried in sunflower oil, lard or duck fat. Duck and rabbit are the main meats. You will find live rabbits and baby ducklings in the large and colourful Saturday-morning market under the plane trees in Lavaur, a long avenue of which follows the line of the original moat.

Dishes are served in a rustic fashion. Pierrette Canonica serves her cassoulets and tripe dishes in large earthenware pots on pewter salvers. Izard's famous rabbit dish is served in his elegant, panelled dining room in a rough country pot. Many of the chefs serve the traditional Albigeois salad in earthenware bowls. This is one of the most rustic and unusual dishes imaginable, and I am finally beginning to get a taste for it. Although some serve it with diced foie gras, the authentic ingredient is salted pig's liver, which is sliced and fried in sunflower oil, together with sliced radishes, and then dressed with a little vinegar.

When I asked at the Lautrec garlic market for the real *soupe à l'ail* recipe, I was told there are as many variations as there are cooks. So if you really like garlic, add more than the ten cloves.

GARLIC SOUP
Serves 4 to 6

2 pints (1.15L) water or vegetable stock
10 cloves garlic, preferably pink Lautrec, peeled
1 large free-range egg, separated
salt and pepper
1 soupspoon mustard
4oz (110ml) sunflower oil
4-6 slices bread, toasted

Bring the water to the boil and stir in the garlic and egg white. The garlic can be sliced, finely chopped or crushed in a mortar. (Each method will affect the taste of the garlic differently.)

Cook for a few minutes. Make a mayonnaise with the egg yolk, seasoning, mustard and oil. Just before serving, thin it down with a ladleful of warm broth, and then stir it gently into the soup. Serve poured over toast.

LAPIN AU CHOUX
(Rabbit and cabbage after Claude Izard)
Serves 4

1 large green cabbage, or 2 smaller ones
1 rabbit, skinned, cleaned and jointed
2 tablespoons sunflower oil
2oz (60g) ham, diced
½lb (230g) carrots, peeled and diced
½lb (230g) onions, peeled and chopped
3 cloves garlic, peeled and sliced
4 tablespoons flour
1 soupspoon tomato concentrate
¼ pint (140ml) dry white wine
¾ pint (430ml) chicken stock
seasoning
thyme, bay leaf, parsley
4oz (110g) pork skin, cut into 1in (2.5cm) squares

Separate the cabbage leaves, wash them and remove the tough central ribs. Blanch the leaves and put to one side. Brown the rabbit and ham in the oil and then add the onions and carrots. Sweat the ingredients for five minutes or so, dust with flour, and stir well, adding the tomato concentrate.

Gradually add the wine and the chicken stock. Season, and tuck in a few herbs. Put the pork skin on top, bring the contents of the casserole to the boil, cover with the cabbage leaves, making sure they are well pressed down, and cook in a pre-heated oven at 200°C/400°F/gas mark 6 for about an hour or so.

The top layer of cabbage can be removed if it has dried too much. Best accompanied by potatoes, this dish, although robust and copious, is surprisingly digestible.

FROM *THE TIMES MAGAZINE* (3 SEPTEMBER 1994)

BUYING AND SELLING

POULTRY MARKET AT FLEURANCE

PIERRE KOFFMANN (WITH TIMOTHY SHAW)

One of the best April memories I have of my grandmother is of travelling with her to the market at Fleurance. The market was held every Tuesday, and Camille went there to sell her rabbits or pigeons or ducks or if she wanted to buy odds and ends for the house, like saucepans, nails, lengths of material, or items connected with her embroidery. She went most often to market in the spring; in summer it was generally too hot, and there was always far too much to do at the farm to lose a day away from Saint Puy. When I was small, Camille quite frequently went to market to sell her poultry, but, as the years went on and she gradually gave up the ducks, she had less and less to sell, and finally she went only to buy.

Whenever possible we travelled on a noisy, jolting local bus, which left Saint Puy at 6 o'clock in the morning and reached Fleurance at 7; we returned by the 3 o'clock bus which got us home at 4 in the afternoon. It was a day packed with all the excitements and uncertainties of trade. The bus had a great roof rack with metal rails and a ladder at the back for climbing up. In the morning the roof was crammed with crates and cages of poultry of every sort, among them Camille's ducks and rabbits. As we rattled into Fleurance we passed the town cemetery with its fine stone wall and its new gates. My grandmother thought this was the smartest cemetery in the whole of the *département* and never failed to remark with a sigh how sad she was that, being an inhabitant of Saint Puy, she would never have the right to be buried there.

The poultry market took place in a great, echoing warehouse which, during the rest of the week, was used as a sports stadium. On Tuesdays it was a cathedral dedicated to birds and to their buyers and sellers. Ducks, geese, guinea fowl, hens, pigeons, cocks, turkeys, all in their magnificent colours, squawked, fluttered and brooded while whistles blew and bargains were struck. Birds were carried away singly, beaks downwards, their wings beating, or were packed into boxes and removed by the dozen. If we did very well and my grandmother had sold everything by midday, we were able to have lunch at her favourite little restaurant near the church. Here, long rows of wooden tables with cast-iron legs accommodated a crowd of hungry market people; conviviality reigned with good soup and local wine and *confit de canard*; the floor was laid out with brown and yellow tiles, and at the end of the room stood a massive old dresser laden with glasses and loaves and lots of ornate little pots for salt, pepper and oil.

Before we set off for home, Camille would buy me a *pain à l'anis* from one of the stalls near the old arcaded market hall, not far from the four fountains of the four seasons, each with a statue of its own particular goddess. The bread was round, like a crown, and the aniseeds scattered on top permeated it with a delicious taste and a wonderful smell, which lingered on in my mouth long after I had finished the last morsel. I do not think I have ever had *pain à l'anis* as good as that anywhere else.

I remember how much we enjoyed the first spring leeks, the first shallots and the first garlic and how good these fresh vegetables seemed after a winter of *confits* and *conserves*. We sometimes ate the garlic and spring onions raw *à la croque-sel*, but Camille also used them in other ways, especially when she cooked spring chickens. I think that garlic and onions have always been popular in south-west France. Certainly, the Romans in Gascony enjoyed them and I have read some wonderful descriptions of the Gascon penchant for these strong-flavoured foods written by the early seventeenth-century court physician, Joseph du Chesne. According to him, the French only ate leeks in the form of soup, while the Gascons took great delight in eating theirs raw, dipped in honey.

Our Gascon forefathers also ate their garlic raw, just as we did at the Oratoire [his grandparents' farm]. The peasants ate it to keep away the plague; apparently vermin also kept their distance from garlic eaters! I love the story of the infant Henri de Navarre: how on the night of 13th December, 1553, when the plague was raging in Béarn, the baby's grandfather, Henri d'Albret, struggled into his fur dressing gown and dashed down the cold stone stairs at Pau to rub a clove of garlic on the lips of his new-born grandson, the future Henri IV, to protect him from the ravages of the disease. Unfortunately, when the young Gascon prince arrived at court in Paris, he was said to exude such a stench of garlic that he could be smelt several yards away and his bride, Marguérite de Valois, refused to share his bed on at least one occasion because his breath was so unpleasant!

This salutary tale did not prevent us from enjoying our raw garlic at the Oratoire, but we also liked to eat it in the less potent form of *l'ail sous la cendre*. Marcel would put a whole head of garlic under the wood embers of the log fire and leave it to cook. Then, when it was tender, he would toast some bread, extract the cloves of garlic, and we would eat them on the toast. *Ce n'était pas gastronomique, mais c'était délicieux à manger.*

FROM *MEMORIES OF GASCONY* (1990)

FRENCH CRUMBS OF COMFORT

RICHARD OLNEY

Inhabitants of neighbouring towns consider the village near which I live to be backward – some say inbred – "because it is off the main road." It is, in fact, but a few metres off the main road, which means that "foreigners" (Parisians) are not driving in a constant stream through the heart of the village. The streets are regularly blocked by the insouciant passage of the shepherd and his troop; the women still beat their laundry along the streams; stuffed aubergines and courgettes are carried through the streets at eleven o'clock in the morning to be installed in the ovens of the local bakery and picked up an hour or so later; the men devote half the year to playing pétanque and drinking pastis and the other half to playing cards and drinking pastis, and if, upon entering the general store, a couple of housewives happen to be discussing with the shopkeeper the various merits of their respective *ratatouilles* or *soupes au pistou*, one may as well expect to wait half an hour before being served. These are picturesque details, perhaps of minor importance, but they are comforting – one is tempted to hope that the reins of stubborn habit are strong enough to frustrate the famous industrial revolution for some time to come.

Comforting also are the fantastic, crowded out-of-door morning markets, of which that in Toulon is exemplary, bearing ample witness to the fact that people still want fresh garden produce and seafood and to the certainty that, on the whole, the French willingly spend a great deal more on food than a similar budget in any other part of the world would permit. There are banks of fruits and vegetables, freshly picked – depending on the season, baby violet artichokes, young broad beans, tiny green beans, peas, tomatoes, fennel, and courgettes with their flowers still clinging; creamy white cauliflower the size of one's fist, giant sweet peppers, and asparagus – white, violet, and green; figs, cherries, peaches, strawberries, raspberries, and medlar; the endless tresses of garlic and wild mushrooms of all kinds (including the divine amanita of the Caesars); and crates full of live snails and crabs, both of which constantly escape and wander in a wide circle around the vendor's stand. There are the odours of basil and *pissaladière*; the mongers' cants, melodic and raucous; and the Renoiresque play of light through the plane trees' foliage, an all-over sense of gaiety and well-being. The concert is a vibrant experience, the beauty of which is breathtaking. The peasants from the near countryside have stands with small quantities of varied produce – a few eggs, a couple of live chickens or rabbits, a dozen or so fresh cheeses from goat or sheep milk, courgette flowers (to be dipped in batter and fried in olive oil for lunch – they will be wilted by evening), and a few handfuls of varied vegetables plus whatever they may have picked wild on the hillsides – shoots of wild asparagus, dandelions and other wild salads, bundles of thyme, rosemary, fennel, savory, and oregano. Hand-scribbled notices inform the customer that the vegetables are "untreated" and that the chickens, whose eggs were laid that morning, are grain fed.

FROM *SIMPLE FRENCH FOOD* (1981)

WHAT'S IN A NAME?

MARGARET VISSER

Just when almost all the ice-cream parlours in America had closed, capitulating in part to the take-home ice-cream brick, Walt Disney opened one, in 1955, at Disneyland in Anaheim, California. This parlour was almost certainly the first of its kind: it was built specifically to be "old-fashioned" and advertised itself as such. True, the establishment was a museumizing recreation of an almost dead past, but Walt Disney, in this as in so much else, had his fingers on the mythic pulse of America. Five years later Reuben Mattus, whose story has been repeatedly described as "a capitalist folktale," began to market Häagen-Dazs Ice Cream.

He packed it in pint-sized round containers, not large bricks, and designed it carefully to satisfy nostalgia and fastidious taste ("an old world delight," the tub calls it, "especially for the most discerning"). There are no additives, emulsifiers, or stabilizers. It melts; it deteriorates if it is not kept frozen solid. Consumers are advised to let it soften a little ("tempering" it) before eating. It is also much heavier than it needs to be to satisfy the ice-cream standard, largely because it contains 16 per cent butterfat and only 20 per cent air.

On the lid appeared a map of Scandinavia; clean, sober, efficient, and technologically advanced Scandinavia, with a star marking Copenhagen and an arrow pointing impressively towards the star. The name Häagen-Dazs is a complete fiction, designed of course to attract the eye, to be seen rather than said: so much shopping is now self-service that buyers would rarely have to ask for it by name; when it became famous enough to be a household word, the pronunciation of it would look after itself. In any case, Mattus said, "the type of people we were looking for, if they mispronounced it, they'd think they were right and any other way was wrong." The name is meant to look vaguely but arrogantly Danish, with its double *a*, its hyphenation, and its impossible *zs*. The umlaut is especially effective, even though Danish has no umlaut. Mattus had absolutely nothing to do with Scandinavia; his factory was in the Bronx and later in New Jersey.

Mattus started small, and jealously guarded the "family business" image, even as his brilliant idea turned out to be exactly what the public had wanted without being able to formulate its desire. The firm prospered and spawned imitators. Frusen Glädjé, a concept created in direct competition with Mattus by his cousin Edward Lipitz, has a genuinely Swedish name which means "Frozen Delight." (The umlaut this time is correct, while the final French accent is a purely artistic touch.) Lipitz took the trouble to incorporate his company in Sweden (his tub has a map of part of Scandinavia with Stockholm marked in black), although his factory was in Utica, New York. The new company's innovation was an improvement in the container's design: not only small and round like the Häagen-Dazs tub, but in more emphatically smooth white plastic, with a raised rounded lid as well. Frusen Glädjé street-vending booths continue the smooth round white theme. The product aims at an extremely restricted market, describing itself as "A gourmet experience for those who prefer the best."
FROM *MUCH DEPENDS ON DINNER* (1989)

ETRUSCAN BRUSCHETTA

DELIA SMITH

The high point of my visit to the Archibusaccis [olive oil producers in Truscia, Italy] happened in the reception area of the old mill. Alongside the international buyers, locals drive up, bringing huge jars from car boots for an annual purchase of the new season's oil. The room was quite small and a fire was burning in an old fireplace. Intrigued, I witnessed the age-old tradition of how the oil is tasted before any transaction is completed.

First of all, the hot coals are raked out flat, then an iron grid is placed over them and then on that thick slices of local country bread. The bread is toasted on both sides then removed to a plate. After that a well-worn penknife is used to make slashes along the surface of each piece of toasted bread, which is then rubbed with an open clove of garlic. Next the olive oil is poured over the bread, making little pools all around the base of the plate. The plate is then passed round. "*Bruschetta signora?*"

I'm here to tell you that this, in all its utter simplicity, is one of the most memorable eating experiences of my life. My first real taste of extra virgin olive oil, not frazzled in a pan or vying with other ingredients in a dressing. Pure and simple, fresh, green and fragrant, but powerfully fruity at the same time.

All I can do now is urge you to try some yourself. So for Etruscan bruschetta, buy some ciabatta bread. If you haven't got an open fire, a grill will do to toast thick slices on both sides. Rub with a cut clove of garlic, make several cuts in the bread and now don't be fainthearted with the Canino [olive oil] – 1 tablespoon per slice or even more! One bite and you'll understand exactly what I mean.

FROM *SAINSBURY'S THE MAGAZINE* (APRIL 1994)

I SNIFFED, I SWILLED, I PONDERED

OLIVER PRITCHETT

The sign on the door said "Sensory Appraisal". This was unsettling. What sinister things took place behind that door? My mouth was dry. I made myself open the door and enter. It turned out to be a plain room with a table and chairs and a few charts on the wall – something between a classroom and a surgery. There was also a rack of about fifty small brown jars, like pill bottles. This, I learned later, is the odour library, which goes from almond, apple and basil to tarragon, turmeric and yeast.

It was not surprising that I felt nervous – my palate was about to be put to the test. Gillian Wright, the senior sensory analyst (who goes to wine-tasting classes in her spare time), welcomed me warmly and offered me a glass of water. Well, you don't mess about with strong black coffee when your taste buds are suffering from pre-exam nerves.

All this took place in the home economics department at Sainsbury's London headquarters. This is where buyers come for a day-long course to educate their palates. I did not realize before how much attention Sainsbury's pays to every detail. It all starts with tests, just to make sure that new recruits are not taste-blind.

Armed with a rather stark diagram of a tongue, showing which different areas are sensitive to the four basic tastes – bitter, salt, acid and sweet – I was ushered next door into a booth. This was getting spooky. For lighting, there was a red glow, so that anybody sampling anything red here, such as a tomato, would not be distracted by its colour. I felt like a being in science fiction, although I could not be sure if I was the evil genius who was about to conquer the universe or the captive spaceman who was about to be interrogated by a suave alien in a silver jump suit. Suddenly, a hatch opened and a hand pushed a white plastic tray on to the shelf in front of me. This was the odour recognition test.

There were six paper smelling-strips, each one numbered, and the idea was to sniff them and identify the smell. It is odd how you recognize a smell and then find you cannot come up with the word for it. I caught myself thinking "toothache, soap, cake, disinfectant . . . " before I realized the answer was "cloves, roses, vanilla, pine". There were also two smells of "aunts", or "peppermint and lavender", to be more specific.

Then the hand pushed another tray through the hatch. There were five little beakers containing colourless liquids. One was sweet, one bitter, one acid, one salty and one tasteless. My palate came through this test with flying colours.

To show how important the sense of smell is to tasting, Gillian told me to put on a tight nose clip and take a swig from a beaker of red liquid, then a blue one. Nothing. As soon as I took the nose clip off, I got a powerful taste of almonds and vanilla.

Panels of expert tasters and panels of Sainsbury's head-office staff come to this department regularly to try out different foods. They sit down and compare all varieties of a single item. It could be anything from paw-paws to bread and butter pudding, bagels to chicken Kiev, rollmops to taramasalata.

It is all a matter of vocabulary — as I was discovering. In sensory appraisal, they don't really approve of people who say "yummy" or "yucky". You won't get anywhere if you put your thumb and fingertip together, express your pleasure through weird grimaces or give ecstatic yelps like Loyd Grossman on *Masterchef*. Here, you are expected to be coolly particular. The purpose is to find the right word to describe the appearance, aroma, flavour, texture (or "mouthfeel") and aftertaste of something, so that everybody has the same points of reference.

I sat at the table with Gillian and Julia Brown, another analyst, to blind taste three different glasses of cola, named 291, 572 and 736. We each had a plastic cup as a spittoon. First, we considered their appearance. I suspected that 572 had a noisier fizz, but I was not sure if this was the right thing to say. Julia said 736 had larger bubbles. "They are also slower; they rise to the surface more slowly," I added. Rather judiciously, I thought. "Less effervescent," said Gillian, correcting me.

We stared, we sniffed, we swilled, we pondered. We took sips of water between tastings and nibbled on dry biscuits. Sometimes I remembered to use my spittoon. "More gingery," we said. "More lemony, more acid." Then Julia said that 736 had a "thicker mouthfeel", which was impressive.

After this, we tackled potato crisps. We each had two bowls of crisps called 382 and 917. We stared at them. "Perhaps 917 are more sort of curly," I ventured. The others said they were more of a rich, orangey colour. And 382 were pronounced greasy. We sniffed. We rattled the contents of the bowls round a bit, like claret in a wine glass, and sniffed again. We tasted. It was agreed that the crisps called 917 were saltier and thinner. I discovered that after a while you run out of things to say about crisps. And it was difficult to co-ordinate the crisp, the dry biscuit, the sip of water and the spittoon.

Now there was a chance to go down to the basement, where the quality control kitchens are, and watch the meat buyers sample meatballs in sauce, meat loaves and prepared joints. The food was lined up on a counter. I hovered in the background with a plastic fork, occasionally diving in to sample.

My spittoon technique was getting better, but my vocabulary needed improving. I picked up a couple of useful words from the buyers – "cookout" for greasiness in the gravy and "pappy" for texture that is not quite right.

"Is the gravy bland?" asked one sampler.

"We need to take another look at the gravy," a colleague agreed.

"The texture is a little tighter than it should be," one of them said.

"I wish I had said that," I thought.

Later, I joined the buyers from the delicatessen team at a sampling of six pizzas. It was like being at a rather hectic buffet – the young women dived in, tasted and crisply delivered their verdicts. As I homed in on the very last piece of mozzarella and prosciutto pizza, I tried to compose my face to look sagacious rather than simply greedy.

"Crispy base and very nice rounded flavour," said one.

"Maybe the twelve-inch party pizza is the route to go," another observed.

"The bacon flavour is not coming through very well today."

"Before, it tasted like Italy; now it tastes more like Blackpool."

"Nice texture, different, visually attractive," someone said.

"Excuse me, could I squeeze through and try the garlic and mushroom one?" I asked.

It was a very educative experience. As I remarked over dinner at home that evening – "These sausages have an excellent mouthfeel, but I think we ought to take another look at the mashed potato."

FROM *SAINSBURY'S **THE MAGAZINE*** (OCTOBER 1994)

CAKE-MAKER ON THE RACK

EMILY GREEN

Linda Riley is not a natural law-breaker. She is a forty-eight-year-old housewife with an eighteen-year-old son. She lives in a Fifties bungalow in an affluent town in the Home Counties. She is a practising Christian Scientist. She pays her taxes. She does not smoke or drink. She has never been arrested (she did, she admits, once get a parking ticket).

Yet, as a condition for our interview, she requested anonymity. She could not be photographed. She could not be named (Linda Riley is not her real name). Such exposure, she feared, could land her and her customers in court and liable to up to £20,000 in fines.

Her crime? She bakes and sells cakes in a traditional manner. Most home cooks would recognize her staple ingredients: Homepride flour, fresh eggs from a supermarket, Tate & Lyle Barbados or castor sugar, and so on.

But she is more than a home cook. As a teenager she trained at a college of domestic science. In her twenties she was assistant cookery editor of a leading food magazine, then taught in a London cookery school for two years before marrying a financial adviser and setting up home.

Four years ago she had some spare time and began baking cakes for craft-centre cafés, historic houses and local coffee shops. She and her son even took a fifteen-week sugar craft course together, learning how to make elaborate rosettes. This enabled them to do wedding cakes, which could sell for as much as £400.

Her kitchen is immaculate, but a far cry from the stainless-steel labyrinths of professional kitchens. It is warm and homely, and betrays its professionalism only by having three ovens.

At the height of her business, Mrs Riley would have needed all three. She had begun baking for pocket money, but her cakes were so popular that she was earning between £12,000 and £18,000 a year. Now, as her husband nears retirement, her cake revenue is becoming an ever more important part of the family income.

So, two years ago, it made sense to spend £8,000 on a new kitchen, one that would comply with Department of Health and local authority regulations for licensed food premises. It had stronger lighting, a double-drainer sink, a waste-disposal unit and two extractor fans. She replaced her worktops, floor and ceiling in regulation washable materials. Chairs were re-covered in vinyl so they, too, were washable. She and her son took a hygiene course, which, she says, "taught all this yucky nonsense, like how to defrost a chicken."

Her son adds: "They told us to wash our hands after going to the toilet. And they seemed to be experimenting with steel-tipped Doc Martens to be worn in the kitchen, in case you dropped a knife on your toe."

They got the certificate of training, which hangs in the kitchen, and registered with their local authority as an official food premises. Last December, an environmental health officer arrived to inspect the kitchen. "He said that, because I had a washing machine, I could only do low-risk food, with no raw dairy, so I stopped doing my gooey desserts – roulades and the like," she says.

Then, in February, the new Food Safety Act came into force. A Department of Health spokesman says this should not have affected Mrs Riley. Regulations governing premises such as hers, he says, have hardly changed since the Food Hygiene General Regulations of 1970.

But in June, another environmental health inspector – this time a woman – came to review the kitchen. "She gave me this list," says Mrs Riley. "She didn't want me using fresh eggs. She wanted me to switch to something called 'liquid sterilized eggs'. But if I did use fresh eggs, I would have to crack the egg into a cup, throw away the shell, wash my hands with a product called Dettox, wash the counter with Dettox and repeat the process for each egg. You can't make a cake that way!"

Dettox, an anti-bacterial cleaner produced by Reckitt & Colman, manufacturers of Dettol, was one of many new requirements on the list. "There were to be no wooden spoons, boards or rolling-pins. I had to change glass storage jars, which can be sterilized, to plastic ones, because glass ones chip. Well, plastic ones chip, too, and they hold the flavour of whatever you put in them. And I was to wear white overalls, with pockets on the inside.

"I was to put in three sinks, because you cannot wash a lettuce leaf in a sink where you wash your hands. Every cake had to have a label on it with the sell-by date of each and every ingredient. The paperwork of it! I had to wear a hairnet, and put up fly-screens on every window. I could not use tea towels, only paper. I had to air-dry cutlery. I had to get a new fridge, because mine wasn't cold enough."

Mrs Riley calculated that all this would cost about another £3,000, and stopped baking. Three months later, a local café begged her simply to ignore the regulations and send over her cakes. Even a senior health and safety officer for the region told her to ignore the regulations in order to get more cakes over to the café of a nearby historic house.

The Department of Health says that Mrs Riley can appeal through the Local Authority Co-ordinating Body on Food and Trading Standards, but she is reluctant to have anything further to do with environmental health officers. "If you fully register," she says, "they come to do a booklet on you. I can't afford £3,000 every time they visit."

The most ironic twist came when, by chance, she met the environmental health officer who had insisted on the latest improvements. "She came up to me and said, 'Linda, are you working?' And I said, 'No, you've made it impossible.' And she said, 'Oh, well, it's not essential to have fly-screens. I think we could do it with only £500. Ring me and I'll come and help you.'"

Mrs Riley did not ring. "They make out that they want to help, but £500 is

£500. And I don't like the sound of liquid sterilized eggs. I make wholesome, honest cakes with wholesome, honest ingredients."

Except that, just now, she has to do it illegally.

FROM *THE INDEPENDENT* (17 OCTOBER 1992)

A DAY OF WINE AND CHEESES

WILLIAM FOSTER

The invitation from Var Export (UK) sounded rather promising. Could they please fly me to Brignoles in Provence to visit their 57th Food Fair and sample something entirely new to France? There would be a great display of Provence wines, red, white and rosé, which would be tasted alongside the best British cheeses.

Every venture of this kind has to have an enthusiast behind it and I met him shortly. Monsieur A L Fontana, the High Commissioner for Industrialization in the Var Chamber of Commerce, had previously arranged a sampling of twenty English cheeses at the Royal Show in Warwickshire. That was a year ago.

He had been deeply impressed. The light, charming wines from Provence had gone perfectly with Cheddar, Wensleydale, Caerphilly, Double Gloucester and Sage Derby cheeses. It was an outrage that the British knew their Camemberts, Bries, Roquefort, Pont L'Evêque and dozens of other French cheeses and the French knew nothing of their British counterparts. It would be put right at once.

And M. Fontana was as good as his word. Both the Banque Populaire and Prouvenco, who market Provence goods in Britain, lent a hand. Posters went up all over Brignoles naming *Food from Britain* as co-sponsors. They were mentioned again in the handsome forty-page brochure for the Fair, and so was David Gladstone, Her Britannic Majesty's Consul General at Marseilles, who turned up, bringing the Deputy Consul with him.

There were prefectures from half of France, mayors from twenty cities, members of French Chambers of Commerce and fifty French journalists from Press and radio. A grand lunch would follow the ceremonial sampling. With more English cheeses, of course.

So at the appointed hour, we trooped over to the fair. The wines were there, the mayors, the prefectures, even delegations from Israel and South Africa. It was even raining heavily in the approved British fashion.

But of British cheeses there were but two Dairy Crest cheddars, one distinctly rubbery, the other an indifferent, mass-produced red. (A third, deep-frozen Blue Stilton joined them later, after a hasty sortie to the French supermarket, Sodim, which luckily had a few British foods.)

Expatriates are no doubt used to the variety of excuses when the mighty British export drive comes yet another cropper. A long phone call from Andrew Colvin, *Food from Britain*, greeted me on my return to London.

No, he hadn't been at Brignoles, though he had sent six cheeses along. It was a pity only two had turned up. But we don't sell any British cheeses in France, apart from Cheddar and Stilton, and he is much too busy encouraging the sale of British beef and Scotch salmon.

And surely Brignoles was a pretty small affair, wasn't it? I told him. Oh, he said.

At lunch, I had found myself sitting next to Serge Thomas of the Franco-British Chamber of Commerce. He was saddened but not altogether surprised at the Great British Cheese Disaster.

"The pity of it is that while Provence has a fine variety of wines, their cheeses aren't up to much. So we had a golden opportunity to show the best of British. But all we have done is reinforce the view that Britain is a country without cheeses."

Mind you, he said, it all went much deeper than that. An organization like *Food and Wine from France* in London spent £54 million in a year. Hence the success of French Golden Delicious apples. *Food from Britain's* budget amounts to £14 million, for five years.

And then again, French businessmen have to belong to their Chambers of Commerce if they want to climb the promotional ladder. They give a lot of free time to putting French produce on the map. They see it as a patriotic duty. But the British businessman regards Chambers of Commerce as mere talking shops.

No French commentator who was at Brignoles that day said a word in favour of British cheeses. We sell them under the Official Secrets Act. But I can – and do – recommend Provence wines, especially those dry, fruity rosés. Pop a bottle into the cooler and take it on a picnic. That is where they really come into their own.

Before the dessert course at the big lunch in Brignoles, they produced the cheeseboard. For a moment, hope flickered. Could they possibly be . . . ? But no. The cheeses were all French. If this was Waterloo all over again, the British had decided to call it a day.

FROM *RESIDENT ABROAD* (OCTOBER 1986)

BREAD AND CHEESE

GOOD BREAD, SAFE JOURNEY

ALICE WOOLEDGE SALMON

You cannot help liking Lionel Poilâne, for whose 8 o'clock breakfast I crossed Paris at an unaccustomed hour. The time was itself an indulgence of orthodox schedules, for Lionel usually breakfasts at 7.00, when his shop is opened by *vendeuses* who prepare coffee and take it down a narrow, precipitous staircase to bakers who have worked half the night and just removed the day's early bread from its wood-burning oven.

Lionel is something like a serene grasshopper, based loosely in a tiny modern office that's been skilfully "larded" into much older premises. He calls for large bowls of coffee, *petits pains au chocolat* and comfortable slices of toasted bread with butter and honey. The bread is just wheat flour, water and salt with a natural leaven, yet because of it the telephone rings from Japan, perhaps China, and at various hours from New York, London and most of France. It is fabulous stuff, the world has discovered it, and forms, at times, a twenty-metre queue that has even been snapped by a Moscow photographer to illustrate the food shortage in Western Europe!

"My passion for bread is overwhelming," says Lionel, whose name, Poilâne (meaning "donkey hair"), turns easily into "*ô le pain*". He takes up a *miche*, the round, 2-kilo loaf of brownish bread in question, crust as thick as his little finger; he cuts it, the crust – floured and marked with the slash of a knife – crackles and flies away from an open-textured crumb of warm-shaded putty. "Smell it," he urges; the crumb is ripe, yeasty, acidly fruity, and literally makes the mouth water. It tastes wonderful, slightly sour, chewy; this is *bread*, it has presence, lasts for days.

The slices are perfect untoasted, with salted butter – perhaps Norman, from the province of Lionel's father, Pierre, who came to Paris in the 1930s and bought this Left Bank bakery, installed above the ruins of a Romanesque abbey. Pierre made his country bread, these *miches*, plus many friends, some of them artists who occasionally put the bread on their canvas and paid for it with the paintings which now cover the shop walls. Lionel, who is not yet forty, spent four years as Pierre's apprentice, learned Russian, wrote a history of the old shop, and came to feel that a baker, far from condemned to a life of small horizons, has access to science and psychology, art, history, philosophy, indeed to whatever he may choose if he knows how to find it.

"The more I explored my profession, the broader it grew," says Lionel, clasping his hands, rising quickly and bounding from the office, hair flying, as he urges you to follow. He holds a pilot's licence, considers "*les super-jets*" as the twentieth-century form of cathedral, has launched his loaves by such means around the globe, lectured in China, made furniture in bread for Salvador Dali, written a generous book on *le pain*, is planning another on ovens, and reckons that the measure of man remains intimate with bread, handmade from the best ingredients.

"That's why anyone who wants can come and see my *fournil*, my bakehouse," he says, preceding me down to the twelfth-century cellars. Two shorts-clad Chinese and a Frenchman are at work in a vaulted room of breadish colour.

"Our grains come from the Brie, the Beauce and the Sarthe, big cereal regions south of Paris, are grown without pesticides, and the wheat then stone-ground to order. With this flour we put sea salt from Guérande on the south Breton coast; its best season is the springtime." He holds out a measure of this coarse, rather grey substance, which smells faintly of violets — or is the whole experience going to my head?

"With these go water, and a leaven from the previous batch of dough to act as fermentation." After a series of operations, all of which — save kneading — are accomplished by hand, the uncooked loaves are turned out of their rising-baskets, slashed, and pushed into a low, century-old brick oven which Lionel had rebuilt seven years ago. There bake some eighty *miches* — behind apple pastries, croissants, and delicate little shortbreads — for an hour in the residual heat of the oven that has first been wood-fired from underneath.

"My greatest problem is in finding good, clean wood; two of my '*garçons*' are employed full-time just to search it out." With an oven fired five or six times a day, every day, I can see the difficulties, and wonder whether Lionel can detect from the bread's flavour a difference in the timbers used.

"No, but I can always tell when a bread has *not* been baked in a wood-burning oven, just as I can sense, without being mystical, when it has been made by hand. And, in the latter instance, so can most people — which is why we keep faith with a certain idea of what all of us, as humans, really need."

I left Poilâne's shop with many breads and a cushion — produced at the end of a Lionel-bound with the cry of "don't eat this one!" — that is a ringer for their famous loaf. Across a stone in the threshold is carved succinctly "*bon pain, bon chemin*" (good bread, safe journey), and the message is accurate.

[Ed: The main Poilâne shop and bakehouse is at 8 rue du Cherche-Midi, Paris 75006, and there is a branch at 49 boulevard de Grenelle, Paris 75015.]
FROM *HOUSE & GARDEN* (APRIL 1984)

IS IT A CRUMPET OR A MUFFIN?

ELIZABETH DAVID

Crumpets, or at least terrible travesties of them, can still be bought in England, although they are more commonly sold packeted by grocers or supermarkets than by bakers. Perhaps indeed they are delivered direct from a plastics recycling plant, and have never been near a bakery.

Muffins one rarely sees – although Sainsbury's sell packets of a thing they *call* a muffin – and hears about only when the spasmodic wave of nostalgia for bygone popular specialities breaks over the British Press and its cookery contributors, when there is much talk of the muffin-man and his bell from feature writers far too young ever to have heard that bell or eaten the wares which the muffin-man cried through the streets; at such times there is nearly always reference to the past glories of the British breakfast (I remember the muffin-man ringing his bell on Primrose Hill when I lived there in the 1930s; it was always at weekends and in the afternoon, in time for tea, so if you wanted them for breakfast you had to keep them until the next day) and also to a solitary surviving muffin-man who still supplies the occupants of Buckingham Palace.

Well, what are or were the crumpets and muffins which Mayhew's muffin-man used to sell for a ½d each? What is the difference between them? Which have holes, which are baked in rings? Which are made from a pouring batter, which from a soft dough similar to the one used for baps and rolls? Is a pikelet the equivalent of a muffin or of a crumpet? What is the relation of an oatcake to either? Should muffins and/or crumpets be split and/or toasted or should they not? Are muffins and crumpets made from identical ingredients? If so, what are they? Flour, yeast, water, salt? Or flour and yeast plus milk, fat and eggs? Or flour, fat and eggs with a chemical raising agent? Anybody who knows the answers to more than two or three of these queries is wiser than I . . .

CRUMPET STREET

As a last word on the common present-day usage of the word crumpet, I quote Philip Oakes writing in the *Sunday Times* of 6 October 1974. (His words may be useful to future students of slang.) The subject is a play called *The Great Caper* by Ken Campbell. The play, the author told Philip Oakes, "locates the crumpetstrassen of the world; thoroughfares where beautiful women can always be found . . . In London, King's Road Chelsea is the crumpetstrasse to note. In Munich it's the Leopoldstrasse; in Rome via Botteghe Oscure . . . In Copenhagen you should try your luck on the Hans Christian Andersen Boulevard."

Mr Campbell, added Philip Oakes, was not recommending pick-up points; he explained that the interest is purely aesthetic.

FROM *ENGLISH BREAD AND YEAST COOKERY* (1977)

FINDING THE RIGHT CHEESE SHOP

PATRICK RANCE

L ook for a shop where openly displayed traditional cheese is cut for each customer from mature cylindrical cheeses, which only emerge from their protective cheesecloth binding for final sale. The only traditional cheeses without this binding are Stilton, Cotherstone, some Swaledale, some of the Gloucesters from Laurel Farm, and most Caerphilly (a few of the farm cheeses are bound). The newer cheeses with chives, onion, beer, wine and pickle flavourings are unbound. Only fresh cream and "cottage" cheeses should be under refrigeration . . .

Once inside the chosen shop, let your nose and eye take you exploring until you have decided on your probable choices for the day. If an unaccustomed, dazzling range of cheeses, or sheer mental exhaustion, has enveloped you in that embarrassing fog of indecision which affects us all at times, just plead for helpful suggestions. Ask what cheeses the counter hand feels most tempted by today. In the right shop you will then be offered tastes until you are suited. In such a shop you need to be patient and interested while others are tasting. Cheese buying cannot be hurried.

When tasting, proceed from mild to strong, leaving blues and most cheeses with added flavours until last. It is important to remember that cheeses of the same name vary greatly in flavour and strength according to the maker, the seasons of making and of selling, and the method and length of keeping. Never delude yourself that you know what some favourite cheese of yours is like without tasting the particular example in front of you. You will save yourself disappointment and money by testing it every time.

The cut face of the cheese from which you are being served should have a fresh look. It should not be hardened, cracked or sweaty, nor harbour surface mould, faults which betray a surface left uncut for a day or so. If necessary, ask for it to be trimmed before your piece is cut, or for your piece to be cut from another more acceptable face of the cheese.

Mould in itself is harmless, and internal mould in a cheese not normally blue is often a sign of richness; indeed it can be a bonus, but only for those who like blue cheese.

Unless you are going to work on a whole small cheese, buy only what you can eat in a day or two. Cheese is always at its best when fresh cut and pieces never improve with keeping. You can no more mature a slice of cheese than you can age a glass of wine. "Little and often" is the best guide for cheese buying.

When you are given your taste take it between finger and thumb, or on the palm of the hand, if the cheese is crumbly. You may have caught the aroma as the cheese is cut; if not, put the piece first to your nose, then on the tip of the tongue, and finally press it up on the palate to test the consistency and the after-taste. If you find the consistency disagreeable, despite pleasant flavour, or have any other doubts, do not buy.

FROM *THE GREAT BRITISH CHEESE BOOK* (1982)

PARMESAN

SIMON HOPKINSON (WITH LINDSEY BAREHAM)

Let's get one thing quite clear: Parmigiano Reggiano is the only cheese of its type to qualify for the title "Parmesan". All other granular types of cheese – which may have similar taste and texture – are collectively called "grana".

Parmesan is made in and around Parma and is unique. The finest cheeses are aged for about four years and can develop a crumbly and buttery texture like no other cheese. Parmesan is made from unpasteurized skimmed milk and cooked until the curd has separated. The whey is fed to pigs which, in turn, provide us with prosciutto di Parma. Aren't we lucky.

It may come as a surprise that not all Parmesan has to be grated. Moreover, it is often preferable to eat it in thin slivers (made using a potato peeler) over a salad or atop the ubiquitous carpaccio. When in peak condition, it is a wonderful cheese to eat on its own, or after dinner with some ripe figs or cherries, or better still, pears.

A well-matured Parmesan develops a sweet and tangy quality when in its prime and can be broken off into chunks with the fingers. It should not be cut, but eased off in a chunk with a special stubby knife designed for the purpose. Any knife will do, of course, but it's nice to use the correct implement. When it comes to grating Parmesan, Reggiano is the finest one to use, but (and expense comes into this in a big way) good quality grana is quite respectable and a good deal cheaper.

Parmesan, for me, is like a seasoning; it is not so much something that you cook with, more something you add after cooking. As we all know, its sweet, salty taste transforms a simple dish of pasta that has been turned in butter. A risotto Milanese is incomplete without Parmesan. The saffron, onion, chicken broth and rice come together to form a glorious, unctuous mass once the cheese is stirred in.

Similar things happen to a bowl of soft polenta. This Italian peasant staple has become a fashionable dish in recent times, but it seems that although many of us, including me, love it, just as many hate it. Perhaps it is reminiscent of school semolina pudding. Who knows? If salt instead of sugar, and fresh Parmesan instead of jam, had been handed around in the canteen, things might have been different.

Shellfish risottos do not require Parmesan; fish and cheese do not go well together. Lobster thermidor is a disgusting dish. I also don't understand the addition of cheese to fish soup. There are times when personal taste is not necessarily the issue. Is it possible that some revered and age-old combinations are simply not right?

I once worked in a restaurant where I was asked to cook a dish called Délices de Sole Parmesan. It consisted of pieces of Dover sole dipped in Parmesan and breadcrumbs and fried in butter with bananas. I was quite new to the cooking game at the time, but even then I thought this was a bit rum.

FROM *ROAST CHICKEN AND OTHER STORIES* (1994)

CAMEMBERT BY ROYAL APPOINTMENT

PATRICK RANCE

The Livarot of 1708 was probably like today's; but we know that at least some of the Camemberts being made as late as the 1790s were only five centimetres in diameter, half their present size, and rather stodgy compared with Brie. It was in that disturbed decade that the excesses of the Revolutionary Terror occasioned the revolution in Camembert's cheese which produced its modern shape and internal texture. The crust retained the traditional blue coat given by the spores of the indigenous mould present in the *hâloirs* and *caves* of Basse-Normandie.

On the evening of 23 August 1792 seven priests died in the Terror at Meaux. A young colleague of theirs, the Abbé Gobert, unwilling to compromise his beliefs, was advised by his bishop to escape to England. He went on his way with an introduction to the bishop's cousin, *née* Marie Fontaine, who had been born in Roiville in 1761, and had worked there, or in the nearby village of Camembert, all her life. She was now married to a farmer called Harel near Vimoutiers.

Marie received the young priest and undertook to shelter him until the political atmosphere had calmed down. In return, the *abbé* watched her making cheese, his interest enlivened by his having observed parishioners making Brie de Meaux. Gobert thought the little Harel cheeses rather under-drained, and sad in their yellow-brown aspect, compared with his native Brie. Marie was receptive and tried the Brie method as he remembered it: patience with the curd, and leaving it unbroken until it went into the mould (draining the moulds on a slight slope may have come in then too). Marie's new, more succulent cheese went well on the market at Vimoutiers, and she decided to have bigger moulds made, eleven centimetres in diameter, thus inaugurating the modern size of Camembert. I have read that when Napoleon first met the cheese in Normandy he kissed the waitress who served it to him.

The Harel's daughter, also called Marie, learned the art of cheesemaking from her mother, and married Thomas Paynel of Champosoult, a parish adjoining Camembert and Roiville. They were very active and must, I believe, have made cheese, or had it made for them, on a farm in the parish of Camembert itself (perhaps one belonging to the Harel family). When Napoleon III opened the Paris-Granville railway in 1863, Marie Paynel presented him with one of her cheeses. Like any true cheese-lover, he asked where it came from. "Camembert" was her answer, and "Camembert it shall be called" was his response, together with the appointment of her son Victor as *fournisseur* [purveyor] to the Imperial Court.

FROM *THE FRENCH CHEESE BOOK* (1989)

THE CHIP BUTTY

NIGEL SLATER

I love chip butties. But there are rules.
• The bread should be white and thick sliced. The "plastic" type is more suitable than real "baker's bread" because it absorbs the melting butter more readily.
• The chips should be fried in dripping, not oil, and sprinkled with salt and malt – yes, I said malt – vinegar.
• The sandwich should drip with butter.
Good eaten when slightly drunk, and the perfect antidote to the char-grilled-with-balsamic-vinegar-and-shaved-Parmesan school of cookery. And so frightfully common.

FROM *REAL FAST FOOD* (1992)

ROSES FOR TEA

ARABELLA BOXER

It was in the country houses that tea reached its zenith. Although only a few were ever served at one time, the variety of dishes was impressive. The sandwiches alone were legion, and quite different in character from those of today. Apart from a very few, like cucumber or tomato, they were made with complex mixtures of different ingredients, all finely chopped and mixed together, similar to the sandwiches we find today in cities like Vienna and Turin. Hard-boiled eggs were never simply sliced, but chopped and mixed with mayonnaise, mango chutney, or watercress. Cream cheese was combined with chopped walnuts, dates, dried apricots or stem ginger, or with honey, or redcurrant jelly. There were many more savoury fillings than sweet, and brown or white bread was used, or a mixture of both, or soft finger rolls. For picnics or shooting lunches, substantial sandwiches were made with meat or fish: smoked salmon with anchovy butter, rare roast beef with horseradish sauce and sliced tomatoes, or cold game with sauce tartare. For the tea table, lighter versions were made on similar lines, using fillets of Dover sole, minced lobster, or potted shrimps. Vegetables were sometimes used in the form of asparagus spears, or a purée of green peas. Fruit, in the shape of sliced dessert apples, made an unusual filling, but the most exotic must be Mrs Leyel's rose petal sandwich [from *The Gentle Art of Cookery* by Mrs C F Leyel and Miss Olga Hartley].

ROSE PETAL SANDWICHES

When made with the whitest of white bread and bright-pink rose petals these are incredibly pretty. Damask roses have the strongest flavour, but even this is faint, though wonderful. The texture is also interesting.

1oz (30g) rose petals, preferably bright-pink Damask or old-fashioned roses
2oz (55g) unsalted butter
4 large thin slices white bread, 1 day old, crusts removed

[*Start 1 day in advance.*] Line a dish with rose petals, then place in it some butter [*loosely*] wrapped in its own paper. Cover the whole with more rose petals, pressing them closely together until the dish is full. Put it in a cool larder [*or refrigerator*] overnight. Then cut thin slices of [*white*] bread and spread them with the butter, make into sandwiches, and place [*a single layer of overlapping*] rose petals on the top of the butter so that the edges of the petals show outside the sandwich. [*Makes 8 small sandwiches.*]
FROM *ARABELLA BOXER'S BOOK OF ENGLISH FOOD* (1991)

PAST REPASTS

SANBUSAK

CLAUDIA RODEN

At a banquet given by the Caliph Mustakfi of Baghdad in the tenth century, a
member of the company recited a poem by Ishāq ibn Ibrāhīm of Mosul
describing *sanbūsaj* (*sanbusak*) as follows.

> If thou woulds't know what food gives most delight,
> Best let me tell, for none hath subtler sight.
> Take first the finest meat, red, soft to touch,
> And mince it with the fat, not overmuch;
> Then add an onion, cut in circles clean,
> A cabbage, very fresh, exceeding green,
> And season well with cinnamon and rue;
> Of coriander add a handful, too,
> And after that of cloves the very least,
> Of finest ginger, and of pepper best,
> A hand of cummin, murri just to taste,
> Two handfuls of Palmyra salt; but haste,
> Good master haste to grind them small and strong.
> Then lay and light a blazing fire along;
> Put all in the pot, and water pour
> Upon it from above, and cover o'er.
> But, when the water vanished is from sight
> And when the burning flames have dried it quite,
> Then, as thou wilt, in pastry wrap it round,
> And fasten well the edges, firm and sound;
> Or, if it please thee better, take some dough,
> Conveniently soft, and rubbed just so,
> Then with the rolling pin let it be spread
> And with the nails its edges docketed.
> Pour in the frying-pan the choicest oil

And in that liquor let it finely broil.

Last, ladle out into a thin tureen

Where appetizing mustard smeared hath been,

And eat with pleasure, mustarded about,

This tastiest food for hurried diner-out.*

FROM *A NEW BOOK OF MIDDLE EASTERN FOOD* (1985)

COUNTRY HOUSE FOOD

ARABELLA BOXER

It took the butler at Chatsworth six minutes to walk from the kitchen to the dining-room. Most of the cooking was still done on Aga-style solid-fuel ranges; a thermostatically controlled gas oven was introduced in 1923, but there was no gas supply in the country. Electric thermostatically controlled ovens appeared on the market in 1933; Mrs Tanner, the cook at Chatsworth, persuaded the Duke of Devonshire to install one near the dining-room, so that she could serve soufflés. But her plan failed, for it took the butler too long to walk around the huge table, and the soufflé collapsed before it could be served. It was not here, in the houses of the mega-rich, that the move towards a new simplicity began, but in the more modest homes of a younger, more fashionable set.

The food in our own home was a good example of Scottish country house food. We lived in a fairly remote part of north-east Scotland, with little social life apart from shooting parties. My father was a purist about food, and liked only the very plainest things. He had a horror of cream and rich sauces, which literally made him ill. My mother is American, but unlike many of her compatriots who came to live in Britain in the 1920s, she had little interest in food at that time, although she learnt to cook after the Second World War, and thoroughly enjoyed it. We lived for the most part on prime ingredients, very simply cooked. We had our own farm, large kitchen garden with greenhouses, salmon river and grouse moor, so that we were almost self-supporting. Each Sunday we had roast beef: a sirloin with the fillet – then called the undercut – still attached. My father was an expert carver, and gave each person a thickish slice of the undercut, with one or two thinner slices of the sirloin. For the next two or three days we ate cold roast beef, rather rare; this was our favourite food. I don't remember ever having it hashed up or reheated in any form. Salmon was always poached; when hot, it came with a sauce made from its cooking liquor, reduced. We ate a lot of salads, for my father loved cold food. He insisted on making the salad dressing himself;

*From Mas'ūdī's *Meadows of Gold*. Translated by Professor A J Arberry in *Islamic Culture*, 1939.

bottles of olive oil and vinegar, salt, pepper, sugar and Worcestershire Sauce were laid out on a side-table. My father was terribly fussy about his food; the only comments I remember hearing were criticisms.

FROM *ARABELLA BOXER'S BOOK OF ENGLISH FOOD* (1991)

ROBERT BURNS AND THE HAGGIS

CATHERINE BROWN

R obert Burns, on his first visit to Edinburgh, has come from Ayrshire seeking approbation from the great and illustrious in the land. Already he has made a good impression on the intelligentsia and they clamour to invite him to their private social functions at the Assembly Rooms and St Cecilia's Hall. But the truth is that, while enjoying the adulation, he finds their affairs unbearably stiff and formal. Though he needs their help, their accolade means little to him – a bubble quickly burst – and he would much rather spend his time socializing in the less sophisticated taverns where the atmosphere is more relaxed, where the homogeneous mix of social classes allows Lord Provost to sit with humble caddie, where people meet on equal terms regardless of who or what they are. It is in such taverns that his genius has picked up so much material for the bawdy lyrics – totally unfit for publication – which capture the riotous spirit of the age.

The tavern fare is more to his taste too, and particularly at Dowie's. Not a claret and French fricassee man, he describes brandy as "burning trash". His drink is ale and the "rascally" Highland Gill, not yet fully nationalized as whisky. Illicit distilling of whisky is rife in Edinburgh: hundreds of displaced Highlanders are making it in improvized stills hidden in the cellars of the city. Dowie's food is noted for its fine quality, as is that of many other Edinburgh taverns. Some are run by characterful tavern landladies, known as luckies, who cook up good things in the kitchen and have poems written about their wonderful hospitality and excellent fare.

Tonight Burns is ensconced with his cronies, Willie Nicol and Allan Masterton, in one of Dowie's recesses known, on account of its shape, as The Coffin. Along with the excellent "Edinburgh Ale" brewed by Archibald Younger they have already eaten some of Dowie's famed, and jokingly named, "Nor'loch trout" – not trout at all, but fresh haddock coated in breadcrumbs and fried in butter (the Nor'loch is a stagnant pond, now Princes Street Gardens). Johnie Dowie takes great pleasure in hospitality and every sort of kindliness and discretion. He is one of the finest landlords Burns has come across; in caring for his customers nothing is too much trouble.

Tonight the smiling John brings in a fine gamy dish of jugged hare, and a rich apple pie flavoured with lemon and cinnamon, raisins, almonds, and some finely chopped lemon and orange peel. They have this around nine o'clock, and then later Dowie tempts them to a tangy Welsh rarebit: his wife melts some ripe hard cheese on a plate in the hot hearth and then mixes it with ale and secret spicing while Dowie toasts the bread in front of the glowing coals.

It is not the hamely (homely) Ayrshire fare that Burns is accustomed to. His family are poor farmers and food is limited to the daily contents of the kail (broth) pot along with bowls of brose (meal and hot water) for filling up and hard oatcakes and ripe cheeses for taking to the fields. But the fare at Dowie's, though much richer, is still hamely enough with good broths and stews, the ubiquitous oatcakes and hard cheeses. It is certainly more familiar than the rich and fancy French dishes which Burns meets on the tables of the wealthy.

He has eaten a number of suppers since he arrived in Edinburgh on 29 November [1786], not all at Dowie's or at the fashionable dinner tables. He has been to the Oyster Cellars, and he has eaten juicy sparerib steaks cooked by cheery luckies – butchers' wives, who get the best steaks from their husbands – in the noisy taverns of the Flesh Market Close. Their fires glow hot from morning to night, gridirons clatter, beef steaks sizzle, and customers wait in anticipation till the wooden trenchers are rushed through steaming with the crisp, browned, juicy meat. These are the less familiar city foods for the Ayrshire farmer.

Not long after he arrives in Edinburgh an Ayrshire friend, the merchant Andrew Bruce, invites him for a family supper. Bruce's wife has made haggis puddings that day specially for the supper. Using the pluck (innards) of the sheep which she bought from the Flesh Market first thing that morning, she has spent the best part of the day boiling, chopping, and then stuffing stomach bags, until the muckle pot is eventually filled full of plump haggis puddings tumbling in the bubbling boil. And they eat them that night, appreciating their quality and feeling the satisfaction of eating something good made out of odds and ends – bits and pieces which separately have no real value. Appearance is not the first consideration: what matters is the taste – a principle which applies generally to tavern food in the eighteenth century.

Tasty food may come out of pots, or turn on spits, or grill over hot coals, but it is served up and eaten, by twentieth-century standards, in a rough-and-ready way. Attractive presentation has no meaning as long-boned chops of mutton are grasped from the broth pot and chewed on unceremoniously. Slices of meat carved off roasts on spits are eaten with fingers, potatoes are eaten in the hand, communal eating from a central pot still goes on, and two people will share a basin of broth. We would have found both streets and table manners a problem, though we might well have enjoyed the taste of the food.

To celebrate the haggis and the special supper with his Ayrshire friends, Burns writes a tribute to the "Great chieftain o' the pudding-race!". "The Address" appears in the December issue of the *Caledonian Mercury* and in the January issue of the *Scots Magazine*.

And now this everyday pudding is elevated by the bard to national importance. He could have chosen other dishes. Haggis, though common enough, was by no means any more of a special Scottish dish at this time than roast beef an English one. English cookery books still give recipes for haggas (*sic*) puddings in the late eighteenth century and the Scots certainly liked a bit of roast beef when they could get it. So why did Burns choose to nationalize the haggis? We can only assume that Burns, the iconoclast, looked around for the best example of Scots ingenuity and thrift, the most plebeian dish that would best symbolize honest peasant food. He needed a worthy challenge to the cityfied food fripperies and their attendant pretentions which he so detested. He found it in the haggis.

FROM *BROTHS TO BANNOCKS* (1990)

SHALL I COMPARE THEE
TO A DUCK-LIVER PÂTÉ?

GILES MACDONOGH

[Grimod de La Reynière (1758-1837) is one of the most intriguing and entertaining figures in gastronomic and literary history. Born thirty years before the French Revolution, he trained as a lawyer and journalist before becoming a dedicated gourmand and writer about food. His Almanach des Gourmands, *in which he wrote on all aspects of the subject, was published eight times between 1803 and 1813. The following extract from the first English translation of his work is by Giles MacDonogh.]*

Is there a woman, no matter how pretty you assume she is — were she to have the head of Madame Recamier,[1] the deportment of Mademoiselle Georges Weimar,[2] the enchanting graces of Madame Henri Belmont,[3] the sparkle and appealing plumpness of Mademoiselle Émilie Contat,[4] the smile and mouth of Mademoiselle Arsène,[5] etc, etc — who could rival those admirable partridges of Cahors, the Languedoc and the Cévennes, the divine aroma of which dwarfs in its magnitude the perfumes of Arabia? Could you compare her to those fat goose- and duck-liver pâtés to which the cities of Strasbourg, Toulouse and Auch owe a greater part of their fame? What is she beside the stuffed tongues of Troyes, the Mortadelles of Lyon, Parisian brawn, Arles or Bologna sausage, foods which have won so much glory for the person of the pig? Could you enter some painted pretty little face in competition with those admirable sheep of the Pré Salé,[6] Cabourg, the Vosges or the Ardennes, which melting in the mouth become the most delectable of meats? Who would dare prefer a woman to the indescribable calves, weaned by the riverside at Pontoise or Rouen, the whiteness and tenderness of which would make the very Graces blush? Where is the gourmand so depraved who would opt for some sickly, scrawny beauty rather than one of those enormous succulent sirloins from the Limagne[7] or the Cotentin, which drench the carver, and cause those who eat them to faint from the very taste? Incomparable roasts! In your vast flanks is the source of all vital energy and genuine sensations; there, the gourmand derives his very being, the musician his talent, the lover his tenderness and the poet his creative genius! Would you rather have some attractive but irregular face than a Bresse pullet, a capon from La Flèche or Le Mans, a virgin cock from the Caux, the beauty, finesse, succulence and plumpness of which exalt all the senses at once, marvellously seducing the nervous crests of a delicate palate? And gentlemen, you will note that in my arguments I do not allude to the lark pâtés of Pithiviers, the duck pâtés of Amiens, the dotterel pâtés of Chartres; robin redbreasts of Metz, the partridges of Carhaix, geese from Alençon, smoked tongues of Constantinople, the smoked beef of Hamburg, Ostend cod, oysters of Marennes, Dieppe, Cancale and Etretat; I haven't even mentioned Breton, Isigny or Prevalaye butter, or delicious Sotteville cream; who could waver at the steely force of arguments of a sweeter or more sugary nature? I shall pass in silence over crystallized walnuts, apple jelly from Rouen, prunes from Tours, Rousselet pears, fresh or preserved,[8] gingerbread and *nonettes* from Rheims,[9] Metz *mirabelles*, redcurrants from Bar [le-Duc], the Cotignac of Orléans,[10] the Epine-Vinette of Dijon,[11] Roquevaire preserves, Malaga grapes, the excellent figs of Olioules, the dried figs of Brignoles, the muscat grapes of Pézénas, royal prunes or candied orange blossom from Agen, sugared almonds, rose and vanilla pastilles from Montpellier, apple and apricot paste from Clermont [-Ferrand], fruit pastes from Beaucaire and Béziers,[12] etc, etc. I shall not speak, knowing the weight they would lend to my argument, of Bordeaux *anisette*,[13] Hendaye liqueur,[14] Danziger Goldwasser,[15] Phalsbourg Kernel liqueur,[16] aniseed oil and Kirschwasser from Verdun,[17] Mocha cream from Montpellier, Colladon water from Geneva, Rose oil from Cette [*sic*],[18] Jasmin oil from Marseille (the best of all indigenous liqueurs),[19] cherry Ratafia from Louvres and Grenoble,[20] Liqueur Saint André,[21] the fine liqueurs made by M Noël de la Serre or M Folloppe, Arabian Cream produced by M Le Moine, M Tanrade's syrops,[22] and lastly that human balm, crème de menthe, sandalwood and other Martinquais liqueurs, etc. Be grateful then gentlemen for my silence on the matter, and see if you can establish any comparison between these delicious foods and drinks and the caprices of a woman, her moods, her sulks, and, let us not be frightened to say, her fleeting favours! Think about the dishes I have enumerated first, prepared by the cooks of our modern France, basted by the roasters of Valogne [sic],[23] and finally carved by German butlers, and will you still hold your original position? . . .

Let us conclude then: accept that the pleasures a rich gourmand procures from the table are the greatest that exist, and a great deal longer-lasting than those one tastes in breaking the sixth commandment of the Decalogue. They lead to no languors, no disgust, no fears, no remorse; the sources of these pleasures never cease to renew themselves, without ever drying up. Far from fraying the nerves or weakening the brain, these pleasures become the happy foundation of a robust health, brilliant ideas, and the most vigorous sensations. Further, far from engendering regrets or fostering hypochondria, something which finishes by making a man intolerable even to himself, and all too frequently to others, these joys are quite the reverse; we owe to them the face of jubilation, the distinctive mark of all the children of Comus,[24] and how different that is to the pale and washed-out visage which is the ordinary guise of the bashful lover.

1: Great society beauty, wife of the banker from Lyon, Mistress of Chateaubriand.

2, 3, 4, 5: Actresses in the contemporary Parisian theatre.

6: Pastures where the sheep develop a salty flavour from their proximity to the sea.

7: Possibly Limogne in the Lot.

8: "The genuine Rheims rousselet. Famous for its pronounced musky scent, it was a little pear, of which the skin, green mottled with grey, became yellowish at the end of August. Once ripe, the side exposed to the sun took on a brick red colour. The watery consistency and very rapid ripening of the fruit made keeping impossible. As soon as they were picked, the pears were dried in the oven to make *poires tapées*, which, once bottled, could be kept for a long time without their losing their exquisite flavour." Now a thing of the past (Sarazin: *La France à Table*). In England it is called the "Katherine Pear", cf., Suckling: "A Ballad upon a Wedding" – "For streaks of red were mingled there/Such as are on a Katherine pear [the side that's next the sun]."

9: Glazed gingerbread made in the local convents before the Revolution. Hence the name.

10: Quince paste much loved by the infant Balzac.

11: I can find no trace of this today.

12: *Patissoun*: little lemon pastes eaten hot, sprinkled with sugar.

13: Then and now made by the firm of Marie Brizard.

14: Even the locals have lost all knowledge of this liqueur.

15: Spirit flavoured with orange peel and herbs. Distinctive for the small gold flakes which float about when the liqueur is poured.

16: From Alsace but, it seems, no longer produced.

17: Vespetro, an aniseed liqueur, used to be made in nearby Metz. Kirsch is now made chiefly in Alsace, the Black Forest and Switzerland.

18: Sète is now only famous for vermouth.

19: No longer made.

20: Liqueur de Cérise. It used to be a cottage industry. An almond liqueur called Mérisette de Grenoble was also made.

21: I can find no trace of this.

22: All Parisian distillers and merchants.

23: Cf. Lesage, *Turcaret*, 1709 – *"Vive Valognes pour le rôti!"*

24: The God of Revelry.

FROM *A PALATE IN REVOLUTION: GRIMOD DE LA REYNIÈRE AND THE ALMANACH DES GOURMANDS* (1987)

THE CONCIERGE AT TABLE

ALICE WOOLEDGE SALMON

The true recipe for miroton *is now known only to three or four very old concierges of the Saint-Sulpice quarter who were once in the service of archbishops.*

Théodore de Banville

Paris changes, like the rest of us, and whatever we may do, said the 1890s humorist Alphonse Allais, the more time passes the rarer grow our meetings with people who were friends of Napoleon III. As modern Paris multiplies its towers and apartments, fewer are built with lodgings for the caretaker-porter-and-door-keeper known for centuries as *la concierge*, formerly the ageing and footsore harpy whose dispositions made every tenant quake, now perhaps a young woman, benign and well-educated, sometimes foreign, with fixed hours, a second job, and regular holidays *comme tout le monde*.

As a breed, the new concierge lacks mystery; I know one or two of the old style who would not look out of place beside the guillotine, but the legend of these women as fabulous cooks, as artists with ingredients whose stews were tawny and succulent, in whose sauces, wrote Balzac, "a mother would unwittingly have eaten her own child", belongs to the past. At the end of the last century, the poet Banville lamented the rarity of *miroton*, an ambrosial leftover from boiled beef, while Colette, whose pen flowed with the honey of nostalgia, evoked in the 1940s "an old lady's voice, telling me the recipe for '*café au lait de concierge*', savoury breakfast, snack for an epicure".

A myth has seeped and swirled, like aromas from a casserole, that these were once the *true* Parisian cooks – though I doubt they were any more authentic than the talented *cuisinières* of good bourgeois households or the chefs in a prime restaurant. But during the first half to three-quarters of the nineteenth century, there developed in Paris social and gastronomic customs that set the tone of life until the First World War, and which remain in many ways vigorous to the present day. It is that distant, formative period whose aromas are most varied and diversely tantalizing.

"Concierge" is an ancient word, derived from the Latin *conservius*, meaning "fellow slave". In medieval Paris it was given as title to the royal officer controlling the prison of La Conciergerie, but came eventually to designate a simple keeper of prison keys or of château lodge, or the caretaker of a house or block of flats. *Concierge, portier, gardien, suisse, pipelet* (from Eugène Sue's novel, *Les Mystères de Paris*), and *bignole* – "cop", more or less, in Parisian slang – have been the marks of derision for Monsieur le concierge, husband to the putative cook of whom successive generations have felt more like prisoners than tenants.

In the eighteenth century, the French capital had changed from outsize village to an elegant city of imposing houses, both religious and secular, which the Revolution kicked down and overturned. Clerics and nobles died or fled, the adventurous grew rich, the unfortunate starved while others ate sumptuously in well-stocked restaurants newly-opened by former chefs, jewellers and gardeners to the *ancien régime*. The Empire (1804-14) sorted out liberty and organized equality, Paris became a boom town, a vertical mass of building and venture to which provincials rushed in search of work, perhaps fortune – a process accelerated during the Restoration (1814-30) of Bourbon monarchy and subsequently continued with waxing and waning fervour.

New blocks of flats, new tenants, more concierges, drawn from the multitudes of failed provincials, retired artisans and former housekeepers, erstwhile cooks and ex-prostitutes – ". . . *et puis, la fin, loge de concierge* (that's the final employment)", writes historian Richard Cobb – often hovering near the breadline. For beneath the superficial and well-documented Parisian affluence of that time seethed poverty, a quarter to one half the population always in misery, hundred of thousands receiving bread coupons from Public Assistance during the famines of 1828, the early 1830s, and the years preceding the 1848 revolution.

City statistics for 1846-47 record 21,092 concierges among the 299,387 *temporarily* needy – out of a population around 1,000,000 – who were issued with such coupons, and 1,116 practising or former concierges shown as heads of household in 1872 were classified as indigent.

This "essential muscle of the Parisian monster" (*encore* Balzac) was housed and heated gratis, paid in proportion to rents, and tipped at the New Year – which meant a decent life in the small number of grand buildings and a skimpy time elsewhere. To augment a meagre income, Monsieur usually worked at home – typically as tailor or cobbler – while Madame, though possibly barely literate, distributed papers and post, collected rent, brought up fuel for tenants' fires and cleaned their quarters, charged extra sums for laundry or sewing or cooking, and being rarely off the premises, acted as watchdog and door-keep. Usually *mal vue* – Simenon, through whose work stride many concierges, describes them in *Maigret s'amuse*, as "ill-natured, sour-pussed sneaks" – she and family were frequently badly-lodged in one or two rooms (*la loge*) beside the carriage entrance, beneath a staircase, or in a semi-basement with little light and bad ventilation worsened by fumes from a stove used for cooking and heating. An unlikely setting for gastronomy – or any eating worth notice.

The Revolution, however, had brought fine casseroles from noble kitchens out to the street, into restaurants, caterers, and all sorts of food shops. In 1789 there were hardly fifty Paris restaurants, and by 1820 almost 3,000. The *nouveau riche* speculator and politician were delighted to fall, in public, upon the sort of dishes served by Robert (ex-chef to the Prince de Condé), heralded by writer and glutton Grimod de La Reynière, or detailed in recipes from chefs like Beauvilliers and Carême.

To eat well, or conspicuously, was a sign of prestige, within reach of the few, desired by the many, and increasingly available to the bourgeois, both middling and petty, as the century passed. Respectable wives, absent from restaurants, hired cooks and read the texts of *La Cuisinière bourgeoise*, *Le Cuisinier impérial* (*royal* or *national*, depending on the nature of government during the many editions of its long life), or *La Cuisinière de la campagne et de la ville*, which had forty-one reprintings between 1833 and 1900. In the view of Jean-Paul Aron, modern chronicler of nineteenth-century Paris eating, it was around the sort of nourishment enjoyed by "this minority which converged the longings and demands of those, unable to afford it, who made the ideal more valuable by reason of its inaccessibility" – an ideal which all but the most straitened among concierges would to some extent have recognized.

So what was the nature of this mighty food? Even before the advent of railways in the 1840s, Paris was engulfed daily by tons of ingredients, from its surrounding hectares of cabbage to Breton oysters to peaches worth several days of a worker's wage. Among throngs of modest fish were skate, cod, and whiting, which Carême introduced to the grandest Paris menus, while offal, the cheapest of popular flesh, was praised in 1803 by Grimod de La Reynière and later distinguished by the Baron Brisse, a gastronome and journalist whose *365 Menus* (1867, with numerous re-editions) can be seen as the summation of nineteenth-century Parisian tastes.

Reading cookbooks of the period one comes to share Jean-Paul Aron's view that finesse and style of preparation (*l'accommodement*) were of far greater importance than components of a dish, with consequent lack of snobbery about service of the humblest materials. The Baron Brisse, for instance, stocked his menus with roast beef, sole, asparagus, and *vol-au-vent de quenelles de poisson*, among frequent suggestions for ways to accommodate ox tongue or tail, various ears and giblets, and the ubiquitous *boeuf bouilli*.

The latter brings us swiftly to the concierge. This *pot-au-feu*, once made weekly by most French families, has been famous to the point of cliché, the meat a selection of inexpensive beef cuts – forequarter flank or silverside, shin, *macreuse*, perhaps an ox-head – simmered in water for several hours with leeks and root vegetables to yield a savoury broth with succulent meat and potential for leftovers.

The concierge was house-bound; her eye would turn easily to the pot as it trembled on a corner of the wood, coal, or, eventually, gas-burning stove, which might well have been a small portable *réchaud* that doubled as a heater. She would almost certainly have lacked an oven, had few utensils, rarely if ever read or needed recipes, and not accompanied her boiled beef with anything like the Baron Brisse's *sauce à la bourgeoise*, with its *glace de viandes*, Dijon mustard, lemon juice, and *fines herbes*.

But from her leftovers, Madame would fix dishes dependent for interest on skill, and a certain knack of preparation: *salade parisienne* (cold sliced beef, boiled eggs and potatoes, raw onions, carrots from the pot, with oil, parsley, and vinegar), *hachis* (chopped beef, onion and garlic simmered down in bouillon and liaised perhaps with mashed potato), and Théodore de Banville's cherished *miroton* (or *mironton*), described in many cookbooks and formerly served by innumerable Paris bistrots.

What a dish, this *miroton*: finely-sliced onions slowly, slowly melted with a little broth or fat, lightly floured, vinegared, simmered into sauce, layered with boiled beef and topped perhaps with fine breadcrumbs. Or the beef might be chopped and put to tremble gently with minced onions and a drop of bouillon till the two form a sort of "cream". Simplicity made delectable by care and experience and lengths of the unrushed cooking time at a *portière's* disposal.

Her domaine might be quite extensive, embrace houses round a courtyard, their stables, and various outbuildings; such a concierge could easily raise the principal ingredients of *gibelotte de lapin*, a fricassee of rabbit, broth, and white wine. Writing in 1841, the caricaturist Henri Monnier described the specimen *portière* as fond of domestic animals like the guinea-pig, whose swarms were culled regularly into *plats du jour* judged both "choice and delicate".

Of course, local tradesmen – butcher, baker, greengrocer – had an interest in holding Madame's good opinion and the custom of tenants she would guide in their direction; heaven knows what tidbits found their way into her basket, what reductions remained inside her purse. When she bought the cheaper cuts of lamb and mutton, the concierge would simmer the sort of stews or *ragoûts*, the *navarins* and *haricots* detailed in the contemporary books for middle-class women, like the truly bourgeoise *Cuisinière de la campagne et de la ville* which gives, without the slightest snobbery, numerous recipes for the even cheaper offal – beef tongue, oxtail, *tête de veau*, kidneys, brains, and *gras-double* (beef tripe). Madame Pipelet, Eugène Sue's wrinkled, tattered, peevish, and good-hearted *portière*, listens to her *marmite*:

> . . . let me take my pot off the fire; she's finished singing, so the stew must be eaten. It's tripe . . . that should help cheer up Alfred; why, he says it himself – for a plate of *gras-double* he would betray France . . . *sa belle France!*

Madame Pipelet's cooking fats would be anything from lard or butter (though rarely the latter) to a ready-bought mixture of drippings, butter, pork and poultry fats, to fat from the horse. Horse meat was current in the nineteenth century; Napoleon's police chief had authorised *viande de cheval* for public sale to certified owners of dogs and cats – a pretext which gave poorer classes an access to low-cost meat without embarrassing squeamish governments. The charade continued until a *banquet hippophagique* was held at the Grand Hôtel du Louvre in 1855, and eleven years later the first Parisian *chevaline* butcher opened shop. Though never conceived as more than inferior, horse meat was found to be versatile. Writing in 1875, the scientist Armand Husson lists many preparations, among them the *pot-au-feu* and derivatives, *"boeuf" à la mode, haricot de "mouton"*, *"bifteck"*, sausages, and several ways with offal. The price then was about half that of equivalent cuts of beef.

On precarious days the ménage would have no meat from its own pots, not even the humbly eccentric "escalope of cow's udder"; there might be soup, bread, vegetables (often potatoes, after mid-century), and bread *encore*, with – more or less frequently – some contribution from other people's leftovers. In Balzac's novel, *Le Cousin Pons*, Madame Cibot, former oyster-seller at the Cadran bleu restaurant in its Restoration days of glory, is by 1844 one of the better-off concierges, with a large, clean *loge* in a Marais building, a well-fed husband, and absolutely no savings. For Schmucke and Pons, the frugal tenants whom she cossets like children while avariciously wrecking their lives, Madame Cibot shops and prepares dishes: a sort of *miroton* "concocted with love" from beef scraps bought at a slightly unscrupulous cook-shop, on which Schmucke dines better than "King Solomon in all his glory",

sometimes scraps of sautéed chicken, or meat in a *persillade* and fish
in a special sauce of Madame Cibot's . . . sometimes venison, all
according to the quality or quantity of whatever the boulevard
restaurants had resold to the cook-shop in the rue Boucherat . . .

Buying cheaply and serving short rations, Madame Cibot pockets ten *sous*, or
half a franc, on Schmucke's daily meals.

In nineteenth-century Paris everything from rags and bones to broken bits
of glass and mirror could be regularly sold and auctioned, and the traffic in *restes*,
or leftovers, was highly developed at this unrefrigerated period. Each day the
kitchens of ministries, embassies, hotels, restaurants and caterers would sell off
their debris. In 1859, a servant of the *frères* Goncourt saw a nun arrive with
handcart at the flashy Maison dorée to collect remains from a lavish supper, but
most frequent heirs to such leavings were the chefs of lesser restaurants and a
race of dealers called *bijoutiers* or "jewellers".

Early every morning the Paris "jewellers" would cross town, filling zinc-lined
carts with kitchen remainders destined for stalls and shops in the marché St-
Honoré, the rue Berger at Les Halles, and other markets around the city. By 9
a.m. each "jeweller" had arranged his stock, as stylishly as possible, onto plates
costing three to five *sous* about 1860, and four to twelve *sous* by the 1890s. Emile
Zola, in *Le Ventre de Paris*, describes "pieces of meat, fillet of game, fish heads or
tails, vegetables, *charcuterie*, even desserts, the cakes hardly touched and the
bons-bons almost whole". The cheapest plates featured stewed meat and many
vegetables, the most exotic offered lobster, sole, or some truffled galantine.
Patrons here were the poor, ill-paid, and the down-at-heel, with many varieties
of Madame Cibot. The ready-processed mixture of diverse fats referred to
earlier would be bought from such a dealer, and at the end of the century, a sharp
operator called, appropriately, Chapelier, made a fortune from *croûtes de pain* –
discarded crusts of bread collected by rag-pickers and recycled as breadcrumbs,
croûtons, and (if burnt or toasted) a sort of poor man's chicory.

Some of the *bijou* was still quite respectable, but worse could be had: the
leftover leftovers turned up elsewhere in the markets and in squalid shops as
the *arlequin*, or "harlequin": a sordid motley of salad, bits of pastry, heads of
woodcock, cutlets, gnawed drumsticks in twenty different sauces, already four
or five days along and rotting, destined for a third- (and even fourth-) hand stage
if still unsold.

But this leftover trade had a curious twist: a fragment of cutlets Soubise, of
quenelles de brochet or of venison fillet was a morsel from the rich man's table which
gave the purchaser a share, however obscure, in the sort of food he could never

afford and is said to have craved. Zola's dreadful Mademoiselle Saget (*Le Ventre de Paris*), snoop and gossip, best friend to a concierge and herself a concierge *manqué*, haunts the *bijou* of Les Halles and one stall in particular, where

> [the] dealer affected to sell nothing but scraps from the Tuileries
> Palace. One day, she had even persuaded [Mademoiselle Saget] to buy
> a slice of mutton, assuring her it had come off the plate of the
> Emperor. The memory of this mutton, eaten with a certain pride,
> remained as a sop to the old maid's vanity.

If the poorer concierge and family, plus tenants, are sure to have eaten more or less of this dubious, sometimes dangerous food, nearly all will have swallowed an unhealthy number of adulterated products. The pharmacist and chemist Alphonse Chevalier wrote, in the 1850s, that there were almost as many fraudulent as pure substances to be had on the French market, and the victualling trade was notorious for its trickery.

Let's take that quintessential dish, the *miroton*: lard in which the onions melt might have been "stretched" with cooked potato, starch, kaolin, or pulverized marble; the flour cut with sand, ground bones – if not pebbles – or alum; the wine vinegar, rather weak in impact, sharpened by wood vinegar (containing arsenic) or sulphuric acid; the breadcrumbs, not just second-hand but made from loaves touched with plaster or copper sulphate. And the wine that washed this along the gullet? Usually *pinard* from the centre or south of France, liberally "baptized" or watered-down and doctored with spirits, chalk, lead acetate, or lead monoxide, known as litharge, to temper excessive acidity. Not all wine was wine; a fermentation of juniper berries, coriander seeds, rye bread, and water, racked and then coloured – if necessary – with beetroot, was one available substitute.

The century boomed forward, with its gains and loss and ultimate rush into war, new freedoms, transports, and means of preservation. If French cooks, at their best, can still get wonders from *trois fois rien*, make whiting the equal of any salmon and pigs' trotters into one of life's joys, few of them, these days, seem to work as concierges. No one can confirm that Mesdames Cibot and Pipelet were the best, the *true* cooks of Paris despite modest means, bad conditions, and multiple hazards, but the story is a good one, and like many good legends, is the better for telling and eludes conclusions.

FROM *WORLD GASTRONOMY* (1985)

IN THE KITCHEN

MIXING IN THE BATH

CLAIRE MACDONALD

In November we begin to unwind after the season. It is generally a stormy month in Skye and we often have our first snow, just to remind us what winter holds in store. When it snows we go tobogganing in the fields, but I hate it when we have to get anywhere by road. Single-track roads (of which there are many on the island) mean that if you skid there is no choice but to slide straight into the peat bog at the side.

November is when I make my Christmas puddings and cake. If I was properly organized I would do them in October, but although my intentions are there each year, somehow I never quite get round to it. We are always stuck for a receptacle large enough to hold the ingredients for the Christmas puds for Kinloch, but one year we solved that problem by mixing them all up in the baby's bath. It is ideal for such things – Hugo has long since grown out of it and so now the baby's bath will undoubtedly become an integral part of the Kinloch kitchen equipment.

FROM *SEASONAL COOKING* (1983)

BOEUF MODE

EDOUARD DE POMIANE

We are going to discuss braising. Now you know that this long, slow form of gentle cooking represents the acme of culinary art. This method of cooking, which requires time, is disappearing from our lives, for we have got into the habit of living in a perpetual flurry. Instant cookery is replacing more and more the good old custom of simmering for long hours. But enough of philosophizing. Back to our saucepans and let us make together an imaginary *boeuf mode*.

For this dish one should use a *cocotte*, which is a heavy iron pan with two ears. It has a heavy lid which forms a hollow on top. You will probably have to use an iron casserole instead.

We shall need 3lb of beef (roll of silverside, for example) cut in the shape of a cube and larded by the butcher.

When the casserole is on the fire we will melt some pork fat, preferably from the back, cut into very small pieces, with a large knob of butter. As soon as the fat begins to smoke it will have reached its maximum usable temperature so we shall put the meat into the casserole.

In contact with the hot fat the meat changes colour. First it turns pale as the albumen coagulates, then it becomes brown as the sugar turns to caramel. We will turn the meat so that it browns on all its six sides, then sprinkle it with salt and add a glassful of hot water, afterwards putting the lid on the pan.

Suppose that we leave the casserole for four hours over a low fire, what happens? It fills with steam, the temperature of which rises rapidly to 212°F. As the lid is very heavy it is scarcely lifted by the pressure of the steam, which accumulates inside.

The meat, when subjected for four hours to this same heat, becomes tender and full of peptone like the meat in a stew. This fragrant peptone exudes through the softened surface of the meat and through the slits made in the process of larding. It dissolves in the liquid in the pan and a gravy is formed. Will this gravy be tasty? No, it will simply have the flavour of peptone. So we must modify our technique, or at least render it more artistic.

So let us abandon this experimental *boeuf mode* and make another. Let us start again at the point where the beef is sizzling in the *cocotte*, browned on all its sides, sprinkled with salt and baptized with the glass of hot water.

Now we are going into action as artists. We are going to add all the fragrances which we can find in the vegetable kingdom: onion, garlic, shallots, thyme, bayleaves, parsley, chervil, tarragon, carrots, pepper, nutmeg, ginger, cloves, rosemary, fennel, coriander and marjoram.

We can improve on things still more and replace the water by burgundy and even add, at the last moment, a glass of *armagnac*.

In the course of cooking, the steam becomes perfumed with all these essences and impregnates the meat with them. As for the gravy, it will be more than fragrant. It lacks one thing, however – a velvety smoothness. We shall remedy this by adding gelatine. To this end, from the outset of cooking, at the same time as the herbs, spices and vegetables we shall add half a calf's foot and some bacon rinds.

During the hours in which the *boeuf mode* is cooking these will yield their gelatine and when the juice is cold it will set in a jelly.

During all these long hours of preparation all you will have to do is to lift the lid every half-hour and add a little hot water if the gravy has reduced too much by evaporation.

But each time you will be rewarded for your pains as you sniff the delicious smell which you have been able to create and blend and concentrate.

Just shut your eyes and let your mouth water as you anticipate the moment when your wonderful *boeuf mode* will melt in your mouth.

FROM *COOKING WITH POMIANE* (1993)

THE PESTLE AND MORTAR

NIGEL SLATER

I am beginning to hate my food processor. Yes, it can whiz a pan of summer tomatoes and basil to soup in seconds, reduce a bowl of strawberries to sauce at the click of a switch and turn a colander full of lightly boiled summer carrots into a smooth purée in the time it takes to say baby food. But somehow the whole effortless process leaves me wanting.

The modern food processor is a cumbersome beast. It takes up valuable space in my small kitchen, is a hassle to put together and a nightmare to clean. Even upside-down in the dishwasher the bowl and lid collect water, which I invariably tip over the clean cutlery. But worst of all, it cannot make pesto.

Of course, the staggeringly sharp blade can reduce fat cloves of new garlic, pots of basil leaves and a handful of pine nuts to a pleasant enough glop with which to lubricate a bowl of pasta. But it's not real pesto. There is something too smooth, too sophisticated, too . . . well . . . processed about the result.

Pesto is traditionally made by pounding. Its name actually comes from the Italian verb *pestare*, meaning "to pound". A food processor chops, whizzes, purées and creams. But it cannot pound. There is something about the action of pushing down while applying pressure that achieves a result far more interesting than a quick whiz from the food-processor blade.

There is something boringly consistent about machine-made pesto – or machine-made anything for that matter. I would also argue that the taste is different. I have made sauces in the machine from basil leaves, grated Parmesan, olive oil and pine nuts that were bitter. This has never happened with the pestle and mortar.

It amazes me that so few homes seem to have a working pestle and mortar. It breaks my heart to see this most ancient and efficient of kitchen implements end its working life as a place to store the dog's lead or the keys to the shed. Few kitchen utensils are such a pleasure to use. Crush a handful of basil leaves and the peppery green scent wafts up. Put a little pressure on a spoonful of dark-purple juniper berries and the unmistakable smell of a freshly-poured gin and tonic will fill the kitchen. Even if you stick your nose down the funnel of a food processor, the aroma will just not be the same as basil leaves you have pounded with a pestle.

Enormous pleasure can be had from using a pestle and mortar. There is something about the way the pounding action releases the herbs' essential oils that is therapeutic and relaxing. After a hard day I find the scent of freshly-crushed garlic and basil lifts the spirits.

Even the most automated of homes will find a stone pestle and mortar of use for the little jobs that are too small to warrant the use of the food processor. Crushing crystals of sea salt, for instance, or grinding a small quantity of spice. A well-made pair will last you a lifetime. I can recommend the plain stoneware variety for pretty much everything. It is especially good for crushing olives, anchovies and garlic, three strong flavours that would impregnate a wooden mortar. Less successful, I think, are the polished marble mortars. Whole spices are inclined to slide round the bowl and the pestle can barely get a grip. Ideally I would like a second one with a ridged bowl or rough surface, like the Japanese or Indian versions, for crushing chillies and oily seeds such as sesame.

If you have only one mortar, let it be a medium-sized one. Smaller ones are fine for tiny amounts of spice, but impractical for pesto or aïoli, the golden garlic mayonnaise. It can be just as infuriating, though, chasing a teaspoonful of coriander seeds around an oversized bowl.

The pestle and mortar must surely have been invented for pesto. There is really no excuse for not making your own in high summer, with good basil so plentiful now. I get more fragrant results from the larger, tougher leaves of my pot-grown basil out of doors than I do from the fleshy fragile plants in the supermarkets. If we have a hot summer, the blazing sun seems to concentrate the herb's essential oils. A lack of water seems to produce a more potent leaf. Even shop-bought specimens harden up when replanted in real soil instead of the brown cotton wool they were grown in. Watered from underneath rather than on top, a trick recently learned from a friend, they keep going for weeks.

A pestle and mortar get more fragrance from the basil leaf than a knife or a processor. As the leaves turn from lush bright green to a darker, deeper colour, their oils are released. You can hold their flavour in suspension with olive oil, where they will keep in a screw-top jar in the fridge for a few weeks. Or better still get out the pestle and mortar, add the new season's garlic, pine nuts and cheese and make a real version of pesto. A hundred times better than that from a bottle, and head and shoulders more interesting than a Magimix version, I suspect pesto is what your right arm is really for.

A FEW POINTS

• Wipe the pestle and mortar out every time you use them. Some smells, particularly garlic, anchovy and capers, can linger on the pestle no matter how many times you scrub it.

• If the pestle is made partially of wood, as many are, do not put it in the dishwasher.

• You may find it easier to place the mortar in your lap rather than on a work surface.

• Wooden versions are unsuitable for mashing salt cod, making mayonnaise or crushing anchovies, whose smells they will absorb.

• Don't be tempted to overfill the mortar. It is easier to use when it is about a quarter full.

• If the food starts to slide around, add a little sugar or salt, whichever the recipe calls for, to enable it to get a grip.

FROM *THE OBSERVER LIFE MAGAZINE* (7 AUGUST 1994)

FLAVOURING THE MEAT

THEODORA FITZGIBBON

One cut from venison to the heart can speak
Stronger than ten quotations from the Greek;
One fat sirloin possesses more sublime
Than all the airy castles built by rhyme.

Peter Pindar

The roast beef of old England needs no introduction to the world. It is justly world famous, although perhaps sometimes somewhat overcooked for our taste. It is, however, still possible to get the juicy succulent underdone cuts in Britain, namely at Simpson's-in-the-Strand, at the Baron of Beef in the City of London, as well as at quite a few places in the country. Scotch beef is still considered the best and the Aberdeen Angus breed the finest. The sheep from the South Downs of England are fat and juicy, but the little lean Welsh mountain lambs are equally delicious in a sweeter way.

The flavour of the food the animal ate used always to be taken into account, and the joint was flavoured accordingly. Thus the mountain sheep which grazed on wild thyme was flavoured with that herb and the berries of the mountain ash tree, the rowan berries, were made into a jelly to serve with the meat. The marsh mutton of Romney marshes and elsewhere had a spicy iodine tang, not dissimilar to the French *pré salé*, and this would be served with a hot laver sauce.

"A capital dinner! you don't get marsh mutton, with hot laver sauce every day!" (Collins, 1875.)

Laver is a smooth fine seaweed which clings to the rocks like wet, brown silk. It is washed thoroughly and then simmered for hours, before it is mixed with butter, cream and sometimes lemon juice. It is still found and served in the remoter parts of the west of England, Scotland and particularly in the west of Ireland. It has an acquired iodine taste, which grows on one as one goes on eating it. Needless to say it is extremely health-giving, and in eighteenth-century Bath, where rich people went for their health, it was sold in little china pots. Samphire is another well-known edible seaweed.

The fat downs sheep had sauces from the orchards, such as redcurrant jelly, whilst the lambs in the valley would pasture by streams with wild mint and wild garlic growing alongside, and so garlic and mint were cooked and served with them.

The pigs roamed the orchards too, guzzling up the windfall apples, and so apple sauce became their garnish.

The lush cattle were kept in the near meadow, and as calves shared the milk of the household, and so the accompaniments naturally have the milk and corn products of the meadow and dairy, the Yorkshire puddings, creamy horseradish sauce, and the wild mustard seed of the good pasture. Likewise the garden herbs such as bay and rosemary should be cooked with them.

This principle is followed all over the world when one looks into it. The peach-fed hogs of the United States often have a sweet sauce with them, and the sturdy little mountain lambs and kids of Greece, Sardinia or Corsica are always cooked with the strong rosemary, wild thyme and wild garlic on which they feed. Therefore one can do no better than follow these age-old rules. No doubt the tasteless battery hens *could* be flavoured with a piece of chicken wire!
FROM *THE ART OF BRITISH COOKING* (1965)

NOTES FOR A STEW

RICHARD OLNEY

A stew without the aromatic support of onion is difficult to imagine – carrots and garlic are usual but not inevitable allies. Thyme, commonly assisted by bay leaf, celery, and parsley, is the constant of all bouquets garnis, but it need not be: oregano, savory, and marjoram are among the very useful herbs too often ignored in French kitchens. Nor is a bouquet, in itself, indispensable; its aim is to prevent the herbs from spreading through the sauce in fragments, making them easily removable in a neat bundle. A sauce that is strained will, in any case, eliminate them, and a simple stew with a rough sauce suffers in no way from finely crumbled herbs being scattered through it. A stalk of celery or a bay leaf is easily removed but, if bouquets of parsley or leek greens are used in quantity, it is obviously less messy to tie them up.

Water, stock, leftover roasting juices (fat removed – lamb or mutton juices should not be used with other meats), tomato, and wines are among the more satisfactory moistening agents (in Normandy cider, sometimes reinforced with Calvados, is often used and, in Flanders, beer). Wine may have transcendental powers but, if improperly treated, the sauce will be "winy" and the flavour raw and harsh – distinctly unpleasant. As the principal moistener in a *daube* that cooks for a number of hours (and may be further improved by being left to cool, gradually returning to a simmer the following day), it will eventually melt with aromatic, succulent, gelatinous strains into a single languid and caressing note . . .

FROM *SIMPLE FRENCH FOOD* (1981)

ROASTED RED PEPPERS
STUFFED WITH FENNEL

DELIA SMITH

This delightful combination of flavours makes a very attractive first course. I love to serve the peppers on a faded antique plate I have, which shows off their outstanding colour. The dish needs lots of really good bread as there's always a profusion of fragrant juices.

Serves 4 to 6 people as a first course.
4 large red peppers
2 small bulbs fennel
1 x 14oz (400g) tin Italian plum tomatoes
1 rounded teaspoon mixed pepper berries
¾ teaspoon whole coriander seeds
½ teaspoon fennel seeds
8 dessertspoons good quality olive oil
juice of ½ lemon
rock salt

You will need a shallow baking sheet (I use a Swiss-roll tin).

Pre-heat the oven to gas mark 4, 350°F (180°C).

Slice each pepper in half lengthways, cutting right through the green stalk end and leaving it intact; though it won't be eaten, it adds much to the look of the thing. Remove all the seeds. Place the pepper halves on the baking sheet, then drain the tomatoes (you don't need the juice), and divide them into eight equal portions, placing each portion inside a pepper half.

Now pare off any brownish bits of fennel with your sharpest knife and cut the bulbs first into quarters and then again into eighths, carefully keeping the layers attached to the root ends. Now put them in a saucepan with a little salt, pour boiling water on them and blanch them for 5 minutes. Then drain them in a colander and, as soon as they're cool enough to handle, arrange two slices in each pepper half. Sprinkle 1 dessertspoon olive oil over each one, using a brush to brush the oil round the edges and sides of the peppers.

Next lightly crush the pepper berries, coriander and fennel seeds with a pestle and mortar or rolling pin and bowl, sprinkle these evenly all over the fennel and peppers, and finish off with a grinding of rock salt. Then bake the peppers for approximately 1 hour on a high shelf in the oven until they are soft and the skin wrinkled and nicely tinged with brown. After removing them from the oven, sprinkle the lemon juice all over, cool and serve garnished with a little finely chopped spring onion or as they are.

Note: If you want to make the peppers ahead of time, cover with foil after cooling but don't refrigerate them as this spoils the fragrant flavour.

FROM *DELIA SMITH'S CHRISTMAS* (1990)

SIROP À SORBET AND SORBET AU CHAMPAGNE

ALBERT AND MICHEL ROUX

SIROP À SORBET

Ingredients

2lb 2oz (1kg) granulated or caster sugar
2½ pints (1.4L) water
6oz (175g) glucose
Preparation time: *5 minutes* Cooking time: *20 minutes*

Combine all the ingredients in a heavy-based pan and set over high heat, stirring occasionally with a wooden spatula. Bring the mixture to the boil and leave to bubble for several minutes, skimming the surface if necessary. Pass through a conical sieve into a bowl and leave to cool. Once cold, the syrup can be used in any fruit sorbet, or it will keep for up to two weeks in a refrigerator.

SORBET AU CHAMPAGNE

Serve this sorbet in well-chilled glass dishes. Add a few wild strawberries in season to make it look pretty; their flavour marries very well with the champagne.

Ingredients
½ bottle dry champagne, preferably pink
12fl oz (300ml) Sorbet syrup (see above)
½ lemon
½ egg white
Serves: 6 people
Preparation time: *10 minutes*

Preparation
Put the sorbet syrup in a bowl, pour over the champagne and stir with a spatula. Add the lemon zest and juice. Beat the egg white with a fork and add it to the champagne. Stir well, transfer to a sorbetière or ice-cream maker and freeze.
FROM *NEW CLASSIC CUISINE* (1983)

BARBECUED SALMON

CLAIRE MACDONALD

This is the most delicious way of cooking salmon that I know. The charcoal flavour penetrates the foil parcel, giving the salmon the most exquisite flavour. My mother was rather dubious about this until one evening when she, my father and some friends were staying. It was pronounced the most deliciously cooked salmon eaten by any of them! Praise indeed . . .

As there are many ways to deal with cold left-over salmon, as well as eating it just as it is, do not be put off if you have a fish rather larger than you need to feed the number of people at dinner.

Put the fish on a piece of foil sufficiently large to wrap the fish completely. Butter the foil, and put two or three pieces of lemon and stalks of parsley inside the fish. Put the foil parcel on the barbecue, turn it over after 15 minutes' cooking, and give it a further 15 minutes. Carefully unwrap the foil, lift a piece of skin in the middle of the fish, to see how it's getting on. It won't be cooked unless it is a small fish of around 5lb (2.3kg), but during the cooking time, which will be between 45 minutes and 1 hour, turn the parcel of fish, so that it cooks for an even time on each side.

I like to serve barbecued salmon with Tomato Aïoli.

TOMATO AÏOLI

1 whole egg
1 egg yolk
1 rounded teaspoon mustard powder
1 rounded teaspoon salt
1½ teaspoons sugar
about 12 grinds of black pepper
¼ pint (150ml) sunflower seed oil
2-3 tablespoons wine vinegar
2 cloves of garlic, peeled and chopped
2 rounded teaspoons tomato purée
3 tomatoes

Into the blender or food processor put the egg, egg yolk, mustard powder, salt, sugar and black pepper. Whizz. Then add the oil drip by drip. Add the wine vinegar. Add the chopped garlic, it will break down in the blending. Add the tomato purée.

Drop the tomatoes into a saucepan of boiling water for 2-3 seconds then nick the skins with a knife and remove them. Cut the tomatoes in half, and remove all the seeds. Cut the flesh into quite small pieces, and stir into the aïoli.

FROM *SEASONAL COOKING* (1983)

DANISH OMELETTE

ALASTAIR LITTLE (WITH RICHARD WHITTINGTON)

The correct name for this lovely dish is "Danish Egg Cake", but for some reason people say they are put off by it. This is a shame, because it is seriously delicious and one of the first things I look forward to eating when each year I visit Faborg, the small town in which my wife grew up. It is also one of the few Danish dishes that does not involve the use of herring and, much as I adore herring, you can have too much of a good thing.

There are eight or nine restaurants in Faborg, none of them – it must be said – Michelin rated, but my favourite egg cake is served at a lovely old pub called Tre Krona, where I like to eat it washed down with a lot of good Danish beer.

Traditionally it is served with *rugbrod*, a bread in my view more akin to floor tiles than anything I want to eat, so I say, "Hold the *rugbrod*, more beer on the side." Bliss.

Egg cake may be cooked as individual omelettes or in a large serving, in which case the pan is brought to the table and people help themselves to thick wedges.

The Danes use a local bacon that they call speck, which it is not, being closer to streaky bacon. You can use either smoked or unsmoked. The tomato in the dish must be raw. There is something about a sweet raw tomato that goes brilliantly with an omelette. You might also like to try the egg cake with a topping of strips of smoked eel mixed in with the bacon, to produce a happy marriage of flavours and textures.

Ingredients (per person)

4 slices of streaky bacon
1 tomato (or 3 cherry tomatoes)
1 tablespoon sunflower oil
3 eggs
1 tablespoon double cream (optional and certainly not traditional)
½oz (15g) butter
handful of chives
1oz (30g) smoked eel fillet (optional)
salt and pepper

Utensils

roasting pan
roasting rack
omelette pan or heavy frying pan with an ovenproof handle for a larger omelette
    (a paella pan would also work well)
pastry brush
bowl
whisk
spatula

Mise en Place

First prepare the bacon: preheat the oven to 200°C/400°F/gas mark 6. Cut the rind off the bacon and place the rashers on a rack in a roasting pan in the oven until it just begins to crisp. Remove from the oven and reserve. (This is a very good way of cooking bacon for other dishes – much better than frying and easier than grilling.)

Reduce the oven temperature to 160°C/325°F/gas mark 3. If not using cherry tomatoes, cut the tomatoes into wedges and reserve. Brush the omelette pan with a little sunflower oil. Beat the eggs in the bowl with a little salt and pepper and the cream, if using, until just amalgamated. Do not over-beat.

Cooking

The cooking technique is somewhere between that of making a classic omelette and stirring scrambled eggs, since what you want to achieve is a layered effect of lightly browned egg and moist creamy egg.

Put the pan over a medium heat, add the butter and swirl it around. Tip in the beaten eggs before the butter is completely melted. The eggs will start to set at once. Using a spatula, push the egg away from the edges. Leave for 60 seconds, then repeat the process. Turn down the heat and cook very gently for 3–4 minutes, until the bottom is set and lightly browned.

If the cake is very large and still liquid, stir the surface and put it into the cooler oven for a further 4 minutes to finish cooking, though remember that it will anyway continue to cook in the pan when taken off the heat. This is a case of practice makes perfect. After you have made it three or four times with a certain number of eggs you will know precisely how to achieve the perfect balance between under- and over-cooking.

While the eggs are cooking, return the bacon to the oven to warm through.

Serving

Arrange the tomatoes round the edge of the pan. Cut the bacon into ¼in (5mm) pieces and use them to cover the top of the cake. Scatter with chopped chives and chopped eel fillet, if using.

FROM *KEEP IT SIMPLE* (1993)

PARSLEY AND GIN SOUP

JEREMY ROUND

This soup, a thick greenish mush, is both cooler and inflamer – eaten in very small portions on hot, humid days by the pool. Behind the cocktail-belt, pan-American touches of canned tomato juice and gin, is a base of onion, celery and green pepper, which Louisiana-born chef Beany Macgregor calls the "holy trinity" of Creole and Cajun cooking. They give a distinctive, slightly bitter, metallic tone to all the area's most famous dishes, from gumbo to jambalaya. The recipe is an adaptation of a Bloody Mary Soup concocted by Ed Keeling, executive chef of the New Orleans Hyatt Regency.

Serves 2-4

8fl oz (200ml) canned tomato juice
2oz (50g) celery, chopped
3oz (75g) onion, peeled and chopped
2oz (50g) sweet green pepper, de-seeded and chopped
4 heaped tablespoons chopped parsley
2fl oz (50ml) gin
salt and freshly ground black pepper

Liquidize. Chill.

FROM *THE INDEPENDENT COOK* (1988)

ORANGE SALAD (*REMOJON*)

ELISABETH LUARD

This salad can be classed as a sort of *gazpacho*: eaten in winter and spring, when there is no fresh tomato or appetite for a *gazpacho*. It is traditionally made with salt cod, *bacalao*, the universal fasting food in mountain districts of Catholic countries. If you have *bacalao*, soak it for a few hours, grill it fiercely for a few minutes, then shred and bone it with the fingers. Salt cod is now so expensive that salted tuna and anchovies, sometimes with hard-boiled eggs, are commonly used as a replacement.

Serves 4 as a starter.

6 oranges
1 small can tuna (about 4oz / 125g)
1 small can anchovies
4 tablespoons olive oil
1 red pepper, hulled, de-seeded and sliced lengthwise
6-8 spring onions (scallions)
1 garlic clove, skinned and crushed with a little salt
1 tablespoon wine or sherry vinegar
2oz (50g) pickled green olives

Peel the oranges with a sharp knife, taking care to remove all the pith, and cut them in fine slices. Drain and flake the tuna. Separate the anchovies, drain them and reserve the oil for the dressing.

Heat the olive oil gently in a frying-pan (skillet). Put in the red pepper strips and let them fry for about 10 minutes, until they soften and caramelize a little. Take care not to overheat the oil.

Put the orange slices in a bowl, and toss with the contents of the frying-pan, the chopped spring onions (scallions), the garlic crushed in a little salt, and vinegar. Finish with the flaked tuna, the anchovies and their oil, and the olives.

Leave the salad to marinate for 1-2 hours. Serve with crisp lettuce leaves to act as scoops.

FROM *THE FLAVOURS OF ANDALUCIA* (1991)

SEASON OF MELLOW FRUITFULNESS

FRANCES BISSELL

Pumpkins for Hallowe'en and for pies are to be found piled outside greengrocers' shops now, and they are well worth buying for their versatility. They make excellent soups, even using the shell as a soup tureen; can be added to beef stews, as is done in South America; and as a filling for pasta, such as you will find in northern Italy.

The first mention of pumpkin pie as we know it today, mixed with cream, sugar, eggs and spices, is in *American Cookery*, written by Amelia Simmons in 1796. Earlier recipes suggest thinly sliced raw pumpkin and apple, well sugared and layered in a double-crust pie. This is good too, but the traditional soft, moist, open pie is better.

The best way to cook pumpkin is first to bake it in large chunks in the oven until tender. This dries it out a little and concentrates the flavour. I used the same method for the parsnips with which I made the parsnip and walnut pasta.

This was inspired by a recent visit to Emilia-Romagna where our friends, the Lancellottis, make a marvellous *tortelloni alla zucca*. I discussed the parsnip version with Angelo Lancellotti and he thought it would work. It does. But next time, I shall add a little blue cheese to sharpen the flavour of the filling.

One of the reasons that I welcome the first cold snap of the autumn is that pasta-making is much easier in a cooler, drier atmosphere. With luck and perseverance, I can roll out the dough to number six on my pasta machine, which is very thin and perfect for stuffed pasta. The lower notch makes for a rather stodgy ravioli, with very thick edges. Hand-rolling, of course, produces even better pasta.

The other welcome addition to my kitchen in the autumn is root vegetables, which begin to be at their best – leeks, fennel, celery, parsnips, celeriac, Jerusalem artichokes and marvellous onions, which I make into soups and gratins, or serve as accompaniments to meat dishes. Root vegetables also add an appealing sweet crispness to salads.

Meat has more appeal in the autumn too. I have just cooked my first Sunday roast beef of the season, a wing rib, which is the very best roasting joint, with exactly the right proportion of meat, bone and fat. For two of us, I chose a joint a little over three pounds in weight, too big for one meal, but the leftovers made marvellous sandwiches and the roasted bone a good stock.

I cooked the joint for 40 minutes in a pre-heated oven at 250°C/475°F/gas mark 9: about 12 minutes per pound for rare meat or 51°C/125°F on a meat thermometer; for medium-cooked meat, it needs 16 minutes per pound, and 18 to 20 minutes for well-done meat.

If you do not have a meat thermometer, the following is a reasonably accurate method of judging the internal temperature of meat: insert a skewer into the thickest part of the meat and count to 30. Then remove the skewer and place it on the outside of your wrist, or the back of your hand if very sensitive. The meat is not cooked if the skewer is cold. If the skewer is warm, the meat is still rare. If quite hot, the meat is medium rare. If the skewer is very hot, the meat is quite well done.

The game season is now well underway, with hare, wild venison, grouse, wild duck, pheasant and partridge available, as well as woodcock and snipe. I like partridge and occasionally, although they roast very well, I pot-roast them at a gentle heat. We drank a 1985 Gevrey Chambertin with them, a perfect match.

PARSNIP AND WALNUT PASTA
Serves 4 to 6

To make pasta at home, allow a good 3½oz (110g) flour for each size-three egg. This is enough for one generous portion as a main course. Use a mixture of strong plain flour and plain flour, or strong flour, which has a high protein content and is firmer to handle.

If you are making pasta in a food processor, simply put in the eggs and flour and process until loosely bound together. Knead by hand until smooth on a floured work surface, let it rest, covered, for 15 minutes and roll out to the thickness of a 20p coin. The resting period is important to let the dough relax and become elastic.

To make the dough by hand, pile the flour on to a work surface, make a well in the centre and slide in the whole eggs. Draw the flour from the edges to the centre, covering eggs, and, working with your fingertips, gradually mix in the flour and eggs until thoroughly amalgamated. Knead the dough for 10 to 15 minutes, until it is smooth and satiny.

Filling

2 parsnips, roasted
3½oz (100g) walnuts, ground
2oz (60g) ricotta
½ a nutmeg, grated
3-4oz (85-110g) freshly grated Parmesan
2 teaspoons orange marmalade, with the peel finely chopped
good pinch freshly ground black pepper
1 tablespoon breadcrumbs

Halve the parsnips, scoop out the flesh and mix to a stiff, smooth paste with the rest of the ingredients. Roll out the pasta dough and cut into rounds or squares; fill and shape into half circles or triangles, sealing the edges after moistening with water. Or spoon the filling at intervals on a sheet of pasta, moisten the spaces between and cover with another sheet of dough. Press down around the filling and cut into squares. Place on a cloth-covered tray until you are ready to cook them.

Drop into a large pan of boiling water and simmer for two to three minutes. Drain, toss in butter or olive oil, which can be infused with lovage or sage. Any leftover filling can be used to make dumplings to serve in a game broth.

FROM *THE TIMES MAGAZINE* (29 OCTOBER 1994)

RAS EL HANOUT

JILL NORMAN

This renowned traditional Moroccan blend of twenty or more spices never fails to intrigue foreigners. *Ras el hanout* means "head of the shop", presumably because the owner mixes the blend to his own taste and to the requirements, including spending power, of the customer. The blends vary from one region to another; those from the bazaar in Fez seem to be the most complex. All contain some aphrodisiacs – *cantharides* (the shiny green Spanish fly), ash berries and monk's pepper – as well as spices and dried flowers. Ras el hanout is always sold whole and ground as required. It is considered warming, and is used with game; in rice and couscous stuffings; in lamb *tagines* (stews), such as *Mrouziya*; and in a sweetmeat of almonds, honey, butter and hashish called *el majoun*.

[A typical blend] could include: cardamom, mace, galangal, long pepper, cubebs, nutmeg, allspice, cinnamon, cloves, ginger, rose buds, lavender flowers,

Spanish fly, ash berries, grains of paradise, black pepper, chufa nuts, turmeric, cassia, nigella, monk's pepper, belladonna and orris root.

ONION PURÉE

Serves 4
4oz (125g) butter
1½lb (750g) onions, finely sliced
1 teaspoon salt
2 teaspoons ras el hanout
3 tablespoons (45ml) honey
2 tablespoons (30ml) sherry vinegar

1 Heat the butter in a pan until a deep golden colour. Put in the onions, salt and ras el hanout and stir to mix.
2 Cover and cook slowly over a heat diffuser for 30 minutes, stirring from time to time.
3 Add the honey and sherry vinegar and cook, uncovered, for another 30 minutes, stirring the mixture frequently.
FROM *THE COMPLETE BOOK OF SPICES* (1990)

A LA CARTE

FISH LIVERS IN SHETLAND

ALAN DAVIDSON

When I went to Shetland it was with an intention so specific and limited as to border on monomania. I wanted to find out about the traditional dishes of fish livers, often combined with oatmeal, there.

The phenomenal scale of this practice arose because the fishermen gutted their fish ashore before shipping them south, and their families frugally made use of the edible parts thus discarded. But I knew that in recent times North Sea oil had transformed the Shetland economy. Hence doubt: would many Shetlanders still do as their ancestors did in this respect? Indeed, as the ship from Aberdeen drew into the small and bustling harbour of Lerwick, my wife and I wondered whether we would easily find people to tell us anything at all about fish livers.

We needn't have worried. Informants were numerous and communicative. Indeed Mrs Hutchison, who provided us with bed and breakfast in her spotless and spacious bungalow, was herself a prime source.

By way of introducing us to the subject, she explained that the fish livers vary not only with the species of fish but also according to the season and the habitat of the particular fish which have been caught. One variation which is important to cooks is in oiliness. The more oily a liver is, the more oatmeal must be used with it. A Shetland cook has to use her discretion in this, not follow a recipe.

Mrs Hutchison went on to give her view that if you cook the livers in "muggies" (the fish stomachs) you get the full force of their vitamins; and that if you cook the livers in a fish head the effect is less concentrated. I wondered about this. An expert at the Torry Research Station in Aberdeen had mentioned that the consumption of large quantities of fish liver could be harmful, precisely because one would have an overdose of vitamins. Perhaps "muggies" would be safer fare.

By this time, however, convinced of our genuine interest, Mrs H was proposing that we make "krappin" together, in her kitchen. This is the liver-in-a-fish-head dish, and she emphasized that it was supposed to be a *quick* dish for busy Shetland crofters. It should only take five minutes to clean a big fish head under running water, and not much longer to prepare the stuffing. Some people sewed up the back of the head after putting in the stuffing. She had one friend who even sewed up the lips. But none of this sewing was necessary. One ought to be able to make the dish in under a quarter of an hour, then just leave it to cook for half an hour to an hour, depending on the size of the fish head. We would see.

Indeed we did see; what is more we were not spectators, but served as apprentices, carrying out the whole operation under her directions. (There seemed, incidentally, to be no problem obtaining fish livers, but it was some time before the small boy who was sent for a suitable fish head came back with one of the right dimensions. Mrs H commented with tolerant disapproval that the fish trade nowadays took less care to keep an array of these in stock for customers such as herself.)

The operation went smoothly, although more slowly than if Mrs H had been doing it herself. As on another occasion, when a Japanese sushi chef invited me to take over from him for a while, I was impressed by the natural, or rather unnatural, stickiness of my fingers, which caused a minor but still deplorable wastage of oatmeal. Anyway, the Krappin Heid (to give the dish its full title) was delicious; and I was able to record the Hutchison recipe in full detail in my *North Atlantic Seafood*.

Fresh from this experience, we met a man who belonged to the sew-up-the-head school. This was Mr J S Ross from Out Skerries, whose recipe was that of his mother. It called for a cod's head and cod livers. The livers are mixed with oatmeal and also, if you like (as his mother did), onion, but you must be sure that liver dominates the mixture. You sew up the back of the head, insert the stuffing through the mouth, then sew up the mouth too (I could imagine Mrs H's reactions to this twofold sewing operation). Boil the head for half an hour, then serve it hot on a very hot plate.

Our single-minded quest now brought us to Mrs Mowat of North Roe, another enthusiast for Krappin and a supporter of Mrs H in declining to sew up the head. She allowed that, if a cod's head big enough for several people was not available, several haddock heads (one per person) would do. She added an interesting comment: if no fish head were to be had, the krappin could be stuffed into a large cabbage leaf. She would use a half-and-half mixture of oatmeal and flour in making the stuffing, which ought to be of about the same consistency as the kind of stuffing which one normally makes for a chicken.

Next, we met Mrs Sinclair, formerly of Sandwick and now of Lerwick. She said that she was particularly fond of Stap, the other of the two famous fish liver dishes, but that fish livers were now hard to come by. Her idea of making Stap seemed to be to stuff a fish head with livers (not mixed with oatmeal or anything like that), cook this, then remove the livers and the fleshy parts of the head and mash all together before adding salt and white pepper and serving. She explained that you could perfectly well cook the livers in a stone jar standing in the same pot which you use for cooking the fish head; the pot is covered and the livers cook by steaming. She also observed that haddock was usually recommended for Stap, though other fish would do quite well.

Mr Willy Fraser, a highly respected Shetland fishmonger, had his own ideas about why fish liver dishes had gone out of fashion. He said that line fishing was what used to be done, and that the fish were then landed ungutted, partly because the fishermen would not have had time to gut them. So the livers were available, and were kept and used. But since the Second World War the general practice had been to fish with nets. The men now had time to gut the fish at sea, and the general demand from wholesale merchants was for gutted fish; so the fish were gutted and the livers thrown overboard with the rest of the offal.

Mr Fraser said that in the old days people would have fish liver in one form or another three or four times a week; it was very rich in protein, he thought, and did them a lot of good. Nowadays, older people would come to his shop and complain that they couldn't get fish livers; but he had noticed that on the rare days when he had some they would make enthusiastic noises but wouldn't actually buy any.

The television show *Pebble Mill at One* now entered the picture. Mr Fraser had seen an item in this programme which showed the preparation of a fish liver dish on the Isle of Skye. Piltocks (saithe) had been stuffed with a mixture which seemed identical with krappin, and the result was much the same as a dish known as Cuids or Liver Piltocks in Shetland (except that the *Pebble Mill at One* people had decorated the dish with slices of lemon, a terrible solecism). To make this dish, gut the fish without cutting them open, stuff them with livers (no oatmeal), put a potato in the gullet of each to keep the stuffing in place, and cook them thus.

Talking about Krappin Heid, Mr Fraser said: "I only had it once, and I wasn't thrilled." But he had views about the choice of fish livers. He thought haddock best of all, followed by cod. These were soft after being cooked. But some people preferred ling liver, which remains hard enough to be sliced like lamb's liver.

Mr Fraser's brother-in-law told us about a man from Whalsay "who lived for food, but didn't live very long." This man used to take a big cod's head, put it in the middle of a large pot, surround it with fish livers, apply heat until the livers melted and then spoon the melted liver over the head as it cooked. He would eat the flesh from the head, with potatoes of course, using the liver oil as a sauce. There was an implication that the appalling richness of this dish contributed to the shortness of his life.

Finally, Mrs Grey told us about making liver piltocks in the island of Yell. The piltocks were laid in a pie dish and covered with fish livers, then put in the oven and baked. The heat melted the livers and the fish were cooked in the liver oil. She also told us about a certain Dr Jamieson, who used to go out and catch piltocks every evening. Then he would gut them and put them in a little wooden tub ("daffick" in dialect) before making Stap with the piltocks and their livers, assuring everyone that this was the most nutritious kind of Stap. Dr Jamieson ate this dish daily; it was reassuring to know that he survived in good health on this regime.

We had, by the time we sailed back to Aderdeen, absorbed a near-surfeit of both information and actual fish liver. But Mrs Sinclair was making sure that we would be all right. Her cottage is on the coast and she made a great point of telling us that she would come out in front of it and wave a sheet in the air as the Aberdeen boat went by, "to wish you Godspeed and safe home". So she did, and we were touched by this simple gesture of goodwill towards inquisitive foreigners, as they headed back towards their own more sophisticated but less civilized part of the world.

FROM *A KIPPER WITH MY TEA* (1988)

SNAIL HUNTING

JANE GRIGSON

When we first went to stay in France, I was amazed to see the village come alive on wet summer and autumn evenings. As the rain grew steadier, the paths of the steep cliff – the houses are layered up and into this cliff – attracted more and more people, old men and children mostly. Wrapped to pear shapes in sacking and plastic, they peered into bushes and walls. In their hands, they carried sticks and those openwork globes of metal normally used for draining salad greens. The snail hunters were out.

Soon converted by the shared and savoury results, I never go out now without keeping my eyes firmly on the crevices of the lane. Returning at night to the garden, I see in the beam of the torch snail after snail moving majestically up the mint plants, or over the wet gravel. When in England, I hear the tap-tap-tap-tap on the paving stones outside the window, I try to startle the thrush into dropping its prey before the shell is broken.

The snail hunter's aim – and occasional prize – is the "gros Bourgogne", *Helix pomatia*, the apple or vine snail, which can measure two inches. This beautiful brown and white creature flourishes in local patches of chalk and limestone country in southern England, and is known here as the Roman snail. In spite of its name, *Helix pomatia* was not introduced by the Romans: it was here to welcome Julius Caesar when he first set his standard on the Pevensey coast. Its most famous habitat is Burgundy, where it may be found in the vines, but more likely in *escargotières*, miniature snail farms which supply the Paris market. (The casual hunter is not likely to be very successful, though things are not as bad in Burgundy as in Neuchâtel in Switzerland where a licence is now required; it's feared that snails may become extinct without these alarming precautions.) Burgundian cooks invented the best way of dressing snails. They send them to table on specially dimpled dishes of pottery, pyrex or metal, sizzling by the dozen in garlic and parsley butter. A great treat.

Local savants, though, in our less opulent Touraine, claim that the Bourgogne's close relative, *Helix aspersa*, the common garden snail, or "petit-gris" has a better flavour. They say, too, that it's less inclined to toughness. I cannot judge between the two in this respect, as I've never cooked or had the good fortune to find Roman snails. And I can't often afford to eat them in restaurants, either. But I do notice that recipe books give a three hour cooking time for Roman snails, whereas the common garden snail takes about forty minutes only. So the local opinion may be right, as size alone would not account for the difference.

Helix aspersa is the snail you're most likely to find in your garden in England. Its markings are dark grey and brown, less glamorous than the Roman markings; the shell is about an inch across. It seems to have a decided penchant for walls and hard surfaces – in Bristol snails used to be sold as "wall-fish" – and I often find a dozen or eighteen of them crawling about the porch and doorstep at night . . .

The French think we're odd about snails. "To the Anglo-Saxon, the snail represents a curious French gastronomic habit," says a recent article in a cookery periodical. But seeing that snails are on sale in tins, with accompanying bags of Roman shells, in quite unadventurous towns, places that no one could possibly regard as swinging or avant garde, I think the French are out of date. These tinned delicatessen snails may be the result of our modern travelling habits, but I suspect that the habit of eating snails, in some parts of Britain at least, has never quite died out, though it is much diminished in the last hundred years. Once glassblowers and glassmakers in Newcastle and Bristol used to consume them in quantity. They believed that the bubbly juice soothed their over-tried lungs. This was not superstition, but the survival of a medical opinion voiced as long ago as Pliny, and still maintained in the nineteenth century. Doctors had for centuries forced decoctions of snails (sometimes mixed with earthworms) on delicate children and chesty patients. As late as the 1880s Francatelli, the royal chef, gave a recipe for

ABOVE: SAVOY CABBAGE
PHOTOGRAPH BY PETER KNAB (*SAINSBURY'S **THE MAGAZINE**, OCTOBER 1994)

FOLLOWING PAGE: POULTRY MARKET AT FLEURANCE
PHOTOGRAPH BY ANTHONY BLAKE (*MEMORIES OF GASCONY* BY PIERRE KOFFMANN, 1990)

ABOVE: GREEN GOLD
PHOTOGRAPH BY MARTIN BRIGDALE
(*BBC VEGETARIAN GOOD FOOD*, AUGUST/SEPTEMBER 1993)

OPPOSITE: ETRUSCAN BRUSCHETTA (SEE PAGE 77)
PHOTOGRAPH BY NORMAN HOLLANDS (*SAINSBURY'S THE MAGAZINE*, APRIL 1994)

NAPA Valley WINE TOUR TASTING

I'm a NAPA Valley Wine Snob.

WINE TRAIN

Ralph STEADman 90

ABOVE: CORKS
PHOTOGRAPH BY PATRICK EAGAR (*THE OXFORD COMPANION TO WINE* BY JANCIS ROBINSON, 1994)

PREVIOUS PAGE: ILLUSTRATION BY RALPH STEADMAN (*THE GRAPES OF RALPH*, 1992)

"Mucilaginous Broth" in his *Cook's Guide*. It included chicken, cray fish and a pint of snails. "This," he said, "is a powerful demulcent" – ie soother and loosener – "and is much in use in France, in cases of phthisis, catarrh, bronchitis, etc."

Less scrupulous dairymen of the time put these foaming gastropods to another use. They'd beat them up with milk and pass the thick result off as cream. Oh happy days, when business initiative and individual enterprise flourished, before food adulteration laws spoilt the fun.

FROM *GOOD THINGS* (1971)

AMERICA'S NO 1 PASSION

JANCIS ROBINSON

Tense? Nervous? Headache brought on by people coming to dinner? Adam Shatz, 13, is the answer to your prayers – if you happen to live in Massachusetts. He's been running his own private catering company for three years now. Starting off with takeout pesto and raspberry coulis, he now specializes in dinner parties, typically serving chilled fresh tomato and basil soup, sole steamed over leeks with lime and chive, grilled marinated lamb with red wine sauce (1976 burgundy actually) followed by chocolate mousse cake, to a dozen presumably thrilled academics and professional persons.

Grave to the point of torpor and witheringly self-assured in his Ralph Lauren tie, Brooks Brothers shirt, blazer and cavalry twills, he takes media attention in his stride. "No, I certainly *didn't* look in any cookbooks." I heard him correct the wine and food editor of *USA Today*, "these are all my own creations." He is not a phenomenon, merely a symptom of one: the food boom in the USA today. His proud lawyer daddy may boast of the Roger Vergé on Adam's bedroom walls, but many more aged – if hardly more mature – Americans have been swept up by the prevailing whirlwind to worship such domestic icons as James Beard, Julia Child and M F K Fisher.

Food has become the most effective medium of upward mobility. You are no longer what you eat but what you serve. Shii-také mushrooms, (*Fantasia* shapes, pronounced "she-tarky"), arugula (rocket, pronounced "aroogerler"), sun-dried tomatoes and sesame oil buy you social status. The "safe" dinner-party menu of roast beef and radicchio (chicory at its reddest) signals merely a pathetic awareness that there is a race to be won, but no knowledge of where the finishing post might be.

Americans now spend a third of their food budget outside the home. Events at the bottom end of the market have lifted the average number of visits to a fast-food joint to nine per person per month; today's all-American kid is a lot more familiar with the Gulp'n'Gallop coffee shop than with mom's mixing bowl. At the top end of the market the gourmet revolution means that chef-patrons, such as Jonathan Waxman of New York, Paul Prudhomme of New Orleans, Jeremiah Tower of San Francisco, Alice Waters of Berkeley and Michael McCarty of Santa Monica are the country's new superstars. As one would expect, they are closer to baby lambkins than mature mutton.

Michael McCarty – a dark Dick Diver of Irish descent – was just twenty-five when he opened Michael's, probably the most successful conjunction of gastronomy and glitz in the western world. His defence against elitism and effeteness in the cult of the chef is telling. "When I began six years ago, no one knew what radicchio or *arico ver* were. Now arugula's *de rigoor*. We've served everyone by demanding a greater variety of raw ingredients." Ingredients in greedy earnest.

To the outsider, having the "*de rigoor*" ingredients sometimes seems more important than knowing what to do with them. Much of what passes for cooking in America (and, increasingly, in Europe?) is easy to confuse with styling, merely perming and arranging what is deemed acceptable by the whirl of fashion. There at least, home-made pasta and goat's cheese soufflé are out: nasturtiums, goat (flesh) and fiddleheads (crunchy green vegetable knobbles available in the Pacific north-west only in early summer – or are they really a crafty spun soya product from the labs of General Foods?) are in. Or at least they were two weeks ago.

The difficulty of keeping up with this whirligig has spawned an epidemic of "specialty" food shops and even companies such as Flying Foods International Inc. Three years ago Walter Martin was twenty-six (getting on) and as personal assistant to the general manager of the Waldorf Astoria, "just schmoozing about with dignitaries an' stuff". Why schmooze with a dignitary when you could be earning a fortune chucking Dover sole at him? He and a couple of even more youthful partners now supply America's culinary geniuses with the exotica they crave for their art. Undeterred by the twin menaces of products doomed to die young and Federal Customs, they ship Malpeque oysters from Prince Edward Island, truffles from Piedmont, green mussels from New Zealand and radicchio ("the kiwi of the Eighties") from what were the tulip fields of Holland to the artful low-rise plates that now decorate America's social battleground. Haven't you noticed how the table has begun to star in American soap operas as much as in French art movies?

Walter and friends have had their problems; like their serious over-estimation of American willingness to eat French scallops complete with roe. Luckily, this was in January though, so they just turned off the heating and opened the windows in Walter's Manhattan apartment. They weren't so lucky with the vanful of mâche they tried to keep from freezing overnight with a blowlamp. They ended up, one difficult police encounter later, with a tenth of a vanful of spinach, cooked.

Over in the urban wastes of the South Bronx, Gary Waldron, ex-IBM, has managed to tackle local unemployment and community problems at the same time as keeping New York's top salads garnished aright with opal basil and caraway thyme by setting up high-tech greenhouses growing what they call 'erbs, though perhaps *urbs* would be more fitting in this context.

Not that exotica is all in modern American foodism. The Fog City Diner, for instance, described by the authority at *USA Today* as, "the most *au courant* restaurant in San Francisco", charges around $35 a head for a meal that might include the ultra-trendy likes of mashed potato, peanut butter and jelly (jam) sandwiches and angel food cake. Don't bother trying to book a weekend night in the next four weeks: they're full.

Of course, what really distinguishes American cooking is its reckless cultural mix'n'match, its ethnic smorgasbord quality as exemplified in such current offerings as tofu yogurt, cajun pasta, taco pizza, Japanese trattoria cooking and even, filtered well down the social strata into the salad bars of Middle America admittedly, cold pasta salad with maraschino cherries and marshmallows.

The difference between their food boom and ours, of course, is that they have more cash, or are prepared to part with more cash in the cause of defying their dieticians. (And food's current allure must surely have its roots in its status as forbidden fruit.) One restaurateur in southern California holds a regular caviare tasting at $95. Would they be queuing up in Surrey? The odd British gastronome has been known to splash and blow out, once, *maybe* twice, at the world-famous restaurant Girardet on Lake Geneva. When the work of scientist Bipin Desai, a new Los Angeles recruit to gastronomy, took him to Switzerland for a month or so, he naturally booked in there – for *28* meals.

FROM *THE SUNDAY TIMES* (10 NOVEMBER 1985)

CAN YOU TRUST A BRITISH SAUSAGE?

COLIN SPENCER

The British sausage compared with its European cousins conjures up an image of British cooking, derisory and unpalatable. Yet we manage to eat about 125 sausages per head per year. It was, after all, the first convenience food, the trimmings from a carcass could be chopped up small, stuffed back into a piece of the animal's intestine, salted, smoked, dried and preserved for the winter, the perfect food for travelling people and conquering armies. In medieval Europe, cities and towns gave their name to their particular product, spiced with the herbs of their neighbourhood, from the Romano sausage to the Frankfurter. Is it significant that we did not bequeath to the world a Durham or Winchester sausage? Our repertoire of sausages is sadly small, black or white, pork or beef. All of them dismally unseasoned.

But now we have the British Sausage Bureau, who brought out a report late last year, keen to re-establish the British sausage as "a well-loved trusted item on the menu". For they feel that the sausage has undergone unfair criticism which has misled the public. We no longer trust our sausage and we have been made to feel worried over its fat content, its additives and the exact nature of its meat.

Food regulations blur the fat issue. The amount of meat is shown upon the label, but meat contains fat and the law does not distinguish lean meat from any other type of meat. This is the nub of the anxiety and I shall return to it. A pork sausage must contain at least 65 per cent of meat and at least half must be lean, while a beef, or pork-and-beef, sausage, must contain 50 per cent of meat and half has to be lean. You are left then with 25 per cent of lean meat in your average sausage. The rest of the sausage is cereal, generally rusk, and water. You can now buy low fat sausages with as little as 12½ per cent fat, but that does not mean more meat. The BSB claim we do not like a meaty sausage, and the low fat sausage will have more cereal stuffed into it. (Only too reminiscent of our lodger in the days of rationing who used to refer to the sausages as "them breads".) We are the only European country to use cereal at these amounts.

The second controversy is the question of additives. Sausages have preservatives, antioxidants, colours and texturisers added. The most common preservative is sulphur dioxide (used, the food industry is quick to tell us, by the ancient Greeks and Egyptians), E221-227. Antioxidants stop fats going rancid. BHA and BHT (E320 and 321) are the most common. They are on the list of additives, with sulphur dioxide, which the Hyperactive Children's Support Group suggest be avoided.

The flavour enhancer MSG is often used while the addition of the colour Red 2 G is controversial. At present this has no E number, just 128, but it is banned in the United States. Not all sausages have it, for it turns the meat a blushing pink. ILEA have successfully banned the colour from the sausages served in their schools. The last group of additives are the polyphosphates which are there to hold the water in. Or, as BSB put it, to "retain the juicy texture". Legally manufacturers are allowed to add as much as 10 per cent water to their products. Around 2,500 tonnes of phosphates are used in the meat industry which means we are drinking vast amounts of water disguised as solids.

All this perhaps is not as unnerving as whether the 25 per cent of meat in the sausage is of genuine quality or is MRM, mechanically recovered meat? The BSB say that MRM is "good quality protein" and "helps make the sausage an economical buy for the customer". True, but what is it exactly? Bones from all carcasses are trimmed by a skilled operator with a powered knife for any lean meat upon them. Left upon the bones are meat muscle and connective tissue with the bone marrow inside. This is extracted in machines under hydraulic pressure and appears as a smooth slurry which the makers call "purée". This nutritious pottage, of course, has to be textured and coloured to make it appear like anything at all. The BSB say that there is no crushed bone in MRM and that these would be used in pet foods. In the United States there exist regulations which strictly lay down the amount of MRM in meat products and how much bone, calcium and fat it contains. There is no legislation here to govern the use of MRM or even the need to specify its presence on the label where under our regulations it appears as meat. As usual, the Ministry has fudged the issue.

We all know local butchers who make excellent sausages with plenty of spices, herbs and garlic. These are the sausages the BSB should be promoting, marketing them with labels giving accurate information on how much fat to lean meat or MRM is in the product.

FROM *THE GUARDIAN* (23 APRIL 1988)

NO SMOKING

PAMELA VANDYKE PRICE

The group of transatlantic tourists in the famous French country restaurant were deferential about the food, knowledgeable name-droppers *re* wines, gentle in their behaviour, piano in their speech. And all of them lit cigarettes the instant they sat down at the table, inhaling with animal enjoyment and allowing the tobacco to burn, unquenched, in the ashtrays while they actually had to take time off to put something from their plates into their mouths . . .

The Englishwoman at my table at a banquet for three hundred guests from all over the world inveighed against the "archaic custom" of waiting for the loyal toast before she could light her cigarette. "Surely", she asserted, in those slippery slate-pencil tones that penetrate other noises like a burglar alarm and cause the Englishwoman abroad to be recognizable by sound, "Surely it's my enjoyment that matters, not a lot of silly old customs?" . . .

The politician of all-but-cabinet-rank, entertaining an obviously equally important party in a London restaurant of a size to warrant its being described as "intimate", and a culinary reputation which makes it one of my personal four "tops" in our capital, lit his pipe at the start of the meal, where he sat exactly underneath a notice requesting that pipes should not be smoked in the room. (I have heard since that his working lunches in Whitehall were of so abysmal a railway station sandwich nature that, after one experience, a colleague brought his own picnic basket from Fortnum and Mason – and I hope he asked them to make his salad with plenty of garlic.) . . .

Now I don't smoke cigarettes, having, at the age of four, eaten half of a cigarette belonging to my mama, who smoked up to a hundred daily, and was the only woman I have ever known who could smoke in the street without looking vulgar. My own family and my in-laws all smoked heavily. (My husband used to say, "Doctors begin when they start doing post-mortems.") So I don't mind smoke. Occasionally I smoke a cigar – a large one – after a very good meal. But I enjoy this as a pleasure on its own, not as something superimposed on anything else. Trying to cram several of the good things of life into the single unforgiving minute reminds me of the advice in an American book on how to conduct an affair in the lunch-hour, and give the man a tasty three course meal as well (I suppose you turn off the stove with your toes). And I simply cannot understand why it should be considered other than revolting for people to smoke while they are eating – personally revelatory of total subjection to a habit, and socially lacking in all consideration for those within the vicinity of their whiffing and sniffing. What, after all, would be said, if I sprayed my armpits or scaled my feet in a restaurant? Yet I prefer the smell of both at their worst to other people's smoky exhalations while I am eating.

There is, I suppose, some excuse for those who want a puff between courses. "Such a good dinner – I should like a cigarette," says one of my wine trade friends. But we have compromised: he doesn't smoke between courses at my table, he asks my permission to do so (and I grant it) when at his. And I do stop people lighting up until all my guests have finished or else I mention that we have another wine to come. When I'm a really terrible old lady I shall order the table cleared – even at the first course – if somebody brings out his case. (Someone once did and asked the staff to serve the coffee, as clearly his guest had finished.) Or else I shall put the decanters on the sideboard as a member of the wine trade did when his most important uncle by marriage lit a small cigar after the first course.

FROM *THE SPECTATOR* (24 OCTOBER 1970)

HOW TO TELL THE AGE OF A GAME BIRD

JULIA DRYSDALE

There are only two tests which apply to most species throughout the whole of the season . . .

All young gamebirds have a small blind-ended passage opening on the upper side of the vent. This passage, commonly known as the Bursa, is believed to play some part in disease control. In all species it becomes much reduced or may close completely when the bird reaches sexual maturity, and the presence of a normal bursa is a certain test for a young bird. Insert a matchstick which is burnt at one end so that it is narrow but not too sharp.

The second method (which unfortunately cannot be applied to the pheasant) is to examine the two outer primaries or flight feathers. In the partridge the pointed, lance-shaped tips of these feathers distinguish the young bird from the old, which has blunt-ended outer primaries. It should be mentioned that when feathers are wet, even blunt-ended ones can look pointed.

FROM *THE GAME COOKERY BOOK* (1975)

MARMALADE: AN UNPUBLISHED LETTER TO THE TIMES

ALAN DAVIDSON

I think it was in 1984 that Shona Crawford Poole, then *The Times* Cook, alluded to men making marmalade. I sat down right away and wrote the Letter to the Editor which appears below. It was never published, because it was never posted. I usually remember to put things in the post, and suspect that what was at work on this occasion was a subconscious fear of being typed as the sort of person who writes letters to *The Times*. If so, the subconscious fear won out, and I have escaped that danger.

Mind you, it may be equally bad to be branded as the sort of person who just never writes letters to *The Times*. But the revelation of this little episode is enough to clear me of that charge. I did write one.

14 February

Sir,

Shona Crawford Poole's advice on making marmalade (*Times* yesterday) included the comment that in many families a man does it. So in this family;

and I have now nearly forty years' experience in the art. I began with my Scottish grandmother's recipe, which the S.C.P. version closely resembles, although my grandmother had one more Ritual. Warming the Sugar, Warming the Jars, Putting the Pips in a Muslin Bag, Skimming the Froth, Fiddling with the Waxed Discs: all these and also Steeping the Cut Fruit Overnight beforehand. Gradually, as the decades have gone by and time has become more and more precious, I have introduced simplifications, cannily checking from year to year that the loss in quality of appearance has not been accompanied by a deterioration of flavour and that it is outweighed by the great saving of time and labour.

Here is my advice, for marmalade-makers of either sex. Forget about warming the sugar and the jars. Don't fret because your muslin bag has been lost; you won't need it. Stop searching for waxed discs of the right size; they too are otiose.

Buy 2lb (1kg) Seville oranges, a grapefruit and a lemon. Rinse them, nip off the tough little "buttons" if they are still there, then quarter the fruit and put it in a large pan with more than enough water to cover. Simmer, covered, for about an hour. When the peel is soft, use a pair of kitchen scissors to chop it (in or out of the pan, whichever you find quicker). Add rather more than 2lb (1kg) sugar and stir until the sugar is dissolved. Then turn up the heat to produce a fast rolling boil. Rapid evaporation will reduce the proportion of water to sugar and fruit and permit the temperature to climb to setting point. It may arrive there quite soon (4 minutes is my record so far). So test for setting regularly, as S.C.P. advises. As soon as you have a positive result, remove the pan from the heat, let cool for 5 minutes, stir and then ladle the contents into clean jars, the kind which have screw-on air-tight caps. Fill them very full (no air, no mould), put the caps on loosely, read the newspaper for a few minutes, then tighten the caps and that's that. When you come to use the marmalade you will find that about every second jar does have some mould on the surface of the marmalade. Lift it off with a teaspoon before bringing to table.

The pips? I eat them; with pleasure.

It is fair to add that whatever law it is which says that for every hour saved in carrying out household tasks at least half an hour is restored by the introduction of new complications has been at work. My compensatory complication is to buy for each batch, from a shop selling South-East Asian fruits, one Kaffir lime (*Citrus hystrix*, normally used for flavouring only, thick-skinned and knobbly). I add this to the oranges etc, finely minced. This refinement brings into play the Sub-law of Counter-compensation. You finish up with more marmalade for yourself. Forty per cent of British people find the flavour too sharp and say "No, thank you." The remainder find the flavour so sensationally good that they will be doubly grateful if given half the quantity.

FROM *A KIPPER WITH MY TEA* (1988)

THE CUISINE OF TOMORROW

ALBERT AND MICHEL ROUX

The cuisine of the future will have made giant strides forward – not always for the best, alas! We believe that certain factors will inevitably contribute to the decline of *haute cuisine*.

The first of these is the shorter working week. In a few years' time, the 35-hour week will be standard throughout Europe. No cook working a mere seven hours a day could possibly attend to kitchen basics as well as cook and serve a meal, in so short a time. The kitchens of the great restaurants will therefore have to adapt and change their working methods. There would be no point in staggering working hours and employing two sets of kitchen staff – the personal touch would be lost and so all hope of producing truly great cuisine.

The character of food will change as well. As far as fruit and vegetables are concerned, the ever-increasing use of fertilizers and bio-chemical additives create produce that is attractive in colour and of great size. Unfortunately, this will taste more and more insipid and have less and less nutritional value. Organically grown and naturally harvested fresh fruit and vegetables will become rarer and less commercially viable. Such produce will be grown only by people who love good, fresh food.

In dairy products, too, the trend towards pasteurization, homogenization, dehydration, sterilization, refrigeration and freezing of milk, butter, cheese and their by-products will continue. These processes are already encouraged by European governments, not only for reasons of health and hygiene, but also because they help to rationalize production.

Shorter working hours will mean more leisure time for hobbies, travel, sport, the arts and so on, but, paradoxically, we believe that less will be spent on food. People will patronize only cheap restaurants, serving fast food, snack bars and take-away cafés and these will proliferate.

So, in twenty years' time, the quality of an *haute cuisine* meal, whether prepared at home or eaten in a restaurant, will be quite different from the meals we expect today. The best restaurants, as far as food is concerned, will be family-owned and run. On average, they will seat only forty diners, so that the *patron* can offer a personal service and be in total control. Some large hotels all over the world will continue to run internationally-renowned restaurants for reasons of prestige, even though they may make a loss.

Let us hope, at least, that eating in the year 2000 and beyond will still be a pleasure, rather than just a necessary means of absorbing protein. Let us pray that "progress" will not make every meal identical, nor stamp out the pleasures of eating.

FROM *NEW CLASSIC CUISINE* (1983)

FINE WINES

JUDGING WINE

HUGH JOHNSON

Why is it a mother's trick to hold her child's nose when there is medicine to swallow? The nose is the aerial for the organs of taste in your tongue, palate and throat. Cut off the aerial and you don't get much of a picture. It makes bad medicine tolerable. But it's a terrible waste of good wine.

Yet in effect this is what most wine drinkers do without thinking. Watch them. They give their glass a cursory glance (to make sure there's something in it), then it goes straight to their lips. The configuration of our faces obliges it to pass beneath the nose. But how often do you see it pause there, for the nostrils to register their message? Not often. The art of getting the most from wine is not complicated. But it does have to be learned.

Lesson one is to give it a chance. Any wine that is worth a premium is worth more than a clink and a swallow. How else do you justify the premium?

The art of tasting has been expanded and expanded to fill volumes. Professional tasters stake their names, and large sums, on subtle distinctions that give grounds for investing in a wine's development far into the future. We, however, are talking about enjoyment, not analysis. We start, then, with a list of wine's distinctive characteristics and pleasures: points not to be missed.

APPEARANCE

The first is its colour, limpidity, viscosity, brilliance; its physical presence in the glass. It is the appreciation of the eye. A potent little pool of amber brandy, a glistening cherry tumbler of a young Italian red, a sleek ellipsoid of glowing ruby from Bordeaux or the crystal turbulence of champagne all carry different messages of anticipation. Each is beautiful. Each means something. Each is worth a close inspection. Gradations of colour can tell a practised eye the approximate age of a wine – sometimes even its vintage and the variety of its grapes. Each wine has an appropriate colour that experience can teach us to recognize. Red Bordeaux, to take one example, is nearly always a deeper red than burgundy. If it looks pale and thin the odds are that it will taste that way.

Texture, or viscosity, can be equally revealing. Fine wines with concentrated flavours, like blood, arc thicker than water. Where they wet the sides of the glass they tend to cling, falling back in trailing drops that the Germans call "church-windows"; the British, "legs".

AROMA

When a professional, a winemaker or merchant, swirls the wine around in his glass before sniffing and sipping he is deliberately aerating the wine as forcefully as possible. Your nose can only detect volatile substances. Some wines are naturally highly aromatic, others less so. The less aromatic it is, the more a taster has to, almost literally, shake the smell out of it.

The aromas of young wines are essentially the smell of the grapes, transmitted and intensified by fermentation. The grapes that make the best wines tend to have the most distinctive and memorable smells (aromas is the accepted word) from the moment they become wine. If the new wine is kept in oak barrels for a time the scent of oak overlays and partially conceals the grape smell for a while. After the wine is bottled and as it ages the components become less distinct and complex new aromatic substances form.

TASTE

Nose and mouth are not separate organs of sensation. The blocked nose impedes the mouth from tasting. What the nose detects by sniffing, the mouth will confirm by sipping. But at this third stage of enjoyment, holding the wine momentarily in your mouth before swallowing, all the elements in the wine that are not volatile reveal themselves. Flavour, as opposed to aroma (the trade term "nose" is quite precise), is built up of acids, sugars, tannins, traces of minerals that can suggest, for example, saltiness. You cannot smell tannin or sugar – even though the aroma may suggest, by association, that they are there. Only the tongue, the palate and the throat can get the full feel of the wine; can judge its "body" – the sum of all the flavours in a wine plus the warmth and potency of its alcohol.

Notice particularly what flavour is left after you have swallowed – and for how long. Poor wines leave either a nasty taste or none at all. Fine wines linger in departing sweetness. And great wines perfume the breath for a full five minutes, maybe more, after each sip.

FROM *HOW TO ENJOY YOUR WINE* (1985)

NO ORDINARY PÉTRUS

ROBERT PARKER

The 1982 Pétrus will no doubt be regarded as one of the great wines of this century. It embodies all of the greatest elements of legendary wines and legendary vintages of Pétrus. Consistently "perfect" from the cask and bottle, words hardly do justice to such a rare achievement. First, the colour is sensationally dark, the bouquet explodes upward from the glass within penetrating aromas of ripe mulberry, blackcurrant fruit, and spicy vanillin oak. The wealth of fruit overwhelms the palate with a luxuriance and richness that I have never encountered before. Even the considerable tannic clout of this monumental wine seems to be buried by what is simply a tidal wave of voluptuous, decadently concentrated fruit. In March 1983, when I first tasted this wine, I thought it was the most perfect and symmetrical wine I had ever experienced. Later that day, Christian Moueix called it his "legacy". In an age when "the greatest ever" seems to lack significance and sincerity, this is truly the best wine ever produced for this remarkable property. Anticipated maturity: 1995-2030.

FROM *BORDEAUX* (1986)

WINE FASHION DOWN THE AGES

JANCIS ROBINSON

Fashion has played a part in wine consumption, and therefore eventually wine production, for at least two millennia. The wine drinkers of Ancient Rome favoured white wines, preferably old, sweet white wines. Indeed throughout much of the modern age sweet, heady wines have been prized above all others. In the early Middle Ages the wine drinkers of northern Europe had to drink the thin, tart, sometimes spiced ferments of local vineyards because transport was so rudimentary, and Rhine wines were considered the height of fashion. But when these consumers were introduced to such syrupy Mediterranean potions as the wines of Cyprus and Malmsey, wines traded so energetically by the merchants of, for instance, Venice, a fashion for this richer style of wine was established. By the sixteenth century, for example, light, white Alsace wine was regarded as unfashionable by the German wine drinker, who was beginning to favour red wines. Many fashions were restricted to one particular district or region, particularly before the age of modern communications. It is clear that the wines favoured by the French court in the medieval period, for example, were considerably influenced by fashion, and, possibly, more pragmatically political considerations.

Towards the end of the Middle Ages, fashion seems to have begun to favour not just residual sugar, but alcoholic strength too. Such wines as sack and tent from southern Spain were valued for their potency, although by the end of the seventeenth century seafaring and exploration brought a new range of drinks to the trendsetters of northern Europe which were very much more fashionable than any form of wine.

A new age demanded new products, and the most durable of these were the so-called New French Clarets, whose initial success was largely due to fashion. In the eighteenth century, however, no wines were more fashionable than a clutch of what a modern salesperson might call "speciality items": Hungarian Tokay, South African Constantia, and Moldavian Cotnari. These were available in necessarily very limited quantities, but the wine styles created during or soon after this period illustrate the wine qualities regarded as fashionable then: port, Madeira, Málaga, and Marsala are all remarkable for their colour, alcohol, and often sweetness.

By the nineteenth century much more detailed evidence of the wines then considered most fashionable is available, not just in the form of classifications and a number of books specifically comparing different wines, but also in the form of price lists – for wine prices have reflected fashions in wine throughout history. It would surprise the modern wine drinker, for example, to see the high prices fetched by German wines compared with the classified growths of Bordeaux in the late nineteenth and early twentieth centuries. The late nineteenth century was also a time in which champagne was considered exceptionally modish in northern Europe, notably in St Petersburg.

In the 1920s and 1930s, wine in almost any form was extremely unfashionable. This was the age of the cocktail on one side of the Atlantic and of Prohibition on the other. These phenomena, together with the marked decline of traditional markets and a worldwide economic depression, threatened many small-scale vine-growers with penury (this was the era during which so many wine co-operatives were established).

It was not until well after the Second World War, when some measure of real economic recovery and stability had returned, that wine slowly re-established itself as a fashionable drink (although of course it had long been a drink of necessity in wine-producing areas). As foreign travel became an economic possibility for the majority of northern Europeans, consumers in non-producing countries began to link wine with a way of life they associated with leisure, the exotic, and warmer, wine-producing countries.

By the late 1970s wine connoisseurship itself was beginning to be fashionable, and the economic boom of the 1980s provided the means for a new generation of collectors. This led inevitably to a fashion for marathon "horizontal" and "vertical" tastings of scores of bottles at a time. Buying wine *en primeur* was particularly fashionable in this decade of superlative vintages.

What has been most remarkable about fashions in wine consumption in the late twentieth century, however, has been how rapidly wine production has reacted to them, and in some cases created them. The speed of producer reaction is doubtless related to the development of wine criticism, and its publication in the more immediate media of newspapers, newsletters, magazines, radio and television, rather than books.

Perhaps the most significant fashion has been for varietal wines, especially but by no means exclusively in the New World. This has led to a dramatic increase in the area planted with international varieties – Chardonnay, and to a lesser extent Cabernet Sauvignon, in particular. During a single decade, the 1980s, the world's total area planted with Chardonnay vines quadrupled, to nearly 100,000 hectares / 247,000 acres. There is hardly a country in which wine is produced that does not at least try to produce commercially acceptable Chardonnay in marketable quantities.

On a much more limited scale, the development of a cult following for the distinctive wines of Condrieu in the northern Rhône has meant that Viognier, the vine variety from which it is made, was introduced to wine regions as far afield as Roussillon, South Australia and several parts of California in the late 1980s and early 1990s.

Such versatility in a crop which usually takes at least three years to establish, and is expected to last about twenty years once planted, has been greatly encouraged by the practice of top working, or field grafting.

There have inevitably been casualties among unfashionable vine varieties. Many workhorse varieties have lost ground, which is no great shame, but so has an often rich diversity of indigenous varieties, which is surely regrettable. Outside Germany and Austria, the Riesling vine was one of the most significant varieties to have suffered a sad contraction of influence during the 1980s.

In the vineyard, there has been a fashion for seeking not just ripeness, but physiological ripeness (and "soft" rather than "hard" tannins), even if viticultural academe denied all knowledge of the concepts.

Another viticultural fashion in evidence around the world has been the long overdue acceptance of the now much-vaunted maxim that "wine is made in the vineyard not the winery". But if wine-makers were so much more fashionable than viticulturists in the 1980s, some of what they did seemed heavily influenced by fashion. The flavour of new oak, particularly French oak, became extremely fashionable in the 1980s, as to a lesser extent did the practice of malolactic fermentation, together in some quarters with an overstatement of the flavours associated with it.

Of course fashions change rapidly, and what is fashionable in southern England, for example, may not be fashionable in Sydney or San Francisco. But for certain periods there are wine types and whole wine regions which can be said to be generally out of fashion outside their region or country of production. Obvious examples early in 1994 included most German wines, Beaujolais, and sherry, although by the end of 1994 at least one of these could once again find itself under the fickle spotlight of fashion.

FROM *THE OXFORD COMPANION TO WINE* (1994)

FOND OF FIZZ

HUGH JOHNSON

We know who was responsible for the prompt modishness of champagne in London at a time when it was still a rarefied taste in Paris. It was the Marquis de St-Evremond, a soldier, courtier and irrepressible satirist who had been threatened with a third sojourn in the Bastille for a malicious letter he had written about Cardinal Mazarin, Louis XIV's prime minister. In Paris, St-Evremond and his friends were known as Epicureans, or laughingly as the Ordre des Coteaux because they would drink nothing but "Coteaux d'Aÿ", "Coteaux d'Hautvillers" or "Coteaux d'Avenay".

In London St-Evremond made himself the unofficial agent of champagne, with immediate effect. In 1664 the Earl of Bedford ordered three tonneaux of Sillery for his palace at Woburn. Buckingham, Arlington, all the grandees of the day took to the new taste. With it they ordered bottles and corks: the new strong bottle invented by Sir Kenelm Digby. Unlike the vintners, they probably did not "use vast quantities of Sugar and molasses". But they did find their champagne, bottled on arrival, was perceptibly fizzy, if not downright frothing, when they opened it months, perhaps even years, later. What is more, to the disgust of St-Evremond, they were delighted with the fizz, and rapidly noticed its uninhibiting effect. The old Epicure was as repelled by bubbles in his favourite wine as we would be by bubbles in our claret. Dom Pérignon was fully in

agreement. It was his life's work to prevent champagne having bubbles.
FROM *THE STORY OF WINE* (1989)

MAD ABOUT THE BOY

CYRIL RAY

No wine has ever earned so many or such affectionate nicknames from the English, who have always been among the greatest consumers of champagne. The United Kingdom imports something like eight million bottles a year, only a few hundred cases short of Italy's total, which makes it one of easily the two most valuable export markets – half as big again as the United States.

The derivation of "fizz" and "bubbly" is self-evident, and "the widow" commemorates the Veuve Clicquot. It came to be called "the boy" by Edwardian and late-Victorian heavy swells after a shooting-party – the story goes – at which Edward VII (when Prince of Wales) was present, at which a lad trundled a wheelbarrow-load of champagne around, packed in ice. It was a hot day, and the number of times the thirsty guns called "Boy!" led to a transference of epithet from the lad himself to what he had charge of.

Not that it always followed, as a late-Victorian social historian primly observed, "that everybody who uses the word nowadays was out shooting that day with the Prince". But who calls it "the boy" today? All I ever hear nowadays is "champers". Which is unimaginative of us, I suppose, but then I doubt whether even the most relentlessly facetious present-day after-dinner speaker would stoop to the early-Victorian toast I came across in *The Toastmaster's Companion: Loyal, Patriotic, Naval, Military, Love, Bottle, Masonic, Sporting and other Toasts and Sentiments*:

Champaign (*sic*) to our real friends, and
Real pain to our sham friends.
FROM *RAY ON WINE* (1979)

CHÂTEAU D'YQUEM

ROBERT PARKER

Yquem is located in the heart of the Sauternes region. It sits magnificently atop a small hill overlooking the surrounding vineyards of many of the Premiers Crus Classés.

Since 1785, this estate has been in the hands of just one family. Comte

Alexandre de Lur Saluces is the most recent member of this family to have responsibility for managing this vast estate of 427 acres, having taken over from his uncle in 1968.

Yquem's greatness and uniqueness certainly result from a number of factors. First, it has a perfect location that is said to have its own micro-climate. Second, Yquem has an elaborate drainage system that was installed by the Lur Saluces family; it includes over sixty miles of pipes. Third, there is a fanatical obsession at Yquem to produce only the finest wines, regardless of financial loss or trouble. It is this last factor that is the biggest reason why Yquem is so superior to its neighbours.

At Yquem, they proudly boast that only one glass of wine per vine is produced. The grapes are picked at perfect maturity, one by one, by a group of 150 pickers who frequently spend six to eight weeks at Yquem, and go through the vineyard a minimum of four separate times. In 1964 they canvassed the vineyard thirteen separate times, only to have harvested grapes that were deemed unsuitable. Yquem decided to produce no wine in that vintage. Few winemaking estates are willing or financially able to declassify the entire crop. In addition to 1964, no wine was produced at Yquem in 1972 and 1974.

Yquem has unbelievable ageing possibilities. Because it is so rich, opulent, and sweet, much of it is drunk before it ever reaches its tenth birthday. However, Yquem almost always needs fifteen to twenty years to show its best, and the great vintages will be fresh and decadently rich for as long as forty to fifty years. The greatest Yquem I ever drank was the 1921, served in November 1983. It was remarkably fresh and alive, with a luxuriousness and richness I shall never forget.
FROM *BORDEAUX* (1986)

WELL PRESERVED

EDMUND PENNING-ROWSELL

When Sir Arthur Evans of Knossos fame died early in the last war, part of his cellar was included in the sale of his house on Boars Hill, near Oxford. By this time Britain was cut off from Continental wine supplies, and prices were rising fast. A friend of mine attended the sale, and while anonymous St-Julien and doubtful Liebfraumilch fetched about 30 shillings a bottle, six or seven times their pre-war value, some old bottles of Burgundy and Sauternes were largely disregarded and went very cheaply. My friend bought five or six bottles of Yquem '93 for 15 shillings apiece, and some Clos de Vougeot '98 for the same price. He passed me a proportion of each, and I also shared more than one of his bottles. When I drank the '93s they were either side of fifty years old, the colour was dark, but the flavour wonderfully complete and luscious.

My few bottles of the '21 – certainly the most celebrated Yquem of this century and on a par with the Cheval-Blanc of the same year – came to me soon after the end of the last war from a doctor friend in Swindon. Swindon, a railway town in southern England reminiscent of the industrial north, is not exactly the place where one would expect to find a small cache of Yquem '21, but it had belonged to the departed husband of a patient, who asked my friend to take eight or nine bottles of this precious wine, along with a few other old Sauternes, including Coutet '21 and '24, in settlement of his account. In due course several of these found their way into my cellar, and I drank the last bottle of this Yquem '21 in 1955. It was still pale and in excellent condition, whereas, according to Harry Waugh who shared in this splendid bottle, a number of examples he had had in Bordeaux in previous years had been *madérisé* (madeira-coloured and having lost its freshness) and past their best. One up for Swindon and its cold climate!
FROM *THE WINES OF BORDEAUX* (1973)

GETTING TO KNOW BURGUNDY

H W YOXALL

I hate those exaggeratedly large goblets, bigger even than brandy *ballons*, that they provide in some pretentious Burgundian restaurants, and also, it must be admitted, in some good ones, for even quite unimportant burgundies. (I was given one recently in Beaune for a young Savigny!) To drink from these you have to lie back in your chair, and risk dislocating your neck. A bottle split among six of such leaves only a faint smear in the bottom of each. But burgundy does call for a reasonably large glass, so that, when it is filled two-thirds full, you can twirl the wine round without spilling it. This rotation will release the volatile essences, even in quite unimportant wines, almost all of which have something for the nose, as well as bring out the voluptuous beauty of the *parfum* of the *grands crus*. Colourless, uncut glasses best reveal the loveliness of the colour of burgundy, from the pale green-gold glint of chablis to the magnificent crimson of the Gevrey-Chambertins.

It would not look very pretty at a mixed dinner, but at gatherings of *copains* assembled to discuss burgundy the wine can be rolled round in the mouth, while the drinker breathes in and out through the nose, in order to get the full savour. Another trick, to prolong the luscious after-taste of a fine burgundy, is to protrude your tongue through your closed lips when you have taken a sip. The relish of the wine then seems to go on re-echoing like distant thunder in a summer storm. This prolonged after-taste is one of the most amiable features of good burgundy.

They tell a story in Beaune of the guest of a famous gastronome, who had emptied his glass of a superb *cru* at one gulp. "Sir," said the host, "when one has the honour to be invited to drink wine like this, one looks at it first, then one takes its bouquet, next one sips it, and finally one talks about it." That talking about it is so important, particularly when one can discuss it with persons who know more about it than oneself (which has not been difficult to arrange in my own case). Well-informed opinion enormously increases one's appreciation of wine. It is based on an immense accumulated lore, the synthesis of the experience acquired by thousands of trained palates. There is no short cut to a knowledge of burgundy, but such symposia (I use the word in its original Greek sense) can save the learner from many detours, and even at times from culs-de-sac.

FROM *THE WINES OF BURGUNDY* (1974)

DON'T ROCK THE CRADLE

JULIAN JEFFS

The cradle is perhaps the most infuriatingly misapplied aid to wine drinking ever to have been invented. It has two uses: to help with decanting, or alternatively to avoid the need for decanting. Generally speaking, if there is time, decanting is best done by bringing the wine up from the cellar two or three days before it is required and then leaving the bottles to stand upright in a still place at the right temperature so that the sediment sinks to the bottom. The wine can then be decanted in the usual way. But sometimes a red wine is needed in a greater hurry and then the host may bring the wine up out of the cellar in a basket, holding it very steadily, so that the wine is not shaken and the deposit remains in the position which it occupied in the cellar. The wine can then be decanted at any time by tilting the basket very gently and stopping before the sediment comes over. To avoid the need for decanting altogether, a bottle may be put into a basket (and this is particularly useful when the wine is very old and may fade rapidly in the glass or even during decanting) and then poured into the requisite number of glasses, holding the basket very steady so that the sediment does not get shaken up. But it is essential to complete the decanting in one operation. Once the cradle is put down, the wine swings back on to the sediment and stirs the whole thing up.

There is nothing more infuriating than the misuse of decanting cradles in restaurants. To put a wine with no sediment in a cradle is an absurd affectation that takes up table space and serves no possible useful purpose. On the other hand, if the wine does have a sediment, it should be properly decanted as the perpetual movement of the basket, as glasses are refilled, inevitably stirs the sediment up. Any wine waiter bringing a bottle of red wine to a dining table in a cradle should have it slung at his head.

FROM *LITTLE DICTIONARY OF DRINK* (1973)

SPARKLING RED BURGUNDY

H W YOXALL

I must confess that I cannot recall ever having drunk sparkling red burgundy before starting this book. I had heard that it was a useful medium for relaxing the inhibitions of young ladies in the provinces, but had not had any occasion to put this to the test. However, since undertaking my contract with the publishers, I have, with proper conscientiousness, tested several bottles of different brands and found them quite unobjectionable, if not very interesting.

FROM *THE WINES OF BURGUNDY* (1974)

WINE MAKERS

ERNEST AUJAS

JOHN ARLOTT

You are on the north road out of Juliénas when you pass the Coq d'Or and Chez la Rose, next door to each other on your left. Tiny as they are, they are two of the dozen best restaurants in the entire Beaujolais. The road, like any other in Beaujolais, never continues straight for more than a few metres; but soon it runs like a shelf let into the hillside of south-east facing vineyards. After perhaps a kilometre, a stream, less than a yard wide, comes sparkling down the hillside on your right. It crosses the road through a shallow conduit and then leaps into the wall of a grey stone house, of which only a single – windowless – storey shows at road level.

This is the home, presshouse, cellar, and bottling shed of the vigneron, Ernest Aujas. There is no footpath; the wide wooden doors at the end of the building give directly on to the narrow road and, when they are opened, the ancient, hand wine press can be filled directly from trucks standing in the roadway.

At the other end, the path just wide enough for the family truck, turns, hairpin, quickly down to bottom floor level of the house, while the hill tumbles on steeply away, so steeply indeed that the plough is drawn up the vineyard slope by a winch. The cellar yard is cut deeply into the hill and on the bank rest the carcasses of a couple of cars, a dozen or so worn out tractor tyres, a heap of gnarled, grubbed-up vine roots, and an orderly mountain of empty, green burgundy bottles waiting to be filled.

The ground floor of the house, its windows looking out across its own hill to others, and the cellar, are one solid, stone-built unit, running far back into the earth. The stream bursts from its under-floor tunnel, across the yard and gushes on, between the rabbit hutches and the dog kennels, through the garden patch and the olive trees, and down the hill.

Ernest Aujas is strongly built, six feet tall, sixty years old; his face weather-beaten to a brick red; a sun bleached beret partly covers his white hair; the frilly stub of a hand-rolled cigarette clings to his lower lip. No spendthrift of words, he answers questions with the quiet certainty of a man who has worked out his problems.

He shares the labour of a six-hectare (14.4 acres) vineyard with his son. They split the proceeds 3½/2½: the son will inherit. Roughly speaking, the son cultivates the vineyard, the father maintains the cellar, vinifies, bottles and packs. This, though, is a harsh workload possible only with family help from wives, cousins, even grandparents, at busy times; a team of as many as two dozen Portuguese – mainly students – in the ten- to fifteen-day vendage.

The cellar is gravity fed from the press at road level; five vast and four smaller, but still mighty, barrels hold the wine. In March 1978, the 1976, big and tannic, was still unbottled. M. Aujas, content that he had a fine vintage, did not propose to hurry it. It was safe in his cellar, where the temperature is safely static, and he takes regular samples of all his wines – and allows them to his visitors – in the traditional tastevin which hangs, worn and gleaming, from a tape about his neck. He never fines nor filters; his is a natural wine that throws a natural deposit.

He bottles it himself – as many as 20,000 bottles in a good year – in his primitive one-man bottling machine. His 1976 was still a big tannic wine last spring. As always, he refused to bottle except when the wind was in the north and the moon on the wane.

Now some of that wine has arrived in England, ready to drink; but it will be better yet. Substantially bigger than a normal Beaujolais, almost of the stature of a fine burgundy, it has the usual Juliénas bouquet of summer fields; and, while the taste is fresh, clean and young in the classic Beaujolais fashion, on the palate it is full and round with a perfumed quality which is by no means usual. It is as if it were the essence of Beaujolais.

It is not cheap; inclusive of transport and VAT, it costs £46.35 per dozen case. Not long ago that would have seemed an impossible figure for Beaujolais, but every year fresh factors inflate the price. The ultimate Beaujolais enthusiast and specialist, Roger Harris, has shipped it. His address is Loke Farm, Weston Longville, Norfolk, NR9 5LG; neither he nor the phlegmatic Monsieur Aujas has any difficulty in selling it. Their problem is to replace it; and, so fine is it, that they may never do that. It is a Beaujolais experience to have tasted it.

FROM *THE GUARDIAN* (OCTOBER 1978)

MAX SCHUBERT

OZ CLARKE

He must have some imagination, that Max Schubert. There he was, sheltering from the torrid vintage-time heat in a bodega in Jerez, the air filled with the intoxicating sweet-sour fumes of fermenting sherry – and he was beginning to formulate a first vision of what would eventually emerge as Australia's greatest red wine – Grange Hermitage. Max had been sent to Spain by the chairman of Penfolds, the company he worked for in Australia, because the feeling was that he made uncommonly good "sherry" from Australian grapes without ever having experienced how it was really done in Spain. The chairman liked "sherry", and certainly looked forward to Max returning to Australia full of ideas which he would then put to good use and further improve the flavour of Penfolds "sherry".

But there he was, in the late summer of 1949, prowling around the sherry vats and not thinking of sherry at all. He was thinking of wood. Because the air was full of another, much more exotic smell – something spicy, smoky and sweet. It was the new American oak that was being used to ferment the wine. And in all his years at Penfolds – he'd joined the company as a sixteen-year-old in 1931 – he'd never smelled the scent of wine fermenting in new wood. In Australia, on the rare occasions when new wood was purchased, it was used for brandy production.

New oak and its heady sweet perfume caught up with Max again a month or so later. He had managed to wheedle a few more weeks' "study tour" out of his boss, and arrived in Bordeaux as the 1949 grape harvest was in full swing. The gradual replacement of wood ravaged by war was proceeding apace, frequently with American oak, and now Schubert could put the two different aromas together – the sweetness of wood, and the sweetness of wine from super-ripe red wine grapes. He was lucky to be in France in 1949, because Bordeaux had experienced a bakingly hot year – the temperature in the Médoc had risen to 63°C (145°F) at one point, and October was turning out to be the driest on record. If ever a Bordeaux year was bringing in fruit of comparable sugar-stuffed ripeness to the grapes Max had at his disposal in South Australia, 1949 was the one.

The thing that struck him most about the young wines was how incredibly deep and powerful they were, when Bordeaux had always had a reputation for delicacy. Schubert was lucky to have a kind and indulgent mentor in the late Christian Cruse, one of the last of the old-school grandees of the Bordeaux trade, who showed him that Bordeaux wines from ripe vintages – 1929, 1928, 1900, 1899 – could last and last, even maintaining some of their youthful structure, as well as developing their bewitching and inimitable fragrance. And Max was not overawed in the least. "I didn't think it was any big deal. If I could get the right material I could do the same in Australia." But would anyone want to drink the wine?

Australia in the early 1950s was not a table wine drinking society. Beer and fortified wine were the main drinks people wanted, and most red grape vineyards were planted with "port" production in mind. Consequently Schubert returned from Europe, his mind occupied with the flavours of France, to find that there were no comparable wines at all in Australia, none whose flavours he could examine, none whose makers he could quiz about methods. So he'd have to do it the hard way. From scratch.

He must have kept the quality of his "sherry" up, because the chairman was enthusiastically behind his decision to try to create a "Bordeaux First Growth" red in Australia. Except that Max didn't have any Bordeaux grapes. And he didn't have any oak. Most red Bordeaux is based on Cabernet Sauvignon, helped out by Merlot, Cabernet Franc, Malbec and Petit Verdot. Well, Penfolds had a few sparse acres of Cabernet Sauvignon and Malbec at their Kalimna vineyard in the north of the nearby Barossa Valley, and they knew some people who had some Malbec in the Clare Valley, two or three hours' drive from Adelaide, but they knew of no sources for the other varieties. So Max decided he'd base his new wine on the Shiraz grape, known in France as Syrah, which grew in abundance all over South Australia. The Australians used to treat it as a bulk-producing grape, but that was underestimating its potential. Shiraz is the great red grape that makes Hermitage, the finest red wine of France's Rhône Valley. When Schubert's few Cabernet Sauvignon vines produced good fruit, he could add that to the blend, and he could run the Shiraz juice over the Cabernet skins to extract Cabernet flavour, but basically, Shiraz would have to do.

Because producers wanted to make port-style wines, Shiraz was planted on the hot, open plains, where the grapes ripened easily. Schubert found two areas far cooler than the norm – perhaps as cool as Bordeaux in a year like 1949 – Morphett Vale to the south of Adelaide, and the Grange vineyard around his own Magill winery, on the hillside right above Adelaide's northern suburbs. Both plots had good plantings of mature Shiraz vines. He decided he would pick the grapes early to keep the alcohol level reasonably low and retain good acidity. Acid levels were rarely even taken into consideration in Australia at that time, but acid levels of about 7g per litre would equate pretty well with the norm in Bordeaux. Schubert's work in the Penfolds chemistry lab in his teenage days had shown him that low acid levels, the result of over-ripening the grapes, caused many of the fundamental problems with Australian efforts at red wine-making.

So Max had found his fruit. Now he needed wood. Easier said than done. Oak isn't one of Australia's strong points, eucalyptus trees are. He did try Australian oak – "bloody terrible" – and he got some barrels made up from Australian kauri, jarrah, stringy bark and casuarina. "Bloody terrible" seemed to be the judgement on most of these too, and eventually he was left with a few precious casks of imported oak – partly French, partly American.

He tried the French wood, but he was pretty sure that it wasn't what he wanted. The fruit he was using was pungent and rich and he reckoned that only

American oak would be aggressive enough to give as good as it got. He was right. Those French experiments never saw the light of day. But the five 300-litre (66-gallon) barrels of American oak he obtained for the 1951 vintage contained what would become the very first Grange Hermitage – named after the Grange homestead and vineyard established at Magill by the first Dr Penfold in 1844.

Schubert didn't ferment the juice in his new oak. He wanted much greater control over the fermentation temperature than this would allow. At that time in Australia, a tumultuous uncontrolled fermentation of about three days' length was usual – get it over with as quick as possible and on to the next batch of grapes. But this had two results – a severe danger of the fermentation grinding to a halt, with acetic acid rapidly forming in the hot, still sweet juice; and a complete failure to extract all the colour, tannin and flavour that was sitting in those dark black skins just waiting to be coaxed out.

Excuse me if this is beginning to sound a bit like a wine-making lesson, but Grange Hermitage was the first concerted, scientifically-based attempt to make modern, top-quality red wine anywhere outside the classic areas of Europe. Remember, this is 1951. Before California, before New Zealand, before South Africa and South America, an obstinate, jowly-faced genius was leading the way in South Australia.

Schubert wanted every ounce of personality his grapes possessed. He crushed them, cooled down the resulting must and pumped it into open concrete tanks. He invented a system of headboards that he'd slot into slats in the concrete, below the surface of the liquid, to keep the skins submerged and each day he'd pump all of the juice over the skins – cooling it on its way through a heat exchanger. In this way, by keeping the temperature of fermentation down, he was able to limit the pace of sugar into alcohol conversion. He was getting far more rich flavour out of the skins than anyone in Australia had before, so much so that he reckoned he'd got enough extract before the fermentation was even finished. So he ran the juice off the skins and finished the fermentation in his new oak barrels. The whole process took about twelve days – four times as long as usual. But the fruit quality was already reminding him of those 1949s in Bordeaux, even if the grape variety was different. Now came the real challenge. He'd made quite a bit more than five barrels' worth of wine, so he ran the rest of it into the vast old wooden vats traditionally used in Australia for maturing wine. Identical wine had been put into the two very different storage vessels. Would the new American oak he had obtained make the difference he was gambling on?

It certainly would. He was quite pleased with the "control" wine in the big old vats, but the wine in the new oak was a revelation. After one month the raw oak and the rich fruit were producing an explosively exciting perfume and taste.

After one year the intensity of fruit being displayed was far greater than Schubert had dared hope.

The wine was tough with tannin too, and traditional Australian wisdom would have left the wine in barrel to soften. But no Australian producer had ever aged a red wine in *new* oak barrels before. Once again Max harked back to what he'd learnt in France, and realized that the tannins would soften with enough time in bottle, but the fruit would be sure to tire if it stayed too long in wood, despite his insistence on keeping every barrel topped up to the bung to minimize oxidation. After eighteen months, he gave the word, and the first Grange was bottled. With the 1952 vintage he got the okay from Penfolds' board of directors, and swung excitedly into commercial production.

Schubert produced increasing amounts of Grange in the ensuing vintages, but because he wanted to leave Grange for a few years to soften in bottle, it meant piling up thousands of cases of costly wine in the cellars. He was delighted at how the wines were progressing, but the Penfolds board were starting to realize that not a bottle of this noble experiment had yet earned them any money. Max marched to Penfolds' headquarters in Sydney, expecting to bask in the praise that would be heaped upon his beloved Grange. But what was supposed to be a triumphal unveiling to the Sydney wine world turned into a disaster. With the exception of one of the younger members of the Penfold family, no one liked the wine.

So Schubert went back to Adelaide. But the Adelaide wine buffs' response was equally damning and the final blow came in 1957 when the Penfolds board forbade him to make another Grange, saying the public humiliation was becoming harmful to Penfolds' reputation nationwide.

But it wasn't just Max who believed in what Grange stood for. It was all the men in the cellar who felt that Grange was theirs too. So a conspiracy developed, with the help of the tacit approval of a couple of senior management members and the 1957, '58 and '59 vintages did get made – without new wood, but it was better than nothing.

And in 1960, one sympathetic board member on a visit to Magill asked to taste those original Granges. At eight and nine years old the 1951 and 1952 were finally opening up, the fruit beginning to rise above the tannin, the sweetness of the oak filling the glass with irresistible perfume. The director went back to Sydney and persuaded the board to reconsider. Just in time for the 1960 vintage the word came through – Grange is on again, new barrels and all.

In 1962, the 1955 Grange was entered in the Sydney Wine Show – one of the major wine events of the Australian year – and it won gold. The wine went on to scoop gold 50 more times; wherever it was shown it came away with awards. It had

been a tortuous birth, but finally after a decade of struggle and doubt, Max Schubert and his Grange Hermitage ushered in the modern age of Australian wine.
FROM *OZ CLARKE'S NEW CLASSIC WINES* (1991)

TAKING THE MOULD OUT OF MOLDOVA

ANTHONY ROSE

"Welcome to Soviet *Moldavia*" announced the Intourist brochure which, like much in the new republic of Moldova, was out of date. Moldova was too busy printing new denominations of rouble notes to worry about tourist brochures. At Chisinau airport, fleets of ex-Aeroflot Tupolevs and Antonovas stood idle on the tarmac. In this tiny former outpost of the Soviet empire, sandwiched between Romania and Ukraine, tourists were few and far between.

We were not tourists but a group of international wine people, visiting at the request of the government to assess Moldova's potential for bringing its wine to the West. At Chisinau we were met by George Kozub, head of Dacia-Fenix, the state viticulture and wine department, and Victor Tutuo, his assistant, plus representatives from state farms.

We checked in at one of Chisinau's few hotels near Victory Square. In the corridors hung the sweet, fetid smell of decay, which sensitive noses traced to the Russian furniture polish. Hungry-looking young men approached furtively with their grandfathers' military medals for sale. Next day – in our rooms only – sandpaper and rough carbolic were replaced by real lavatory paper and little bars of hotel soap.

The grim reality of inflation soon became clear. Ten years ago the rouble was, notionally, as parity with the pound. Today there are 450 roubles to £1. To have a shirt laundered costs 5p. But to send a fax costs £35. The vast department store had little to sell other than mass-produced madonnas, plastic shoes and nylon clothes. I bought two records of Eastern European folk music for 3p each.

Sixty-five per cent of Moldova's population is Romanian and this is the official language. By virtue of the Molotov-Ribbentrop pact of 1939, Moldova, formerly Bessarabia, was annexed by Russia the following year. Independence was declared on 27 August 1991, but, as a result of Communist centralism, there is still no banking system and the country depends on others for medicine, petrol and two-thirds of its electricity. It even has to buy its sausage casings from Belarus.

Moldova is poor but it has lots of wine. In fact, its wine industry is known as the "Golden Branch" of Moldovan agriculture. Until the mid-Eighties, 260,000 hectares of state farms and collectives were producing the equivalent of 580 million bottles of wine and 13 million bottles of brandy. Most of this was destined for the former Soviet Union. And most of the latter's consumption of sparkling wine – around 320 million bottles annually in 1988 – came from Moldova, the rest from the ten other wine-producing states.

Then the Gorbachev anti-alcohol drive took its toll. With echoes of the Ottoman occupation of sixteenth-century Bessarabia, nearly 200,000 hectares of vineyard were uprooted. Last year, Moldova finally turned to the West.

But how do you interest anyone in an antiquated industry churning out, for the most part, tired and old-fashioned wines, and where even the paraphernalia of such things as corks and labels is scarce? It was hard for us to believe that Romaneshty, a showcase winery on the outskirts of Chisinau, was only built in 1982. With its joyless concrete and primitive installations, it looked more as if it was ready to be closed down.

At Cricova, a cavernous subterranean wine village renowned throughout the former Soviet Union for its champagne-method sparkling wines, they were surprised when we complained that the wine tasted mouldy. Hygiene may be able to correct it, but the Moldovan palate has apparently become inured to the taste of mould in its fizz.

In need of a partnership with the West, Moldova put out feelers. Enter Joop van de Kant, a Dutchman successful in the fine wine business. He rashly remarked that, at 49, he would like the challenge of developing wine in one of the new CIS states. On his first visit he took to the Moldovans. He admired their resilience; they felt they could trust him. The first of many a toast – *norok*, as they say – was drunk.

It became immediately clear to Mr van de Kant that Moldova was potentially suited not just for making wine, but for producing the kind of light red and white table wines capable of appealing to Western palates and pockets. On the same latitude as Burgundy, Moldova is a country of undulating hills and river valleys with a moderate, continental climate ideal for grape growing.

Thanks to the tsars, it has a tradition of wine made from the classic grape varieties of the West, notably cabernet sauvignon, merlot, pinot noir, chardonnay, sauvignon blanc and riesling. In addition it has its own native varieties such as saperavi, rkatsiteli, rara niagre and fetiaska. The raw material was there. All it needed was a period of political stability and a minor miracle.

Mr van de Kant's three-point plan was to bring in a trio of French winemakers with experience in the styles of wine already being produced; to organize a tasting to select wines suitable for sale in the West; and then to advise on a programme of improvement. He had to explain to Moldovans impatient for Western hardware and cash that to build factories to supply wine bottles was not the answer; the process of improvement had to start in the vineyard and on the floor of the winery.

The old borders of individual communities are slowly being reintroduced. Families are to be given land quotas. Growers will work with producers and the profits of their association will be shared. By moving from the old state farms to a co-operative system, the government aims to give growers the incentives they previously lacked. Plans are also being drawn up for an *appellation contrôlée*-type system that would give formal recognition to superior sites at, for instance, Purkari, Choumai, Taracliya, Charda-Lunga, Cahul, Romaneshty, Staucheni and Comrat.

For his winemakers, Mr van de Kant enlisted the support of two brothers making wine in Bordeaux, Jacques and François Lurton, and Alain Thienot, who also produces champagne. The Lurtons' first job was to look at the vineyards and assess how they could be improved, by means of pruning and harvesting at the right time, reducing a tendency to excessive acidity and coping with disease.

Hygiene was the first priority in the cellar, along with the ageing of the wines and their storage. Most Moldovan wines are kept longer in cask than the modern European palate is used to. They are also pasteurized at the bottling stage – presumably for stability – which tends to remove all character. This year the Lurtons will make their first wines.

From the tasting of wines chosen by Mr van de Kant, reds in the bordeaux style made from the cabernet sauvignon grape were the most successful. The best were medium-bodied, fresh and fruity, without a trace of oak, echoes of a bordeaux of yesteryear. Dry white wines were markedly inferior, with one or two successes from the native rkatsiteli grape (hard to see a wine with a name like that becoming an overnight success). There were some excellent fino and oloroso-style sherry-types from the Yaloveni winery, and a number of interesting muscat-based sweet wines.

Despite their evident quality, neither the sherry types nor the sweet wines were felt likely to stand much of a chance in the West. But the majority of the table wines chosen were highly promising, especially if the prices could be kept in the £2.50-£4 range. Most were red table wines and we chose too many. Mr van de Kant did not want the Moldovans' heads filled with delusions of grandeur. As it was, they appeared to have no shortage of confidence in the viability of their products.

Perhaps a dozen of the wines we chose will end up being bottled in the Netherlands and sold initially to Western Europe, giving Moldova the necessary hard cash it will need to buy new equipment. Amid much singing, dancing and *norok*, accompanied by Moldovan brandy, a contract was duly signed. The flying Dutchman will be bringing Moldova to the West.

FROM *THE INDEPENDENT* (16 JANUARY 1993)

TIPPLERS' TALES

JUNK DRINK

CYRIL RAY

I was once relaxing after a hearty Irish breakfast at the Shelbourne Hotel in Dublin, when into the lounge walked a bright yellow suit with a loud black overcheck, a double-breasted waistcoat, jewelled tiepin, heavy watch-chain, yellow carnation and, inside it all, a chubby American gentleman who proceeded to give an order to the waiter that made me doubt the evidence of my ears. The waiter disappeared to return with two tall glasses on a tray, each filled with a viscous-seeming liquid the colour of uncooked brains. The waiter told me later that yes I *had* heard aright: there was one raw egg in each glass beaten up into a glass of port and a glass of brandy. And having vouchsafed this information, he then hurried off to fetch the third glass of the same that the chubby American gentleman was urgently signalling for.

The following morning (wearing a bright green blazer, fancy waistcoat with contrasting lapels and pocket-flaps, and a white carnation), the chubby American gentleman was clearly concerned not to have to waste his time over sending for second helpings: the initial order was for three, not two tall glasses of the mixture, and yet, even so, there came peremptory signals for a fourth. The waiter confided in me later that in his opinion the customary breakfast – if I may so describe it – had got off to a rather late start, and the chubby American gentleman had decided to carry on with the same rather than switch over at eleven, as was his wont, to his usual mid-morning snack of double Tio Pepes.

Between the two breakfasts, I had seen him at Jammet's preparing the way for dinner with champagne cocktails – this time he was in pale grey, with a pink carnation – and on each of the three occasions he carried a different walking stick. Each stick, according to the waiter at the Shelbourne, contained a long thin flask of Irish whiskey.

It was a few days later, on the other side of Ireland, at my hotel in Galway, that I actually made the acquaintance of this flamboyant character. I had been deeply interested, I told him, in his Dublin breakfasts.

He nodded weightily and said, *"Better than cornflakes."*

Was I right, I asked, in understanding that the proportions were quite simple – one egg, one port, one brandy? Quite right, said the chubby American gentleman: quite right.

And then he flushed deeply, his voice rose, his hand shook: there were those, he exclaimed – I would hardly believe it, but there were those who put sugar in the mixture, and nutmeg on the top: "Junk!" he cried: "JUNK!"

FROM *RAY ON WINE* (1979)

WIDOW CLICQUOT'S EXPORT DRIVE

HUGH JOHNSON

Napoleon's last defensive battles before his abdication brought the Russian and the Prussian armies in force to Champagne. The region had suffered as a camp and crossroads in many wars, but for three weeks in the early spring of 1814 it was the bearpit in which the retreating Emperor fought and won skirmish after skirmish with generalship as brilliant as he had ever displayed. In the words of Victor Hugo, he "wrote with the local names of Champagne the last pages of his prodigious poem: Arcis-sur-Aube, Châlons, Reims, Champaubert, Sézanne, Vertus, Méry, La Fère, Montmirail. So many combats; so many victories".

He had no forces left, though, to face the massing allies marching inexorably west. Reims and Epernay fell to the Russians and the Prussians. The day before Epernay fell, taking his leave of his loyal friend Jean-Rémy Moët, the Emperor pinned on his breast his own cross of the Légion d'Honneur, then left for Paris and his abdication.

The Russians undoubtedly had the best of the occupation and the French, though terrified of the Cossacks and Kalmucks, found that the pillage might have been worse. As it happened the Russian commander in Reims was one of St Petersburg's most polished officers; Prince Sergei Alexandrovich Wolkonski. The Prussians, no doubt envious of the Russian billet, proposed to enter Reims and extract tribute and supplies. "I have received orders from the Tsar", wrote back Wolkonski, "not to exact any requisitions from this town. As for your insolent threat of sending troops to Reims, I have plenty of Cossacks here to receive them."

If the legends are true, requisitions did not need to be extracted. They were carried up willingly from, amongst others, the cellars of the far-sighted Widow Clicquot. "Today they drink", were her somewhat tight-lipped words, "Tomorrow they will pay".

Nor did she hesitate for a moment before putting her maxim into effect. She ignored the fact that the borders of Russia were still officially closed to French goods. The occupying forces left in May 1814. By the beginning of June, scarcely giving them time to reach home, she had a ship chartered, a 75-ton Dutch "flute", the *Sweers Gebroeders*, loaded with Mr Bohne [her salesman] and as much champagne as it could carry (and that the Russians had left undrunk), and sailing for the Baltic. 1811, the year of Halley's comet, had been a wonderful vintage. She sent as much as she had. The ship reached Koenigsberg (today's Kaliningrad) on July 3rd, to find that French goods were no longer excluded. Bohne had the field to himself. There .was not another voyageur from Champagne within 500 miles.

"It is with infinite satisfaction", wrote Mr Bohne, "that I have examined the samples. Spring water is infinitely less limpid than they are. Everyone is agog at the idea of tasting them." The Tsar himself had arrived back in Koenigsberg; even the Imperial door was not closed to Mr Bohne. "You see", he wrote again to the widow in Reims, "what authority one has when one has good merchandise to provide. I had only to let drop the number of my hotel room, and a queue formed outside my door."

FROM *THE STORY OF WINE* (1989)

WHAT DO CHANCELLORS DO FOR CHRISTMAS?

WILLIAM FOSTER

When R A Butler was Chancellor of the Exchequer, I was once despatched by the *Sunday Times* to interview him in his gloomy office at the top of the Treasury building. It was just before Christmas and, as I was working for the "Atticus" column, I kept off such morbid subjects as the balance of payments and the state of the pound, and asked where he was spending Christmas.

"Winston has asked us over to Chartwell," he said. He sounded faintly depressed at the prospect. I gathered that, given his choice, he would have preferred a short break on the island of Mull, where he had a house.

"But Mull out of season," I countered, "compared with Churchill's hospitality . . . ?" And that, it seemed, was the trouble. Butler's capacity for Pol Roger, the PM's favourite champagne, was strictly limited. So much so, in fact, that he always packed an extra pair of slippers, two sizes too big, for Operation Chartwell. "Winston takes offence if you try to abandon a full glass when dinner is announced. So, when the moment comes, I quietly pour the contents of the glass into my slippers and squelch into the dining room."

(Molly Butler, Rab's widow, confirms this was standard drinkmanship practice.)

But no matter where else they put their drinks, you will notice that when Christmas approaches, no photographs are seen in newspapers or on TV of a politician with a glass in his hand. It is supposed to be tactless to be seen carousing with the annual drink/drive campaign raging away.

I first met this taboo when Atticus sent me round to see one of Butler's successors, Reggie Maudling. Few Christmases went by without my inviting a Chancellor to Tell All.

An old-fashioned London fog had seeped into that now-familiar office and when I was shown in, there was no desk where Butler had sat and a distinct shortage of Chancellors. "I'm over here," boomed Maudling, who had moved his desk to the other end of the room and was lost in a peasouper.

He was a genial chap, deft at fielding awkward questions. "What about a drink, as it's Christmas?" he asked. There was another desk within reach, with a handle in front. Maudling tugged at the front, which was hinged on the base and fell forward to reveal a secret drinks cabinet.

"I'm on the Macallan 12," he announced. "What about you?" I decided this was an Atticus-worthy item and began taking notes. "Oh, please," said Maudling, "don't put this bit in. We're having a go at drunken motorists this Christmas and it wouldn't look good. Why not say we had a surprisingly strong cup of Civil Service tea?" Which is what I did.

I thought I had got away from Christmas with Chancellors when I switched from the *Sunday Times* to the job of features editor of a woman's glossy. I was wrong.

"I've got a marvellous idea for you," said the editor brightly. "What about interviewing the wives of both Denis Healey, the Chancellor, and Geoffrey Howe, the Shadow Chancellor? As it's for our December issue," she added, in one of those moments of heady inspiration to which editors are subject, "why not find out what their plans are for Christmas?"

In view of Denis Healey's wood-aged port wine complexion, I half-expected Government hospitality might turn up trumps at No 11. But Edna, his wife, simply produced coffee in a silver coffee pot and said they had tickets for Covent Garden over Christmas.

Elspeth Howe was made of tougher fibre. She was delighted to be taken for lunch to l'Escargot in Greek Street. We knocked back Chambéry as an aperitif, and the Palmer 1971 was also a hit, much to the editor's chagrin when my expenses were signed.

In the summer, Elspeth Howe played cricket in a women's team. But her plans for Christmas were remarkably similar to the Healeys'. Christmas always meant an outing to the opera. So that was two successive Chancellors (as it turned out) with a passion for absurd plots, extravagant posturing and unnecessary verbosity.

Except that it goes deeper than that. If you look back on the duties imposed on wine during Denis Healey's term as Chancellor (up by 200 per cent in little over a year) or Sir Geoffrey's (VAT up in his first Budget, duty in his second), a sinister pattern begins to emerge.

It is opera that is giving Chancellors the wrong idea about wine. The more productions they see, the more they will be tempted to raise taxes on the elixir of life. The demon drink is at the bottom of every disaster.

Take *Fledermaus*, where the stage is literally awash with champagne from beginning to end. It lands Rosalinde's lover in prison, causes everyone to flirt outrageously behind their masks with all the wrong people and ends up with Rosalinde's husband putting the blame squarely on the king of wines.

Then there is *Carmen*, the tragedy of the soldier who deserts the army for love of the girl with the rose between her teeth. You know where he declares his love? In a tavern, that's where. With a glass of red wine in his hand, what's more.

Faust sells his soul to the devil after drinking a potion and you can bet it wasn't Sainsbury's Dealcoholised Own Label. Then there is the fatal passion between Violetta and Alfredo in *La Traviata*, sparked off when the tenor breaks into a drinking song.

Any Chancellor would conclude that students have far too much money to spend on riotous living if he sat through the taproom scene in *Tales of Hoffman*. He'd cut their grants at once. Then there is *La Bohème*, where Rudolfo might well have slipped a wedding ring on Mimi's tiny frozen hand and settled down to yuppiedom if the bohemians had not distracted him in every act by dragging him off for a liquid lunch. (Stage directions from Act III: Mimi appears coughing and shivering from the adjoining tavern . . .)

If you need further evidence, Rigoletto's daughter is slaughtered by mistake in an inn in Mantua during what appears to be an extended power cut. The potency of the local Lambrusco was probably responsible. And you can't tell me Lucrezia Borgia would ever get a job as PRO to Victoria Wine or Peter Dominic after souping up those wine cups.

You might argue that no self-respecting Chancellor would base his fiscal policy on what he sees on stage. I think he might. The way they knock it back in opera rouses the most puritanical instincts.

Note how the well-proportioned lady in the toils of love clutches a papier-mâché goblet and waves it dramatically from side to side, keeping a wary eye on the conductor. (The goblet is fortunately empty, or the tenor would have most of the contents down his frilled shirtfront by now.)

She reaches the end of the aria. At this point you or I might sniff the wine questingly. We would hazard a guess that it travels well from side to side in papier-mâché goblets. We might sip it delicately.

But not the large lady. With a mighty gulp, she drains the flagon to the depths and hurls it into the wings, missing a stagehand by inches. If she did that on the football terraces, the police would clap the bracelets on her.

On second thoughts, I'm not sure that the Chancellor waits till he gets back to his Christmas tree in No 11 before raising the tax on wine. I think he pulls his pocket calculator out of his tailcoat pocket and works out the increase there and then.

FROM *WINE MAGAZINE* (1984)

JUDY'S PUB

MICHAEL JACKSON

The folks in the town figured maybe they were to blame. They had been offered two upright citizens as candidates for mayor, but they had voted for Brad's dog, Bosco, who ran as a Labrador. Could just as well have run as mastiff, really. Seemed a little uncertain of his precise allegiance.

Folks liked Bosco's campaign slogan: "A bone in every dish, a cat up every tree, a fire hydrant on every corner." Trouble is, Bosco never fixed the fire hydrants. If he had, maybe Judy's pub would not have burned to the ground.

After the fire, Bosco ran away for a while. Sort of laid low. When he did turn up, he was saying nothing about anything, even though some smart-ass TV news crew came out from San Francisco to try and interview him.

The night Judy's pub burned, people came from miles around, just like they always did. From San Francisco – and that can take an hour – from San José, on the peninsula, even from Sacramento and Chico, up in the Sierras. Of course, there weren't many people left in Sunol to drink a beer or watch a fire. Even Judy had moved from her place in the woods and taken a house down in the Amador Valley.

Sunol had been a railroad town, but the trains didn't stop there any more. In the old days, the railroad had brought beer from a brewery – called Lyon's – in the East Bay, and unloaded it at Sunol for all the saloons along the canyon. The old brewery depot eventually became a bar.

Used to be a kind of cowboy place. People say Willie Nelson hung out there quite a bit. Then it got to be a bikers' bar. It was a long-neck Budweiser bar when Judy started there. She worked there as a bartender, then business got so poor that the owner sold the place to Judy. Let her pay him bit by bit, as she turned a dollar.

Judy put back the old name, Lyon's Brewery Depot. She fixed it real nice. The old loading dock, where the trains left the beer . . . she turned that into a back porch. She even trained some hops to grow around it. You could sit on that back porch and watch the trains rattle by, along the single track. Heck, you could just about touch the trains.

People would sit there, drinking a beer, and raise a glass as the train passed. The engineer would toot his whistle to say, "Hi!" Then somebody gave Judy a bell from a San Francisco cable car. Judy would be inside the bar, serving a beer or shooting the breeze, when she would hear the train tooting. Right away, she would answer, ringing her bell as hard she could.

She even had an engineer from the railroad as one of her part-time bartenders. She needed quite a bit of help, the place got so popular. According to the law, you could only fit sixty folks into that place, but sometimes Judy had twice as many people there. Even then, someone had managed to put a bullet hole into one of the booths.

You could say it was home brew that made Judy's pub into a special place. The day Bob Hufford gave Judy some of his home brew, she flipped. She said it made her feel like she was running naked through a field of flowers. Heck, Judy can be very poetic at times. Said she never knew what real beer was like before.

Next thing you knew, Bob had her getting all these imported beers from England. Some folks had heard of Bass but, sure as hell, no one knew about Newcastle Brown, Young's Special London Ale and Fuller's Extra Special Bitter. They liked them, though, when Judy put them on tap.

Then these kids over in Santa Cruz started a little brewery, making ales and porters. Judy got into the way of driving over the mountains every week and picking up kegs. She didn't have a truck, but that was no problem. She would just yell over the bar that she needed to go fetch some beer from Santa Cruz, and right away there would be two or three customers out of the door and revving their pick-up trucks.

So far as anyone knows, nobody ever put the make on Judy. Wouldn't have dared I guess. She's a good-looking woman, though. Even if she does have a broken nose from playing soccer with her kids. She was putting a couple of kids through college when her pub burned down. Folks knew it was tough for her – divorced, with her only source of income gone up in flames.

Judy's a feisty woman, of course. When she got all that imported beer, and the ale from the new breweries in Santa Cruz and Modesto and Devil Mountain and the like, she had a "Farewell to Budweiser" party. Someone even made a sign to put behind the bar. It was like a "no entry" sign, only the line went straight through a bottle of Budweiser.

She kept Coors for anyone who wanted one of them lawn-mowing beers, but she insisted the customer get it in a brown-paper bag. One time a bunch of fellers from the city came in and all ordered Coors. When they got the brown-paper bags, they couldn't believe their eyes. Turned out they were big shots from the brewery, come to see if it was really true about this crazy broad in Sunol. Crazy! By then, she had more than two hundred beers, and a dozen or twenty of those were on tap. The whole town only had eight hundred people, and there wasn't much sign of them.

There was Judy's pub, then a feed store, then a general store, then another bar – the hard-liquor place the bikers switched to when Judy got rid of the Budweiser. They were all in one long, wooden building, painted in a cream colour that had gotten faded by the sun. There was a wooden sidewalk, with hitching posts. No way could you insure a building like that against fire. Even the insulation in the walls was sawdust. The railroad track cut behind the building and across the main street, as the road bent into the canyon. On the other side of the track was Addie's café, a gas station, and the post office.

That was, you might say, the downtown area of Sunol. One time, Charlie Chaplin had made some films in front of the wooden sidewalks and out in the canyon. That was the biggest thing that happened in Sunol until Judy's pub burned.

Seems like the railroad made Sunol and darned near destroyed the place. People figured the rumble of a passing train might have broken a gas pipe in the feed store. That's where the fire started. There was a fire hydrant – just one – but it was across the railroad track. With the trains still running, the firefighters had to dig under the track to connect their hoses.

The fire started at three in the morning, and soon the whole canyon was out of bed to watch. There were people who remembered the place sixty years back. The firefighters didn't get the blaze under control until 4.30, then they called Judy at her place in the Amador Valley, about twelve miles away.

When she arrived, she just got out of the car and started picking her way over the embers to what was left of the back wall. The big, walk-in cooler was still standing, giving off smoke and steam. She felt for the door and opened it. Then she yelled to tell the people that the beer was not lost. It was even still cool. She took a tap hose attached to one of the kegs and sprayed beer like a fire-eater, and hosed the beer down her throat. She shouted to the people to step right over, and handed every man and woman a bottle. They started the wake there and then.

A pick-up truck came along the road, heading towards Oakland, then stopped and reversed so that the driver could check out the scene. Someone gave him a beer. People were beginning to pass on their way to do a day's work somewhere or other in the valley or the city. They pretty much all stopped for a while. Most of them knew Judy.

Not many people ever got to work that morning. By the time the fire had been on the morning TV news in San José and San Francisco, there was a steady gathering of more than a hundred people. There was still a crowd by mid afternoon, when a truck arrived with fresh beer from the mourners, donated by the brewery.

The fire had started on the morning of 22 December, and there were plenty of Christmas wreaths around. People began to show up and leave wreaths, or just bouquets, among the ashes of Judy's pub. They would leave flowers in bottles of their favourite beer. Or even leave full bottles, in home-made shrines. Mostly, they put Anchor Liberty Ale or Sierra Nevada Big Foot Barley Wine in the shrines. Nobody stole the bottles, out of respect. Even the bikers from the hard-liquor bar didn't touch the bottles.

There always seemed to be a knot of people there, standing around in the ashes, staring at the empty space where Judy's pub had been, thinking a few thoughts about the times they spent, exchanging a few words, leaving a memento or so . . . until Christmas and New Year had been and gone.

In the first week of January, twenty of Judy's regulars – her "Connoisseur's Club", she called them – showed up at her house to start talking about a new pub. People started working on a benefit for Judy. Didn't take too much time to whip up support.

They held it on Valentine's Day, at a golf club. Darned near a thousand people showed up, at $25 a pop. All the beer was donated, by a couple of dozen breweries. There were breweries from all over the state, and one from Colorado. They called it a national benefit. Heck, they could have called it international. There was even beer donated from England. They auctioned some of the best beer. One feller paid $250 for a straight five years' set of single bottles of Anchor Christmas Ale.

When they counted the money, it was enough to keep Judy afloat, so to speak, until she could get a new place. No way would the insurance companies let her open a place on the old site. By March, she had a new site, in the Amador Valley, near San Ramon, in a place called Dublin.

The railroad engineer, Scott, was able to get his hands on a little money. He and Judy's brother, Gary, helped her finance the new place. Judy was worried, though. It would take a few months to fix up the new place. After all that time, would people come back? Also, the site was in a shopping strip. She thought the Connoisseurs would never forgive her for that. One day, some of the guys went to take a look. They had to ask the way. They asked some local guy:

"Where's the shopping centre?" He scratched his head, then figured he knew where they meant. "Oh, that's them shops by Judy's pub."

In July, they started fitting up the new place. Judy, Gary, their mum and dad, who were both retired, and every friend who could spare a hand, set to work. For three months, they worked fourteen or fifteen hours a day.

Judy didn't smile much until she saw the walk-in cooler finished. She looked at it and said, out loud: "It's beautiful. I could make love in there." The frame was made of fir. The cooler was lined with sheet plastic, then styrofoam, then more sheet plastic, then plasterboard, with seams filled and taped. Then it was panelled in ash, with oak trim on the seams, fixed with rust-resistant, countersunk, screws. The whole thing was finished with two coats of marine varnish.

The best bit was yet to come. The cooler was divided into two boxes, one for ales and the other for lagers. With that kind of insulation, Judy could serve the beers just the way she wanted: "warm" for the ales and chilled for the lagers. The beer would be perfect . . . if the customers came.

In the fall, the new place had its official opening. By midday, there were a couple of hundred people in the place. All day, they came and went, but there were never less than two hundred people in there.

They presented Judy with a new bell, to replace the one buckled in the fire. By mid-evening, she was standing on the bar, ringing the bell, ready to make an announcement. She looked at the prettiest boy in the place and said: "Come with me, into the walk-in cooler."

The crowd shouted: "Go with her! Go with her! Go with her!"

Just then, the 101st Airborne Ultimate Frisbee Team walked into the bar, followed by the entire staff of Judy's favourite sushi restaurant. She jumped down off the bar and started serving pints of Devil Mountain Railroad Ale.

Maybe she went into the walk-in cooler later. Crazy Dave says he thinks she was missing for a while, but no one is really sure. Everyone was having such a good time.

[Ed: The new Lyon's Brewery pub is at 7294 San Ramon Road, Dublin, California.]
FROM WHAT'S BREWING (DECEMBER 1988)

VINTAGE SIN

CYRIL RAY

The 1921 Yquem has become a legend. I have drunk it twice since the day when it washed down my mutton in the Sauternais, but on both occasions in London and with fruit, and therefore with greater enjoyment. But what I remember best about the 1921 Yquem is the story I was told by a woman acquaintance, early in the war, who had just been divorced and to her great surprise, by her much older and, hitherto, complaisant husband.

They had lived, she and the husband, in a stately Sussex home, the park of which had been turned by the War Office into a tented field, and its greater rooms into the officers' mess of a smart and rather rakish regiment.

Its subalterns were not indifferent to the lady's charms; the lady herself not unduly prim, nor hard to please. It was somehow understood that neither the colonel nor the cuckolded husband would complain; so long as certain decencies – or to be more precise, certain reticences – were observed.

And yet . . . the blow fell. The lady and that evening's lover were discovered, when on other evenings with other young men, her adventures had gone carefully unnoticed. She was turned out into the black-out at little more than a moment's notice, and divorced as quickly as a lady can be.

It was long before she could understand why, she told me. Why that evening, and not on any other? And then it had dawned on her. Until that particular evening, she had dispensed her favours, by previous and prettily planned arrangement, in boudoir or in bedroom. It was an understood thing, and the eyes both of martial and of marital authority had winked at it. But on the particular, the fatal, evening she was showing off the house to a recently joined young officer, and they had reached the wine cellar which, in that house, was very properly a show-place. A look in his hostess's eye overwhelmed the boy; his ardour would not wait; and they were heard, and thus discovered, in such a position, she shyly intimated, as to be agitating the bin of Yquem 1921.

FROM *RAY ON WINE* (1979)

WATER OF LIFE

COOKING WITH SCOTCH

ELIZABETH DAVID

Whisky is still, to many Englishwomen, a man's drink, tough masculine tipple. Advice to splash it into the sauté pan strikes a rough rude note. Cognac, being foreign and French, is altogether more glamorous and elegant-sounding, therefore more appropriate to the refinements of good cooking. I wonder if deep down that peppery gentleman's irritation might perhaps have been due to fear that once the gaff about whisky not being suitable for the kitchen was blown the master's bottle would no longer be quite sacrosanct. The little woman, instead of having to explain the spending of twenty-five shillings of the housekeeping money on a half bottle of "cooking" brandy, would be at liberty to raid the Scotch for a few tablespoonsful at any time, and nobody the wiser.

In France, whisky was once a very smart and snob drink; it is now astonishingly popular. In 1961, it is estimated, 682,000 gallons of whisky were consumed by the French, and that was twice as much as in 1960. How many hundreds or thousands of those gallons were tipped into the saucepans the report does not reveal, but certain it is that in these days it is not at all uncommon to find dishes of chicken, langouste or lobster *flambé au whisky* on the menus of French provincial and Parisian restaurants. (For chapter and verse without going to France look at the lists of specialities given by the starred restaurants in the guide books.) An establishment at Arras even serves a speciality of *andouillettes flambées au whisky* – a faint echo of the haggis ritual . . .?

I find the French development encouraging, for I have myself for years been experimenting with whisky in the cooking pots. One of the circumstances which drove me to these experiments will be familiar to most home cooks. It was simply that a bottle of brandy, even of the kind intended only for the kitchen (by which I don't mean something not fit to drink, I mean something one *prefers* not to drink), somehow always turns out in fact to have been drunk by somebody just when it is needed for cooking and hasn't been replaced, while whisky is a supply which is more or less automatically re-ordered as soon as it runs out. And not only have I found whisky successful as an alternative to cognac and armagnac in many fish and poultry dishes, but it has frequently had to do duty instead of Calvados in Norman dishes of veal, pork, pheasant and apples. Calvados isn't always easy to come by in this country and such as we can get is usually one or other of the commercial brands which in spite of their high prices are pretty crude. So, for that matter, are all too many three-star-quality cognacs.

Obviously, the flavour which whisky gives to a sauce differs from that produced by cognac, armagnac or Calvados; certainly the aromas coming from the pot while the whisky is cooking are also very different; but by the time the alcohol has been burned and cooked away I wonder how many people would spot what precisely the difference is.

Not that that is quite the point. There should be no attempt to deceive. To take the simplest example, *faisan à la normande* would be understood, by anybody who knew a little about French regional cooking, to imply a dish of pheasant with a cream sauce and apples, blazed with Calvados. If the dish is blazed with whisky instead it is possible that nobody will know the difference; but a point of principle is involved; once the wedge is in how long before the apples have been replaced with carrots and peas, and the cream with tomato purée or pineapple juice? So all the restaurateur has to do (in the privacy of one's own kitchen one can, after all, call one's inventions what one pleases; until they leave the house one's guests are in no position to pass remarks) is to follow the French example and describe his dish as *faisan flambé au whisky* or alternatively pheasant *au Scotch*. And if he feels that the French have an unfair advantage in that to them the words "whisky" and "scotch" are good selling points whereas to us they are just rather blunt or evocative in the wrong way then he can invent some totally new name.

FROM *AN OMELETTE AND A GLASS OF WINE* (1984)

SMUGGLING SCOTCH

DEREK COOPER

In the early nineteenth century, illicit whisky distilling had reached its peak and smuggling was endemic. It took two forms. The oldest tradition was the importation of contraband cargoes from the Continent. In the Shetland and Orkney isles, smuggled casks were frequently deposited in churches for safekeeping and there were few ministers who asked questions when an anker of brandy was left at the manse door.

So respectable a part of trading life was the running of dutiable goods into the fishing ports of Scotland that Coutts, the merchants and bankers of Edinburgh, had a colleague in Rotterdam whose principal activity lay in providing goods for the smugglers who sailed between Holland and the ports of north-east Scotland.

Those who dealt in contraband stood high in public esteem. Not only were they keeping prices down, they were also, by evading excise duty, cocking a snook at "our auld enemies of England" . . .

The stories handed down by word of mouth always case the smuggler in the role of hero. He or she is quick-witted, generous in defeat, good-humoured and eternally lucky. The excisemen are invariably depicted as plodding dimwits, arriving in the wrong place at the wrong time, subjects of public mortification and universal derision.

On 4 June 1817, the *Aberdeen Journal* revealed to its readers the enterprising ruse adopted by a Kincardineshire woman who was one of the busiest distillers in a remote glen in the Highlands. A neighbour found out that the Excise knew what she was up to and an officer was on his way to apprehend her in the act.

There was no time to dismantle her still and hide it, so in desperation the good wife lugged her infirm and bedridden husband to the door of the hut and put him in a chair so that he was blocking the entrance. When the exciseman arrived, he found the old woman standing over her apparently dying spouse and anointing his lips with a feather and some balm.

"For the love of Jesus," she said with a melodramatic cry, "if you are a clergyman come and pray for my dying husband." The officer declined the invitation, saying that prayer wasn't one of his particular skills. "In that case," implored the woman, "would you be kind enough to go as quickly as you can and send my neighbours to pray." The officer agreed and departed. As soon as he was gone, the old man was dragged back to bed and distilling was resumed.

Dissembled mortality played a role in another popular story of the times. A smuggler who was not in the distilling business, but who indulged in the wholesale distribution of illicit spirit, got word that the gaugers were on their way to search his premises. As he had a big stock of full casks ready to be shipped, there seemed no escape from discovery. But once again invention saved the day. A tailor happened to be in the house and he agreed, in return for a suitable bribe, to be laid out on a table and covered with a white sheet.

As the officer knocked on the door the women of the house broke into an impressive lament, the smuggler intoned piously from a Bible and invited the revenue men reverently into his house of mourning. Discountenanced, they made their excuses and left.

An even more preposterous tale comes from Kirkwall in the Orkney islands, where a smuggler called Magnus Eunson, by hobby a church elder, used to keep a stock of illicit whisky under the pulpit. On hearing that the church was to be searched for whisky, he had the casks removed to his house where he arranged them in the shape of a bier and covered them with a white cloth.

When the officers burst into the room, Eunson was kneeling at the head of the bier with his Bible open and the rest of the family were keening lustily for the departed. "Smallpox!" whispered one of the mourners to the nearest exciseman. They fled.

Many of the tales of thwarted detection have a quality reminiscent of the brothers Grimm. The one most repeated tells of the officer who stumbled upon a smuggler at work in his bothy.

"Did anyone see you coming here?" asked the smuggler.

"No one," replies the officer.

"Then," says the smuggler reaching for an axe, "no one will see you leave!"

FROM *THE WHISKY ROADS OF SCOTLAND* (1982)

THE LEATHER-SCENTED LUCK OF THE IRISH

MICHAEL JACKSON

Having always made it my practice to marry Irish women, and now sharing my life with a lady called Paddy, what else can I expect? At this time of year, I have grown used to the gradual rise of a siren song that urges me to make sure we do something together on 17 March, St Patrick's Day.

As to what we shall do, the decision is between toasting St Patrick in stout or in whiskey (the Irish spell it with an "e"). Last year, we had stout, so this year I will plump for whiskey.

It is not necessary to be Hibernian, or even celebrating St Paddy's day, to savour Irish whiskey. I keep a bottle of each of my two favourites, Jameson's 12-year-old and Black Bush, at all times, alongside my collections of Scotch, Canadian and American whisk(e)y. You never know where the spirit will move you.

Jameson's has recently been running an advertising campaign asserting "The Smoother the Irish", illustrating its point by comparing the style of Yeats with that of Burns. The comparison of two quite different styles of verse and two quite different styles of whisk(e)y is somewhat simplistic, but perhaps it will encourage a few timid souls to try a taste of Irish.

The characteristic accent in Scotch whisky is that of peat, which is used in the kilning of the barley malt – a principal raw material. This hint of smoke is absent from Irish whiskey; for, surprisingly, the Irish do not use peat in their kilns.

In a country where the great obsession is with horses, it seems apposite that experts sometimes talk wistfully about the aroma of saddlery, or new leather, when they seek to define the nose of Irish whiskey. It may be a romantic analogy, but it does seem to pinpoint the most emphatic characteristic of the whiskeys made in Ireland.

One evocation leads to another, much as whiskeys do. Is it the aroma of linseed oil, perhaps? Or is that an even more deeply subconscious rationalization – with the seed of flax and thus the thought of Irish linen?

This pleasantly smooth oiliness derives from the exclusively Irish custom of using a portion of unmalted barley in the still. This is mixed with the malted barley, and it all goes together into a pot still which, though large, is much the same as those used to make single malt Scotch. The Irish use three stills, ganged up together, while the Scots usually let two suffice. The Irish thus start off with a heavier charge of raw materials, but distil them more thoroughly, producing a clear, rounded, spirit.

All Irish was a pure pot-still product in the days when it was the principal whiskey in the English market. Sad to say, the Irish began to lighten their pot-still spirit with a vatting of grain whiskey after England was "invaded" by blended Scotch at the beginning of this century.

Perversely, it was a court case – over trading standards and the definition of whisk(e)y – in the heavily Irish London borough of Islington, in 1905, that led to the way being cleared for Scottish blends.

Occasionally, an old bottling of pure pot-still whiskey finds its way out of a warehouse, but these veterans of thirty or forty years – however interesting – tend to be rather woody.

There are still some Irish whiskeys that have more pot-still character than others. That is why I like Jameson's 12-year-old best. In Jameson Crested Ten, the pot-still character seems to lose out to the sherry-wood finish. Should the name (which is originally Scottish) rhyme with James, or Jam? In Ireland, it always sounds like "Jemmison" to me.

My second-favourite whiskey from Ireland is the big-bodied Power's. Both Jameson and Power's were Dublin distillers. The Jameson distillery, in Bow Street, still does some blending, and has a museum and tasting room called The Whiskey Corner. The John Power building has now been taken over by the National College of Art. Both whiskeys are produced at Midleton, near Cork.

Tullamore was once a renowned distilling town, but its whiskey, too, is now made in Cork. The very light Tullamore Dew is especially popular in France, where it is pronounced "*Tout l'amour*".

The most famous Cork whiskey (which, confusingly, used to be spelt without the "e") is Paddy, named after the salesman who peddled it in the cask in the 1920s – "Send me some of Paddy's whiskey", bar-keepers used to demand.

In Cork, you will still spot the fruity Hewitt's, but there is no longer much of the light Murphy's or even the lighter Dunphy's to be found. In recent years, the distillery has produced a very smooth, malty whiskey, aged in Bourbon wood, under the name Midleton Very Rare. This is produced in numbered limited editions at a very high price (£55-£60). A fine whiskey, but a little too sophisticated for my taste.

There is a theory that the Irish were distilling before the Scots. They are more likely to have used grain than potatoes – contrary to folklore, the word poteen is derived not from the raw material but from the vessel used.

Bushmills, licensed in 1608, is the oldest whisk(e)y distillery in the world. It may be the oldest distillery of any spirit. As the little town of Bushmills is in Co Antrim, it might be expected that the whiskey produced there would have a suggestion of a Scottish accent, like the people. It does.

Bushmills distils exclusively from malt, albeit only very lightly peated, and in three stills. The basic Bushmills is unique in that it is a blend of just one malt whiskey and one grain (the latter made in Cork). Bushmills also makes by the same means a lighter blend called Coleraine, and a rightly celebrated rich, sherryish one known as Black Bush. It also does a Single Malt Whiskey (spotted at a distance by its green label).

One local legend has it that an Irish giant took the secret of distillation with him when he crossed the rock formation that forms stepping stones to the western islands of Scotland. Once, after a Bushmills too many, I set out after him, across the Giant's Causeway, heading for Fingal's Cave, on Staffa. Falling in the sea is a great way to sober up.

FROM *THE INDEPENDENT* (3 MARCH 1990)

SINGLE MALT ON THE MENU

PAMELA VANDYKE PRICE

Gastronomy abounds in old wives' tales: cheese at bedtime gives you bad dreams, port and champagne at the same meal gives you a hangover, women shouldn't walk through mushroom caves at certain times of the month, when they can't make mayonnaise anyway . . . The lot are untrue, though the more backward mushroom cave keepers do tend to keep women out, I believe.

But one old saw has stuck longer than most – the assertion that single malt whisky is "too strong, too heavy, too definite, too heady" to be drunk except on the moor, up the glen or alongside the loch. Now single malts are, in a vague way, the first-growth clarets of Scotland: each is an individual whisky, with the characteristics of its region and pot still. The malts of, say, Speyside are different from the Campbeltowns or Islays, varying according to what they are as the great bulk of whiskies, products of the patent or continuous still, and blends in which a certain proportion of malt is bound to be included, can never do. You buy "scotch" in general according to the brand you like, you use it straight or in mixes. You buy single malt because of the distillery you prefer and you drink it – ideally – only with the addition of water, Malvern if you're remote from Loch Katrine.

The first time I was introduced to single malt I admit I was cautious. (I am not one for uncomfortable and only supposedly health-giving outdoor exercise of any sort.) Would the tasting of fourteen single malts to which I was invited by the Scotch Whisky Association prove too much of a strain? It merely resulted in my deciding that certain malts appealed to me more than others (at least then) and in my now filling my travelling flask with malt instead of brandy, because whereas you can almost always get some sort of brandy, there are times when you want a sound strong drink, either by way of talking point to share with the fascinating character marooned with you at an airport, or else to offer to bandit chief or foreign wine potentate for diplomatic and strategic reasons – and single malt is still something of a special treasure.

Another relevant old wives' tale is that of never mixing grape and grain – obviously you don't stun your palate with spirits before attempting to appreciate fine wines, but a single malt is a wonderful digestive after a good dinner and, with its special elegance and character, I think it can even come closer to the meal than that. I was once asked to arrange a luncheon for William Grant, who love fine wines as much as they do good scotch, and we had champagne as the apéritif, then a hot consommé of beef, followed by the kipper pâté which the Connaught Hotel say they mix with a little scotch anyway, and which on this occasion was accompanied by a small glass – straight – of Grant's Glenfiddich. I certainly didn't hear any comments that this spoiled the white burgundy and the two clarets that we went on to drink . . .

As the haggis are flying low the noo – and existence in the strike-threatened, bill-sodden, transport-complicated south is quite as strenuous as in Highland or Island, you could sustain yourself with the sort of meal that was planned to defy the elements in the north.

A single malt, with water, by way of apéritif, may be followed by either cock-a-leekie soup or kipper pâté (or both) then haggis. (Selfridges have good ones if you lack a source of supply north of the border.) If you balk at the traditional bashed neeps, then spring cabbage is excellent. End with Dunlop cheese (accent on the last syllable to show you're not referring to the tyre) and perhaps the oatmeal-rolled cream cheese, Caboc, and then a syllabub (a tip, as the cookery queens are always giving out – you don't have to make this under the cow). More malt and, possibly, a choice of Prince Charles Edward's liqueur, Drambuie, or the other whisky-based liqueur, Glayva.

FROM *THE SPECTATOR* (16 JANUARY 1971)

LAST ORDERS

HARVEST FESTIVAL

SIMON LOFTUS

Burgundians approach every vintage with a mixture of joy and trepidation. The sense of imminent relief at a harvest safely gathered is clouded by anxiety. A tempest could still destroy the crop which has been nurtured with such constant care while another storm, inevitable and feared, exhilarating as thunder, whirls its unpredictable way through the quiet habits of rural life: the arrival of the harvesters. Like a sudden wind which sets the leaves swirling in the street, bangs doors and shutters and is followed at once by a lull in which you hear inexplicable laughter from an upper room, or a child crying, the pickers are a social tornado. Their breath is anarchy.

Camaraderie and exuberance are fuelled by hard work and wine. Liaisons which at other times would seem inconceivable flower for a moment of madness. Days of exhaustion roll into nights of reckless oblivion until the final day, when the pickers roar back from vineyard to village in a cacophony of triumph; the final night, celebrated with songs and ribaldry at a harvest feast, the *paulée*; and the sudden sobriety of the morning, dispersal and parting.

Most of the villagers forget their habitual wariness of strangers and smile with indulgent complicity at the antics of these invaders. A few grudge the vagrants their gaudy licence and batten their doors against threatening disorder. Behind shuttered windows they wait for the harvest to be over and their dogs growl at every passer-by. But there are others for whom the vintage is a seasonal fever, eagerly anticipated. They await the pickers as liberators, and harbingers of excess.

Vintagers arrive singly, in couples and groups from the poorest regions of rural France, from the cities, from abroad: students chasing the harvest from one wine district to another, criss-crossing the continent before heading towards the east; a truck-driver and his girlfriend, taking a break from the road; a cluster of high-spirited nurses from a hospital in Rouen; the unemployed, glad of work and companionship. Some are returning for their third or fourth season working for the same domaine, while others come without engagement and simply proffer their services to anyone in need of extra labour. For most it is a working holiday and all have an air of carnival, unconstrained by familiar circumstance and social obligation. They relish the vintage like Mardi Gras, as a time of celebration and licence. With dormitories in tempting proximity "*nuits blanches*" are common, followed by a grey awakening.

For their employers, the growers, it is a matter of hard work. The traditional habit of regarding the harvesters as a necessary bane meant that in the old days they were often provided with the most basic accommodation and furnishings, in ruinous hovels; not simply out of meanness but because it was thought that if you put them in a proper house they would only wreck it. And the food was simple. Most growers would fatten a few rabbits before the vintage, to fill out the pot-au-feu, because meat from the butcher was far too expensive. Old Pierre Ramonet is said to have been confronted by his pickers, years ago, with the demand that he provide them with a hot shower, and meat once a day. "I don't have a shower and I eat my meat on Sundays," Ramonet replied, and sacked the lot. Nowadays expectations are higher. Houses which stand empty for the rest of the year must be made habitable, dormitories swept and someone organized to cook the pickers' meals. And their equipment (now provided by the domaines) must be checked and prepared. Innumerable pairs of secateurs have to be cleaned, oiled and sharpened, baskets and buckets washed and counted, squeaky piles of waterproof clothing taken out of store. Mechanical things need servicing: tractors and trailers and presses and cooling apparatus. The cellars are cleaned, tanks sterilized and sacks of sugar stockpiled against anticipated need. Are there enough casks and have they been steamed and sulphured? These and uncountable smaller tasks must be remembered now, because once the vintage begins nobody has time for anything but the job in hand.

FROM *PULIGNY-MONTRACHET*
  JOURNAL OF A VILLAGE IN BURGUNDY (1992)

LAMBIC BEERS

MICHAEL JACKSON

It is the use of wild yeasts that gives such a vinous aroma and palate (reminiscent of fino sherry, or vermouth) to the lambic family of beers. No other style of beer in the developed world is intentionally made with wild strains as the principal yeasts, and it is this procedure, where fermentation occurs spontaneously, that defines a lambic. All beer – and wine – was once made in this way, with the wild yeasts producing a slightly different result each time.

Its definition also insists that lambic be made with a proportion of at least

30 per cent raw wheat, the rest of the grist being malted barley.

These beers were originally the local brews in the mainly Flemish valley of the small River Zenne (spelled with an initial "S" in French), to either side of the city of Brussels, Belgium. The surviving producers in this area, ten or a dozen at the most, are all on the west side of Brussels, in a district known as Payottenland.

Beers of the lambic family became the dominant local style of Brussels itself from the 1750s to World War I, and they are still the speciality of some cafés there. They are now widely known elsewhere in Belgium, and to some extent in the bordering nations of the Netherlands and France. Only recently have they become available in countries further afield, in some of which they have developed a small but devoted following.

Efforts are being made to establish a European Community *appellation contrôlée* that would restrict the term lambic to brewers working with wild yeasts in the traditional area. One brewer in France (Brasserie du Bobtail, at St Séverin, in the Perigord) and one in Britain (All Saints, in Stamford, Lincolnshire) have in recent years experimented with spontaneous fermentation.

In its basic form, lambic is almost still, something between a fino sherry and a hard cider. This version is sold in some cafés in the Zenne Valley, but even there is not always easy to find. A more widely available member of the lambic family is gueuze (spellings vary). This is a naturally carbonated, champagne-like blend of young and old lambic beers. A lambic sweetened with candy sugar is known as a faro. A diluted version of this was called mars. It vanished some decades ago, but may well reappear as traditions are revived.

Among the immense complex of flavours to be found in many of the lambic family is one reminiscent of rhubarb. This flavour is created in fermentation; rhubarb is not added to lambic (although it is an ingredient of some vermouths – which may explain that note). Other fruits often are added, especially cherries or raspberries. In Belgium, if a lambic is used as the base for a fruit beer, this will be indicated on the label. A kriek lambic is made with cherries, a frambozen (or framboise) lambic with raspberries . . .

Traditionally, lambic is brewed with aged hops. Some lambic-makers buy old stocks of excess hops from merchants and other brewers, but economy is not their motivation. This being such an old method of brewing, the hops are employed as a preservative. I know of no other commercially brewed beer in which this is still their principal role. In this function, large quantities are required, and the aging, typically of around three years, reduces their flavour and prevents them from intruding on the palate. Assertive hop flavours do not combine well with the tartness of wheat beers or the intentionally sour notes in some very old styles.

After the boil comes the most remarkable feature, the one central to lambic brewing. The brew is run into a "cool ship", an open vessel like a shallow swimming pool made of copper. This is in the attic of the brewery. The windows are left open, and there may be the odd slate missing from the roof. As the brew cools overnight, it is visited by wild yeasts.

Even a brewer who bends the rules by pitching in a little cultured yeast (top-fermenting) may still leave his beer to spend more than three years undergoing a chain reaction of fermentations in wooden barrels. Many of these barrels were made in Portugal, Spain or France. They were either discarded in the 1920s, when the *bodegas* or châteaux began to use stainless steel, or they were used to transport wines to Belgium. Once, all the beers were fermented in wooden barrels. Today, lambic is the only style in which this is still the normal procedure.

There are seventy-odd microorganisms at work in the valley's breweries, two of which have been given taxonomic names identified with the area: *lambicus* and *bruxellensis*. These are both *Brettanomyces*, the type of yeast that is said to give leathery or "horse blanket" aroma and flavours. There are also four oxidative yeasts not unlike the *flor* which appears on sherry. Several styles of sherry seem to be echoed in a number of different beers, but it is more than chance that compares finos with lambics.

The winy dryness of the two drinks lends them to similar purposes. In Spain, especially Andalucia, I have been served lightly chilled fino sherry with *tapas*, a snack often featuring local seafood. In Belgium, it would have been a lambic or gueuze with cheeses such as the salty Brusselsekaas, the fresh-curd Plattekaas or the acidic Pottekaas with silverskin onions, radishes, sausages and brown bread.

FROM *MICHAEL JACKSON'S BEER COMPANION* (1993)

OPENING VINTAGE PORT WITH FIRE AND FEATHER

HUGH JOHNSON

Bottles of vintage port can present special problems in opening. They are designed to be stored for many years for the raw grape juice and brandy to "marry" and mellow. There is still a convention (more honoured in the breach than the observance) of laying down a case of port when a son is born, to be drunk on his twenty-first birthday. The neck of a vintage port bottle is tall and slightly bulging, and is fitted with a very long cork. If the bottle is stored for longer than about twenty-five years the cork can become soft and crumbly, tending to break up when you pull on it with the corkscrew. In this condition a cork is virtually impossible to extract in the normal way. Sometimes the technique of inserting the corkscrew at an angle will work, but otherwise more extreme measures are required.

You can, of course, resort to the "decapitation" procedure . . . But a less violent and more elegant way is to use a pair of port tongs. You heat them in an open fire or gas flame until they are red-hot, clamp them around the neck of the bottle and leave them there for half a minute. Then wipe the same spot with a damp cloth or – for a touch of style – a feather dipped in water. A faint snapping sound will be heard, and you will know that the neck has split in a neat circle. Then you just lift off the top like a stopper, bringing, unless you are unlucky, the whole cork with it. An impressive trick – but the main thing is that it works.

FROM *HOW TO ENJOY YOUR WINE* (1985)

SHERRY TO THE RESCUE

What have Adnams, Hidalgo and the RSPB got in common? Answer: the Coto Doñana.

Last year Javier Hidalgo was full of gloom. Despite rising sales of his wonderful sherries, life was clouded. Whenever he looked across the Guadalquivir estuary from his home near Sanlucar de Barrameda, gazing towards Spain's largest nature reserve (a vast unspoilt expanse of wetlands, woods and wilderness) Javier's heart sank at the threat of imminent ecological catastrophe. Accustomed as he was to riding through this ornithologist's paradise, a pair of binoculars slung across his neck, Hidalgo shared the mounting worldwide concern for the future of the Coto Doñana. For reasons which remain mysterious (but stank of corruption in high places) developers had gained permission to build a vast new holiday complex on the empty coastline of this supposedly protected region. Apart from the aesthetic horrors of high rise hotels and beaches littered with sun tan oil and souvenir stalls, there was a practical consideration of immense significance. The huge surge in daily demand for fresh water, necessary to service this development, would have had the effect of lowering the water table to a level which would have drained the wetlands – rendering them uninhabitable by the hundreds of thousands of migrating wildfowl which frequent this precious habitat, then would have followed a grim environmental demonstration of the domino theory, as one catastrophe precipitated another.

Southwold, like Sanlucar, is on a river estuary surrounded by marshlands and we too had been threatened by destructive development, so the plight of the Coto Doñana was close to our hearts. I contacted the RSPB and suggested that we organize an offer of Hidalgo sherries through *Birds* magazine, with a contribution from sales going to the Coto Doñana fighting fund. We raised £1400 by this means and when Javier Hidalgo came over to collect the cheque he was able to give us the tremendous news that the international outcry had been so successful that the threatened development was halted, the Coto Doñana was saved and the regional government of Andalucia had been given a major shake up. Moreover the entire Spanish nation had been jolted into a new awareness of environmental issues.

FROM *ADNAMS WINE LIST* (1991)

THE MORNING AFTER AND THE NIGHT BEFORE

PAMELA VANDYKE PRICE

"Only Satan," says Kipling, "can rebuke sin. The good don't know enough." So when efficient young interviewers begin to stumble as to whether I have ever – been unfortunate enough to – been tempted to – I know quite well what they *don't* mean. They want to ask me if I've ever been drunk. And of course I have. Awful indiscretions, double vision, aggressiveness, that terrible swirl when one does get to bed that we used to call "pillow spin", nausea and total lack of remembering what one did, said, where one went and with whom – and the horrors of the aftermath, of which the remorse and apprehension are almost worse than the headache, the eye ache, the stomach ache and the white-hot wires in every joint . . . I've had the lot.

But not for a very long time.

If life has taught me anything, it has taught me to come to terms with my limitations. I never drink any mysterious mixtures. I remember how we used to slosh in the pure alcohol and take our personal tipples from a hidden jug. Usually, the simpler the potion the better. If you treat your stomach like a Regency punch bowl, it's fair enough that the result will be that you feel like a Regency rake – and *they* were pre-Alka-Seltzer and aspirin, poor things. If you drink without eating anything, or only salty things that increase your thirst, the alcohol will obviously have its way with you faster and for longer than if you give it some interior cushioning, which is why I applaud drink party hostesses who serve onion soup, kedgeree, the endless and enjoyable variations on potato pie or gratins, succulent risottos and even such humble blotters as toasted garlic bread with a choice of toppings, pumpernickel piled with cheese, meat, vegetables and eggs or fish, or the blessed baked potato in its jacket, plus plenty of butter, salt and some kind of stuffing to add the protein that one needs when one is tired to avoid succumbing to the alcohol, and must have when one has already succumbed and needs to recover. (My mother-in-law always insisted on one eating a cooked breakfast and having a brisk walk on 1 January before she would allow any lying back with codeine, eye-packs and gallons of water, and maybe the fact that I had to face many a kipper then makes me intrepid now.)

As the elimination process is at least half of the secret of avoiding or minimizing the consequences of imprudent eating and drinking, those of us who've learnt the hard way take several aspirin, some fizzy salts and at least a pint of water (more if possible) before we fall into whatever kind of sleep we're able to get. My doctor husband used to recommend a repeat of all this when one first crawled into consciousness about 5-6 a.m., before one had to get up, and one worldly member of the wine trade placidly advised, "Always champagne as the last drink of whatever evening, darling – then, in the morning, one whoosh and all is well!" Some people swear by the alkalinity of milk before they drop off, but I warn the inexperienced as to the unwisdom of pouring the acidity of a lot of fruit juice onto what may already be an acid-burdened stomach; stick to fizzy lemonade or soda if you don't want to be extra curdled.

The traditional "revivers" are headed by Fernet Branca, which to many is so nasty that they have to be at the stage of forgiving their enemies before they can take it – and then they know that death packs a preliminary sting just before they begin to feel that perhaps life isn't so bad after all. I drink it if, having awakened feeling fine, I suddenly, around midday, have that curious sinking sensation, the result of tiredness, excessive talking and laughing in frenziedly social atmospheres, and the prospect of the sort of luncheon where I have to be efficient as well as actually eating and drinking (usually this is the result of my having finished the last of the dessert wine while doing the washing-up at 2 a.m.). Ferro-China and the German Underberg all do the same admirable job, and so does the sinisterly-named French Arquebuse (it marches into the shrinking stomach *just* like an arquebusier). Some people consider these bitters are aphrodisiacs, but I think one problem at a time is enough for them to cope with. If you really do just feel exhausted through every texture of your being, then Nelson's Blood – port and brandy, half and half – is a comfortable cushion for anything that's got to go inside you, and a foody sort of drink as well, and so is a brandy-based egg nog.

One of the best and simplest mixes, for morning or late-night entertaining is still the famous Buck's Fizz – champagne and orange juice. For the younger members of the party, keep the proportion of juice high and wine low, others may prefer half and half, or, as I do, one-third juice to two-thirds wine. You can individualize your version by a drop of Angostura, a little sugar, or drops of Cointreau or orange-flavoured liqueur, and of course a good dryish sparkling white wine can be substituted for the non-vintage champagne. But you *must* have freshly squeezed orange juice – I've tried most versions of frozen, canned and bottled and there simply isn't the "lift" given by the real fruit, however good (or indifferent) the bubbly. But do a comparative tasting – and see for yourself. Remember that the fruit juice will make the wine foam up vigorously when poured, and when you open whatever sparkler you use, don't point the bottle at anyone or anything, put a napkin round it, hold it at an angle (lessens the pressure inside) and, when you've removed the wire muzzle, turn the bottle, not the cork, and hold on to this so it doesn't fly. If the cork *really* sticks, and you haven't any champagne nippers, hold the neck of the bottle for a few seconds under the hot tap – the pressure inside will be increased and the cork (hold on to it) will begin to rise. If you've already broken off the top of it, pierce it with a skewer or needle to release the gas, then – and *only* then – use an ordinary corkscrew.

Plan for the aftermath – and you don't usually get it.

FROM *THE SPECTATOR* (26 DECEMBER 1970)

PLAIN WATER AND COMPLEX TASTES

KEITH BOTSFORD

What comes out of the tap is water, a liquid colourless but not tasteless. As anyone who cares for his tea knows, the water you use is the major ingredient and the soft water that makes for good shampooing does not make for good tea. Good hard water, limestone water, seems to make the flavour of certain teas explode. Correspondingly, one does not make tea or any other beverage with water from the hot-water tap or with water that has been previously boiled: the process of heating removes the flavour of the water and makes it inert.

Most of us have lived with different types of water and I suspect all of us are sensitive to a change in the taste of it. When I was a young, impecunious academic, I made an alternative living by wagering on two things with my students: first that I could beat them at pool (that required only the skills acquired in a misspent youth), and second, that I could tell them where their Pepsi was bottled. As all soft drinks are locally bottled, with local water and regional variations in taste, this was not as difficult as it sounds.

My students sought to confound me by bearing bottles from Alaska and Brazil, but I seldom failed. The point is that water is a very positive ingredient. He who today slakes his thirst from a tap is a fortunate man indeed. In most cases, our water is not for drinking, but for bathing. It is treated, protected, chlorinated, flouridated and softened until it is awful stuff. Anyone who has been to America, for instance, will know that the ice (made from treated water) is enough to destroy the flavour of most drinks.

There is water for drinking and water for cooking. Of the former, it can only be said that tastes differ. In France and on the Continent in general, where mineral water has been the rage since doctors created the anxious eater, and their commercial partners developed medicinal spas to cure gluttons of their self-indulgence, the variety of mineral waters available is truly awesome. I am urged to drink vast quantities of the stuff, yet in my family we are hereditarily anti-liquid people. My mother, who is ninety-one, seldom manages more than a pint of liquid a day: not the required one litre minimum. I am the same, and my doctor insists, alas, that wine is not, in that sense, a liquid.

There is only one water which I will drink in quantity and that is Vichy: and not Vichy St Yorre, but the old Celestins, which is now hard to obtain. I like Yugoslav mineral water and some Italian waters; not the Spanish. I spurn Evian, Vittel, Contrexéville and all such flavourless waters. I like sulphur and a little natural fizz. My true hatred is for Perrier: I no more wish to ingest artificial gas than chlorine, nor can I understand how others can absorb such aggressive bubbles. You might think that the water we use in cooking is unimportant, flavoured by what we cook in it. Not so. To poach a fresh salmon in processed water is to destroy a delicate balance of flavours. There is no doubt whatever that one of the many reasons why pasta is seldom edible in America is that the water in which it is cooked imparts its own deplorable taste. The rule is very simple: if the material cooked is to retain the purity of its own flavour (steamed fish or vegetables, a delicate soup) be wary of your water.

An easy solution is to use bottled waters for such dishes; a more sensible and less expensive one is to make extensive use of stock, that is a water in which an ingredient of the same sort has previously been cooked. Fish may be steamed by a fish stock, beef boiled in a beef stock, etc. Number three son, a fine cook, taught me how a single clove in the water over which vegetables are steamed will both add perfume and wipe out the chemical taste of big city water.

It is not that water used to cook delicate ingredients should be tasteless; it is important that such flavour as it has (and all water has a taste) derives from geological factors and should not be antagonistic or assertive. Cooking should be intentional. There are wines one uses for a *coq au vin* and wines one would not dream of using. One might drink Vichy but would not cook in it unless one wanted the taste of sulphur, the devil's flavour.

FROM *THE INDEPENDENT* (10 DECEMBER 1988)

LITERARY ENDORSEMENTS

H W YOXALL

Some of the French writing in particular, about wine, is apt to be too highly coloured. Ecstasies on this subject can have an effect on the reader opposite to that intended. But finally enthusiasm will break through. However, in conclusion, I shall let famous men speak for me rather than provide my own peroration.

Rabelais, though a Tourangeot, made Panurge rhapsodize about Beaune. Huysmans, quoted by Morton Shand, has a character proclaim that the great Côte de Nuits *cuvées* made abbatial processions file before his imagination, princely festivals, opulence of robes sewn with gold and afire with light. Meredith has one who exclaims that the second glass of an old Romanée or Musigny will be "a High Priest for the uncommon nuptials between the body and soul of men". Erasmus, defending himself against a charge of drinking Pommard on a fast-day, said more prosaically that his heart was Catholic, but for such wine his stomach was Protestant. An otherwise unknown bishop of Lyon, accused of using expensive *têtes de cuvée* from the Côte d'Or for sacramental wine, replied that he could not be seen making a wry face when he confronted his master. Another prelate, Bossuet (himself from Chenove, a famous field in his time), described burgundy as the *source de force et de joie*. Finally Brillat-Savarin, father and foremost of gastronomic writers, called it "the most beautiful eulogy of God".

On that note, I think, I can leave it.

FROM *THE WINES OF BURGUNDY* (1974)

ACKNOWLEDGEMENTS

William Grant & Sons Ltd gratefully acknowledges the generous permission of authors, publishers and agents to quote from the following works and publications:

The Adventurous Fish Cook by George Lassalle (Macmillan 1976/Papermac 1987); *North Atlantic Seafood* by Alan Davidson (Penguin Books 1980), copyright © Alan Davidson 1979, 1980; *Fish Cookery* by Jane Grigson (Penguin Books 1975), courtesy David Higham Associates; *Culinary Tales* by Niki Hill (Blackstaff Press 1974), courtesy of the author; article by Michael Raffael in *The Sunday Telegraph* (22.8.1993), courtesy of the author; article by John McKenna in *The Irish Times* (11.7.1992), courtesy of the author; *English Seafood Cookery* by Richard Stein (Penguin Books 1988), copyright © Richard Stein 1988; article by Philippa Davenport in *Country Living* (January 1995), courtesy of the author; *Particular Delights* by Nathalie Hambro (Jill Norman Ltd 1981), courtesy of the author; *Real Fast Food* by Nigel Slater (Fourth Estate Ltd 1992), courtesy of the author; *Jane Grigson's Fruit Book* (Michael Joseph Ltd 1982), courtesy David Higham Associates; article by John Tovey in *Sainsbury's* **The Magazine** (October 1994), courtesy of the publishers; *Roast Chicken and Other Stories* by Simon Hopkinson with Lindsey Bareham (Ebury Press 1994), courtesy David Higham Associates; article by Colin Spencer in *The Guardian* (26.11.1988), courtesy of the author; article by Humphrey Lyttelton in *Harpers & Queen* (November 1970), courtesy of the author; article by Craig Brown in *The Sunday Times* (13.10.1991), courtesy of the author; article by John McKenna in *The Irish Times* (22.10.1994), courtesy of the author; *The Bad Food Guide* by Derek Cooper (Routledge Kegan Paul Ltd 1967), courtesy of the author; *The Flavours of Andalucia* by Elisabeth Luard, published by Collins & Brown (1991), £9.99; *Cooking With Pomiane* by Edward de Pomiane (Faber and Faber Ltd 1993); *Memories of Gascony* by Pierre Koffmann (Mitchell Beazley 1990), text © Pierre Koffmann and Reed International Books Limited/Amazon Publishing Limited 1990; *Picnic* by Claudia Roden (Jill Norman Ltd 1981/Penguin Books 1982), courtesy David Higham Associates; *The Legendary Cuisine of Persia* by Margaret Shaida (Lieuse Publications 1992), courtesy of the author; *Classic Indian Vegetarian and Grain Cooking* by Julie Sahni (Dorling Kindersley 1987); *Classic Chinese Cookbook* by Yan-Kit So (Dorling Kindersley 1984); *Step-by-Step Japanese Cooking* by Lesley Downer and Minoru Yoneda (Macdonald & Co Ltd 1985), courtesy of Quarto Publishing plc; article by Frances Bissell in *The Times Magazine* (3.9.1994), courtesy of the author; article by Philippa Davenport in the *Financial Times* (10 December 1994), courtesy of the author; *Simple French Cooking* by Richard Olney (Penguin Books 1983), copyright © Richard Olney 1974; *Much Depends On Dinner* by Margaret Visser (Penguin Books 1989), copyright © Margaret Visser 1986; article by Delia Smith in *Sainsbury's* **The Magazine** (April 1994), courtesy of the publishers; article by Oliver Pritchett in *Sainsbury's* **The Magazine** (October 1994), courtesy of the author; article by Emily Green in *The Independent* (17.10.1992), courtesy of the author; article by William Foster in *Resident Abroad* (October 1986), courtesy of the author; article by Alice Wooledge Salmon in *House & Garden* (April 1984), courtesy of the author; *English Bread and Yeast Cookery* by Elizabeth David (Allen Lane 1977/Penguin Books 1979), courtesy of Jill Norman; *The Great British Cheese Book* by Patrick Rance (Macmillan [Papermac] 10.11.1988); *The French Cheese Book* by Patrick Rance (Macmillan [cloth] 11.9.1989); *Arabella Boxer's Book of English Food* (A John Curtis Book/Hodder & Stoughton 1991), courtesy of the author; *A New Book of Middle Eastern Food* by Claudia Roden (Viking 1985/Penguin Books 1986), courtesy David Higham Associates; *Broths to Bannocks* by Catherine Brown (John Murray Publishers Ltd 1990); *A Palate in Revolution: Grimod de La Reynière and the Almanach des Gourmands* by Giles MacDonogh (Robin Clark 1987), courtesy Quartet Books Ltd; article by Alice Wooledge Salmon in *World Gastronomy 1985*, courtesy of the author; *Seasonal Cooking* by Claire Macdonald (Century 1983/Corgi 1986), courtesy of the author; article by Nigel Slater in *The Observer Life Magazine* (7.8.1994), courtesy of the author; *The*

Art of British Cooking by Theodora Fitzgibbon (Phoenix House/J M Dent 1965), courtesy David Higham Associates; *Delia Smith's Christmas* (BBC Books 1990); *New Classic Cuisine* by Albert and Michel Roux (Macdonald Orbis 1983), courtesy of Little Brown & Co (UK); *Keep it Simple* by Alastair Little and Richard Whittington (Conran Octopus 1993), courtesy of Reed Books; *The Independent Cook* by Jeremy Round (Barrie & Jenkins 1988); *The Complete Book of Spices* by Jill Norman (Dorling Kindersley 1990), courtesy of the author; article by Frances Bissell in *The Times Magazine* (29.10.1994), courtesy of the author; *Good Things* by Jane Grigson (Michael Joseph 1971/Penguin Books 1973), courtesy David Higham Associates; article by Jancis Robinson in *The Sunday Times* (10.11.1985), courtesy of the author; article by Colin Spencer in *The Guardian* (23.4.1988), courtesy of the author; article by Pamela Vandyke Price in *The Spectator* (24.10.1970), courtesy of the author; *The Game Cookery Book* by Julia Drysdale (Collins 1975/Papermac 1983), courtesy of the author; *A Kipper With My Tea* by Alan Davidson (Macmillan London Ltd 1988), courtesy of the author; *How To Enjoy Your Wine* by Hugh Johnson (Mitchell Beazley 1985), courtesy of the author; *Bordeaux* by Robert Parker (Dorling Kindersley 1986); *The Oxford Companion to Wine* edited by Jancis Robinson (Oxford University Press 1994), by permission of Oxford University Press; *The Story of Wine* by Hugh Johnson (Mitchell Beazley 1989), courtesy of the author; *Ray on Wine* by Cyril Ray (J M Dent & Sons Ltd 1979), reprinted by permission of the Peters Fraser & Dunlop Group Ltd; *The Wines of Bordeaux* by Edmund Penning-Rowsell (The International Wine & Food Publishing Company 1969/Penguin Books 1971), courtesy of the author; *The Wines of Burgundy* by H W Yoxall (The International Wine & Food Society 1968/Penguin Books 1974), courtesy of Lindsey Pietrezak; *The Little Dictionary of Drink* by Julian Jeffs (Pelham Books 1973), courtesy of the author; article by John Arlott in *The Guardian* (October 1978), courtesy of *The Guardian; Oz Clarke's New Classic Wines* (Websters/Mitchell Beazley 1991), courtesy of the author; article by Anthony Rose in *The Independent* (16.1.1993), courtesy of the author; article by William Foster in *Wine Magazine* (1984), courtesy of the author; article by Michael Jackson in *What's Brewing* (December 1988), courtesy of the author; *An Omelette and a Glass of Wine* by Elizabeth David (A Jill Norman Book/Robert Hale 1984), courtesy of Jill Norman; *Whisky Roads of Scotland* by Derek Cooper (Jill Norman Ltd 1982), courtesy of the author; article by Pamela Vandyke Price in *The Spectator* (16.1.1971), courtesy of the author; article by Michael Jackson in *The Independent* (3.3.1990), courtesy of the author; *Puligny-Montrachet* by Simon Loftus (Ebury Press 1992); *Michael Jackson's Beer Companion* (Mitchell Beazley 1993), courtesy of the author; Adnams Wine List (1991), courtesy of Adnams Wine Merchants; article by Keith Botsford in *The Independent* 10.12.1988, courtesy of *The Independent*; article by Pamela Vandyke Price in *The Spectator* (26.12.1970), courtesy of the author.

Illustrations

Photographs by Kevin Summers *(The Observer Life Magazine*: 14.8.1994; 7.8.1994; 27.2.1994), courtesy of Kevin Summers; photographs by Robin Broadbent (recipes: Joy Davies; art direction: Robin Harvey), *Harpers & Queen* (June 1991), courtesy of Robin Broadbent; photograph by James Murphy from *Delia Smith's Christmas* (BBC Books 1990), courtesy of BBC Worldwide Publishing; photograph by Peter Knab *(Sainsbury's **The Magazine**,* October 1994), courtesy of the publishers; photograph by Anthony Blake from *Memories of Gascony* by Pierre Koffmann (Mitchell Beazley 1990), courtesy of Anthony Blake; photograph by Martin Brigdale (*BBC Vegetarian Good Food*, August/September 1993), courtesy of the publishers; photograph by Norman Hollands *(Sainsbury's **The Magazine**,* April 1994), courtesy of the publishers; illustration from *The Grapes of Ralph* by Ralph Steadman (Ebury Press 1992), reproduced by kind permission of Ralph Steadman, Ebury Press and Oddbins; photograph by Patrick Eagar from *The Oxford Companion to Wine* by Jancis Robinson (Oxford University Press 1994), courtesy of Patrick Eagar.